JOURNAL FOR THE STUDY OF THE NEW TESTAMENT
SUPPLEMENT SERIES

7

Consulting Editors

Ernst Bammel, James Dunn, Birger Gerhardsson, Anthony Hanson
David Hill, Barnabas Lindars, Howard Marshall
Robert Tannehill, Anthony Thiselton, Max Wilcox

Executive Editor

Bruce D. Chilton

Publishing Editor

David J.A. Clines

Department of Biblical Studies
The University of Sheffield
Sheffield S10 2TN
England

SYNOPTIC STUDIES

The Ampleforth Conferences
of
1982 and 1983

Edited by
C.M. TUCKETT

Journal for the Study of the New Testament
Supplement Series 7

Copyright © 1984 JSOT Press

Published by
JSOT Press
Department of Biblical Studies
The University of Sheffield
Sheffield S10 2TN
England

Printed in Great Britain
by Redwood Burn Ltd.,
Trowbridge, Wiltshire.

British Library Cataloguing in Publication Data

Synoptic studies : the Ampleforth Conferences
    of 1982-1983.—(Journal for the study of
    the New Testament supplement series, ISSN
    0143-5108; 7)
    1. Bible. N.T. Gospels—Commentaries
    I. Tuckett, C.M.   II. Series
    226'.06   BS2555.3

    ISBN 0-905774-80-9
    ISBN 0-905774-81-7 Pbk

CONTENTS

PREFACE

The essays in this volume represent papers which were given at two conferences held at Ampleforth Abbey in 1982 and 1983. These conferences were not isolated gatherings; they were organized as part of a series of meetings designed to further discussion on the relationships between the gospels. In this introduction, therefore, it may be worthwhile to sketch in some of the background and to explain why the conferences were held.

The last thirty years or so have seen a great revival of interest in the Synoptic Problem. In the first half of this century it was believed that the Synoptic Problem had been satisfactorily solved by the so-called 'two-document hypothesis': Mark's gospel was the first to be written and had been used as a source by Matthew and Luke; further, Matthew and Luke had access to other source material, usually called Q. Details within the hypothesis might vary slightly (e.g. on the precise nature of Q) but in general the theory was believed to be securely grounded, and it could be used as the basis for further research in the areas of form-criticism and redaction-criticism.

Recently, however, severe doubts have been raised about the manner in which the hypothesis was established in the past, and quite different source theories are now proposed. In 1951 B.C. Butler published his *The Originality of St. Matthew* (Cambridge, 1951), defending the older, so-called 'Augustinian' hypothesis: Matthew's gospel was written first, Mark was dependent on Matthew and Luke came third. Probably the most influential alternative today to the theory of Markan priority is the revised version of the so-called 'Griesbach hypothesis', i.e. the hypothesis that Matthew's gospel was written first, that Luke used Matthew, and that Mark's gospel was written last conflating Matthew and Luke. The theory was seriously revived for the first time in the modern debate by the publication of W.R. Farmer's *The Synoptic Problem* (New York–London, 1964), and since 1964 a number of other scholars have lent their support to this revival of the Griesbach hypothesis. Other criticisms of the standard two-document hypothesis have come from those who, whilst accepting Markan priority, would regard the theory of a lost source Q as unnecessary. Following A. Farrar's celebrated essay of 1955, 'On Dispensing with Q' (in D.E. Nineham [ed.], *Studies in the Gospels. Essays in Memory of R.H. Lightfoot* [Oxford, 1955], pp. 55-88), some have tried to show that Luke's gospel can be satisfactorily explained if Luke derived his non-Markan material directly from Matthew, without postulating an otherwise unknown source Q. The theory of the existence of a Q source would thus become redundant. Others have sought to refine this further, claiming that extraneous source material is unnecessary to explain not only the Matthew-Luke agreements but also the existence of virtually all Matthew's non-Markan material: Matthew's extra material is due to his own creativity and so his gospel is a kind of 'midrash' of Mark's gospel. This is above all the theory of M.D. Goulder in his study *Midrash and Lection in Matthew* (London, 1974). Other, more complex, theories about synoptic interrelationships have also been proposed: e.g. the French scholar M. Boismard has consistently maintained that the relationships between the gospels can only be satisfactorily explained by a number of pre-redactional, related stages in the tradition.

It is clear that the problem of the relationships between the gospels has become a matter of genuine scholarly debate, and the two-document hypothesis is no longer the firm bedrock of gospel study which it was once thought to be. As in all scholarly work, the debate has proceeded on the basis of individual publications, in books and journal articles. However, in recent years, there has been a growing recognition that further progress could perhaps be made by a more corporate approach. As a result, a number of international conferences have been organized at which fruitful discussions have developed from prepared papers. Such meetings have been valuable as a forum, not only for discussing and clarifying views already held, but also for initiating and coordinating further study to help achieve a deeper understanding of the gospels. One of the first of these conferences was the 'Festival of the Gospels' which was held in Pittsburgh in 1970. The success of the venture led to the organization of another international conference in 1976 in Münster, held in celebration of the bicentenary of the birth of J.J. Griesbach. In 1977 a 'Colloquy on the Relationships among the Gospels' was held at Trinity University, San Antonio, Texas, at which various aspects of gospel study were discussed in four seminars. One notable feature of this gathering was the dialogue between NT scholars and those of other disciplines (e.g. classical studies and English literature). The logical successor of the Münster conference was another Griesbach conference, held in Cambridge in 1979. Many of the papers from all these conferences have been published, in conference volumes or in separate articles,[1] and are now readily available. The series of meetings is planned to be continued in a major international symposium on the gospels to be held in Jerusalem in Easter 1984. In order to prepare for this, a number of smaller conferences in various centres have been arranged. The first Ampleforth conference was one such venture, and the fruitfulness (and enjoyment!) of it led to the organization of a second conference a year later. The present volume contains most of the papers which were given at the two conferences.

One major topic for discussion, suggested by the planning committee of the Jerusalem conference, was the value of the witness of the Church Fathers regarding the order of composition and/or the authorship of the canonical gospels. Some time was devoted to this topic at the first conference. Papers were given by J.B. Orchard (on 'The Authenticity of the Traditional Ascriptions of the Gospels') and by A. Meredith (included here). Another general area proposed by the planners for the Jerusalem meeting was the investigation of possible analogies to the gospels in contemporary non-Christian literature. The importance of this was also recognized in view of appeals by some gospel critics to the phenomenon of 'midrash' to explain the form of, for example, Matthew's gospel. With this in mind, papers were presented at the first conference by P.S. Alexander on 'midrash' (part of which is included here, the other part of the paper being published separately in *ZNW* 74 [1983], pp. 237-46) and by R.T. France (in a paper entitled 'Jewish Historiography: Midrash and the Gospels', the substance of which has been published elsewhere, in R.T. France and D. Wenham [eds.], *Gospel Perspectives III* [Sheffield, 1983]). The remaining papers at the first conference focussed on the problem of the relationship between Matthew and Luke, and the necessity or otherwise of appealing to a Q source. Three papers were presented, all arguing that Luke's gospel could be adequately explained on the basis of Luke's use of Matthew and Mark. These included papers by M.D. Goulder ('The Order of a Crank'), H.B. Green ('The Credibility of Luke's Use of Matthew') and J. Drury (a paper entitled 'Luke's Use of Parables' which will form the substance of a fuller treatment to be published elsewhere).

The second conference picked up many of the ideas generated by the first one. Goulder's first paper had concentrated on the differences in order between Matthew and Luke. This led to a desire to consider the phenomenon of order, and the argument(s) from order, in more detail, and as a result two papers (by C.M. Tuckett and D.L. Dungan) were presented on this topic. It was felt desirable to devote some time at the second conference to a detailed discussion of specific passages in the gospels with different source hypotheses in mind. This led to the presentation of Green's second paper (on Matt. 12.22-50), analysing this passage from the point of view of a Farrer-type position; further, part of Farmer's paper was useful here, discussing the synoptic apocalypses from the point of view of the Griesbach hypothesis. The value of continuing to consider contemporary literature was recognized and two further papers were presented: one by Alexander (on rabbinic biographies) and one by F.G. Downing considering evidence from the Greco-Roman background.

The executive secretary of the planning committee for the Jerusalem conference, David Dungan, very kindly travelled across the Atlantic to attend both conferences. Also Professor W.R. Farmer, who has played such a leading role in reviving discussion of the Synoptic Problem today, was able to come for the second meeting. His paper (included in this volume) gave rise to some useful debate on methodological issues. Finally, Professor G.D. Kilpatrick was invited to give the closing paper of the second conference and spoke on 'Matthew on Matthew', raising further issues and criteria not previously discussed at the two meetings.

It would be foolish to pretend that the two conferences produced any startling changes of mind. By the end there were probably as many differences of opinion as before. Further, the views expressed in the papers presented were not always representative of majority opinion at the conferences. For example, the papers on the external attestation about the gospels by the Church Fathers appeared to argue, explicitly or implicitly, for the reliability of this attestation (at least in part). Others, however, were firmly of the view that such evidence was of little value. The papers on order produced some useful discussion (though again no unanimity!). In particular, Dungan's presentation led into a discussion of the nature of gospel synopses and their possible inherent bias. Again there was a division of opinion: some maintained that the standard synopses were useful and adequate to illustrate different source hypotheses; others maintained that no synopsis could be neutral in relation to the Synoptic Problem. In this discussion, it was very useful to have the contribution of Bernard Orchard who had recently published his own, unashamedly biassed, *Synopsis of the Four Gospels* (Edinburgh, 1983), produced to illustrate the Griesbach hypothesis. The papers on contemporary analogies were also useful. Alexander's 'midrash' paper was clearly critical of appeals by Goulder to the phenomenon of midrash to explain the genesis of Matthew's gospel. In discussion, Goulder argued for a looser definition of the term 'midrash' and appealed to the example of the Chronicler's rewriting of the Deuteronomic history as an analogy for Matthew's alleged rewriting of Mark. Downing's paper also provoked useful discussion, in particular his claim that he could find no parallels in Greco-Roman literature to what a Griesbachian Mark, or a Farrer-type Luke must have done at times to his sources. Certainly all who participated benefited enormously from the opportunity to exchange ideas, to discuss issues of common concern, and to clarify arguments and positions held.

There was, however, unanimous agreement amongst the participants on at least one issue: the conferences were extremely enjoyable and fruitful. Credit for this must primarily go the monks at Ampleforth who provided a warm welcome to those who came, and above all to Dom Henry Wansborough, who did all the hard work behind the scenes to organize the conferences.

Funds for the conferences were provided by a charitable trust. All those who participated in the conferences would like to take this opportunity publicly to express their gratitude for the generosity of the benefactors whilst respecting the latters' wish to remain anonymous.

It is hoped that the papers presented here, and made available for publication through the kind offices of JSOT Press, will assist in the on-going discussion about the gospels, their nature and interrelationships.

NOTE

1.   Papers from the Pittsburgh conference were published in *Jesus and Man's Hope* (2 vols., Pittsburgh, 1971). Some of the papers given at the Münster conference were published in B. Orchard and T.R.W. Longstaff (eds.), *J.J. Griesbach: Synoptic and Text-Critical Studies. 1776-1976*

(Cambridge, 1979). Other papers from this conference include W.R. Farmer, 'Modern Developments of Griesbach's Hypothesis', *NTS* 23 (1977), pp. 275-95; G.D. Fee, 'A Text-Critical Look at the Synoptic Problem', *NT* 22 (1980), pp. 12-28; F. Neirynck, 'The Griesbach Hypothesis: The Phenomenon of Order', *ETL* 58 (1982), pp. 111-22. The papers from the San Antonio meeting were published in W.O. Walker (ed.), *The Relationships among the Gospels* (San Antonio, 1978). Finally, some of the papers from the Cambridge Griesbach conference are included in W.R. Farmer (ed.), *New Synoptic Studies* (Macon, 1983).

Participants at the conferences were as follows:

Dr P.S. Alexander	Manchester
Revd F.G. Downing[2]	Manchester
Dr J. Drury[1]	Cambridge
Professor D.L. Dungan	Knoxville, Tennessee
Professor W.R. Farmer[2]	Dallas, Texas
Canon J.C. Fenton	Oxford
Dr R.T. France[1]	London
Professor S. Freyne[1]	Dublin
Revd H.B. Green	Mirfield
Professor S.G. Hall[1]	London
Revd A. Hodgetts[1]	Canterbury
Professor G.D. Kilpatrick[2]	Oxford
Professor Barnabas Lindars SSF[1]	Manchester
Professor J. Mackey[1]	Edinburgh
Dr A. Meredith SJ[1]	Oxford
Revd G. Murray OSB	Downside
Revd J.B. Orchard OSB	Ealing
Revd H. Riley	London
Dr C.M. Tuckett	Manchester
Revd H. Wansborough OSB	Ampleforth
Revd J. Wenham	Oxford

1. Present at the 1982 meeting only.
2. Present at the 1983 meeting only.

MIDRASH AND THE GOSPELS*

Philip S. Alexander

Department of Near Eastern Studies,
The University of Manchester, Manchester M13 9PL, England

Since the pioneering work of Renée Bloch and Geza Vermes, the importance of early Jewish Bible exegesis for the understanding of Christian origins has been widely recognized by New Testament scholars. The term 'midrash' now occupies a secure place in the vocabulary of New Testament scholarship, and is constantly being invoked to categorize and explain a variety of New Testament phenomena. Attention to the Jewish milieu of early Christianity is, of course, always laudable, but a survey of recent contributions to New Testament studies has forced me to conclude that the nature and function of midrash is often misunderstood by New Testament scholars, and as a result the term midrash is tending to generate more confusion than light. I suspect the reason for this misunderstanding is rather simple: New Testament scholars have had insufficient exposure to midrash itself; they have not spent enough time wrestling with midrashic texts. Their knowledge is largely secondhand, being derived from the general discussions in the handbooks and introductions. My purpose in the present paper is twofold. First, I shall make yet another attempt to define midrash. In my definition I shall stress those aspects of the phenomenon which I feel are being widely ignored. Second, I shall consider the relevance of the idea of midrash to one area of New Testament studies, viz. Gospel criticism, and in particular give my reactions to Michael Goulder's elaborately argued thesis that midrash holds the key to the Synoptic problem.

Most New Testament scholars who offer a definition of midrash begin by defining the word 'midrash' itself. Thus Raymond Brown: 'In Biblical Hebrew the verb *darash* means to "seek, inquire, investigate, study"; and according to the pattern of the Hebrew noun formation *midrash* should designate the product of such study or investigation'. More colourfully, Michael Goulder: 'The word midrash derives from *darash*, to probe or examine. Revelation is a bottomless mine of wealth: no pious man can be content to take what merely lies on the surface—he must *darash*, dig and bring up treasure. There are seventy faces to scripture: we must *darash*, examine it, and find it revealed from glory to glory.'[1] I find this a most unpromising place to start. It leads to vague talk about 'midrash in general'; it smacks of the etymological fallacy; and it tends to open the way for anachronistic explanations of the rare, pre-Rabbinic occurrences of the word midrash. The fact is that, if, as we should, we play down etymology and insist on contextual definition, then we can have little idea of the meaning of the term midrash in Chronicles, Sirach and the Dead Sea Scrolls.[2] The correct procedure in the definition of midrash should be to isolate a corpus of midrashic texts; to examine those texts in order to discover their characteristics; and then to consider the question of whether there are texts outside the corpus which possess the same features.

In establishing a corpus of midrash on which to base our investigation, priority should be given to early Rabbinic literature. This seems to me inevitable. Midrash as a technical term in modern scholarship was borrowed from Rabbinics, having been first applied to Rabbinic literature. Rabbinic midrash is entirely suitable for our purposes: it is very extensive, and we can avail ourselves of an unbroken tradition of Jewish scholarship on it extending from the middle ages down to the present day. So then, the definition of midrash which I shall offer is based on a knowledge of such early Rabbinic texts as the Mekhilta of Rabbi Ishmael, Sifre, Sifra, Bere'shit Rabbah, Tanhuma, Pesikta Rabbati and Pesikta deRav Kahana. This is hardly a controversial procedure. We may disagree over whether or not we should call Philo's Bible commentaries or the Qumran *Pesharim* 'midrash', but we will surely not quarrel over calling the texts which I have just listed 'midrash'.

It is necessary to make a distinction between midrashic form and midrashic method. Texts such as Bere'shit Rabbah are in midrashic form and exemplify midrashic method. There are, however, other texts which exemplify midrashic method but do not have midrashic form. The Aramaic Targumim are the most obvious example of this latter category. It would strike me as odd to deny that the Targumim are in some sense midrash. On this point I am in agreement with Le Déaut and others who would classify them as such. On the other hand I am not happy, as some seem to be, to dismiss form as of minor significance in the definition of midrash.[3] In my view it is vitally important. Midrashic form is a very real thing, which was clearly recognized by the early scholars. This fact may be brought out by comparison with the Targum. Targum is thoroughly midrashic both in content and method, but formally it belongs to the category of translation. The *meturgemanim* go to great lengths to preserve this illusion. Often the material in the Targum runs exactly parallel to that in midrashim like Bere'shit Rabbah, but it is presented in a very different way. Even at their most expansive the *meturgemanim* do not cite Rabbinic authorities by name, or quote Scripture. (There are, to be sure, very occasional lapses, but they are the exceptions which prove the rule.) Clearly both the *darshan* and the *meturgeman* were working to certain pre-set guidelines as to the literary form of their works. The importance of midrashic form lies in the fact that it provides us with our best chance for narrowing the definition of midrash, an aim which I would regard as crucial in the present state of debate. For the moment I would suggest a simple ranking of texts: those which display *both* midrashic form *and* midrashic method are midrashim in the fullest sense of the term; those which display only midrashic method are midrash only in a qualified, limited sense.

1. *Midrashic Form.* The basic literary form of midrash is BIBLICAL LEMMA + COMMENTARY. The lemma may come from a continuous section of Scripture, such as the book of Genesis (cf. Bere'shit Rabbah), or it may be from a catena of Scriptural passages, such as the festival lectionary (cf. Pesikta deRav Kahana). The lemma identifies the segment of Scripture under discussion and 'keys in' the commentary to Scripture. If we ignore the use of *ve-khulleh* and *ve-gomer* (= etc.) at the end of abbreviated lemmata, then as a rule lemma and commentary are not visually or functionally separated. There is a formal contrast here with the Qumran *Pesharim* which quote the Biblical text in full (as against its frequent curtailment in midrash), and use the formulae *pesher ha-davar* and *pishro* as 'spacers' to demarcate lemma and comment.[4] In practical terms, however, there is no danger of confusing Scripture and commentary in Rabbinic midrash, and it would be a very serious mistake to imagine that Rabbinic midrash 'dissolves' Scripture in the commentary in the way in which Jubilees carries Genesis 'in solution'.

The commentary reveals the following formal features:

(i) It quotes freely verses of Scripture as proof-texts, introduced by standard citation-formulae, the most common of which in the Tannaitic period was *she-ne'emar*.

(ii) The *darshan* is particularly fond of stringing Biblical verses together, and in general he is an expert in 'Listenwissenschaft'.

(iii) He quotes named authorities—Rabbi Ishmael, Rabbi Akiva, Rabbi Joshua, and so on.

(iv) He cites different and sometimes contradictory interpretations of the same verse, word, or phrase, often introduced by the formula *davar aher*—'another interpretation'.

(v) He commonly employs *meshalim* ('parables'), especially to resolve theological problems. These are commonly introduced by the formula, *mashal le-mah ha-davar domeh*—'A parable. To what may the thing be likened?'

Is this set of characteristics sufficient to set off midrash from the other Rabbinic literary genres? On the whole I think that it is. Certainly it serves to differentiate midrash from Targum, as I hinted earlier, and from Mishnah, though some of the features listed may be found in both these genres. Comparison with Mishnah is instructive. Mishnah lacks the form of Biblical lemma + commentary which is essential to midrash. Mishnah does indeed presuppose Scripture, but the systems which it develops are more or less free-standing, and not closely keyed in to the Biblical text. Conversely, the standard Mishnaic formulae are absent from midrash. Midrashic style is certainly clipped and formulaic, but it is much looser and closer to everyday speech than that of the Mishnah. It is more problematic whether we can differentiate midrash and Gemara (the commentary on the Mishnah in the Talmuds) on the basis of the formal characteristics which I have listed.[5] This fact rather disturbs me, for I sense that there are (or ought to be) some differences. The formal similarities between midrash and Gemara are, unquestionably, very strong, and this fact at once suggests some reflections. It may indicate the elevation of the Mishnah to the status of a canonic text. On the other hand it may be a timely warning that—contrary to the view which I shall advance presently—midrash does not necessarily presuppose a very high view of Scripture, nor did the *darshanim* necessarily regard the text or language of Scripture as unique. Midrash is a species of interpretation, and we must remember that the canons of criticism, interpretation and philology in the ancient world were not the same as our own. It is possible that the Rabbis would have interpreted *any* authoritative text in broadly the same way as they treated Scripture. Certainly many of their methods were common to scholarship in late antiquity and can be paralleled in the exegetical practice of the Greek schools.

2. *Midrashic Method*. Defining midrashic method is much more difficult than defining midrashic form. The character of midrash is determined by the fact that it is an activity related to Torah, and so to understand midrash it is essential to consider the nature and function of Torah in the Rabbinic scheme of things. According to classic Rabbinic theology—and I must stress that what I am about to assert becomes explicit only in comparatively late sources—Moses received the Torah on Sinai in two forms, as Written Torah (*Torah she-bikhtav*) and as Oral Torah (*Torah she-be'al peh*).[6] The former is embodied in Scripture, the latter in Tradition. The effect of this doctrine is to enrich and complicate the concept of Torah by absorbing Tradition into it. Torah is not simply co-extensive with the Five Books of Moses, or with Scripture as a whole: Torah = Scripture + Tradition. By classifying their traditions as Oral Torah, and by tracing them back to the same revelatory event which gave birth to the Written Torah, the Rabbis were giving divine sanction to the extensive body of laws, customs and teachings which they had received from their predecessors. In no uncertain way they were raising Tradition to the same status as Holy Writ. They were not suggesting that the whole of the Tradition had been transmitted orally unchanged from Moses down to their own day. They were perfectly aware of the fact that much of the tradition had come into being long after Moses' time. What they were implying was that the principles and dominant ideas of the tradition could be traced back to Moses. To put it another way: only those belonging to the circles of the Sages and scholars who stand in a direct line of succession leading back to Moses himself can be regarded as the recipients of authentic tradition; no one else qualifies. The Rabbis sought to justify this claim historically by tracing the line of tradents through whom the Oral Law had come down from Moses to themselves. The most famous of these Chains of Tradition is, of course, contained in Pirkei Avot, ch. 1, where it may be intended to provide validation for the Mishnah as a whole.

For the Rabbis, then, Torah was to be found in two places—in Scripture and in Tradition. As we shall see, this notion has certain important advantages over asserting that Torah resides only in

Scripture, but it also has an obvious drawback: it endangers the unity of revelation. Somehow a way had to be found of meshing Scripture and Tradition which would make them in a sense one, while at the same time preserving their individual identity. The Rabbis achieved this by presenting Tradition in the form of midrash on Scripture. By so doing they were implying that Scripture has priority over Tradition. It is important to understand correctly the nature of this priority. It was not really a priority in time, since both Scripture and Tradition were supposed to have originated at Sinai; nor was it in the last analysis a priority in authority, since both Scripture and Tradition were Torah. The priority was logical or symbolic: formally at least it was Tradition that was brought into relationship with Scripture, and not vice versa. Tradition was reduced to the condition of commentary on Scripture. In Judaism the Written Torah is not merely a source of law or doctrine: it also functions as a symbolic centre, it is the 'still point' at the heart of the Judaic universe. New ideas and developments within Judaism have to be legitimated by being brought into relationship with Scripture: it must be shown that they are somewhere present in Scripture.

At first sight this condition imposes severe restraints on the development of Judaism, it limits its options for change. In practice, however, the only limiting factor has proved to be the ingenuity of the interpreter, and as the history of midrash shows, ingenuity has not been lacking. Scripture has been forced to receive some astonishingly alien notions. In some types of midrash it is reduced almost to a system of arbitary signs and symbols to be manipulated by the exegete at will. So although at a formal, superficial level it is Tradition that is accommodated to Scripture, at a deeper level Scripture is accommodated to Tradition. Midrash becomes the means whereby Scripture can be made over in the image of the Tradition. The great advantage of the doctrine of the two Torahs is that it allows the Rabbis to ascribe to Torah two vitally important but contradictory attributes—immutability and change. In its written form Torah is fixed, unchanging, inviolable: it constitutes an absolutely bounded and defined canon of Holy Writ. In its oral form Torah is open-ended, undefined, continually evolving: it is responsive to life. Midrash is the link between the two; it is the flexible joint which keeps the Oral and the Written Torah in constant alignment. It enables the sacred text to be brought to bear upon and made relevant to changing historical circumstances. It allows the Bible to be brought up to date, without having to resort to the dangerous expedient of endlessly re-writing and altering the Biblical text itself.

So then, a major aim—perhaps one might say *the* major aim—of the *darshan* was to find ways of convincingly validating Tradition in terms of Scripture. He had other aims as well, related specifically to his view of the nature of the Written Torah. Scripture contained God's supremely authoritive revelation to Israel: above all other texts, therefore, it was worthy of study and meditation. Its teachings had to be searched out, explained, and applied to the heart and conscience of the Jew. It was divine utterance, and its content had originated in the mind of God. It was, in consequence, not like other texts. The *darshan* was continually looking for evidence of Scripture's unique character, and trying to draw out its glory and beauty. From his belief in the divine origin of Scripture the *darshan* made three important deductions. First, the text of Scripture is totally coherent and self-consistent. This meant that any one part of Scripture may be interpreted in the light of any other part and harmonized with it. Contradictions in Scripture can only be apparent, not real. The *darshanim* spend much time weaving together diverse Scriptures, and reconciling Scripture with Scripture. Second, the text of Scripture is polyvalent. It contains different levels and layers of meaning. It is not a question of finding the one, true, original meaning of Scripture: Scripture can mean several—sometimes seemingly contradictory—things at once. The *darshan* attempts to draw out its various meanings. In a very real sense he considers that all truth is present in it: it is simply a matter of finding out where it lies hidden. Third, Scripture is inerrant. It is the *darshan*'s business to explain away any apparent errors of fact.

From a detached, purely descriptive point of view, the *darshan*'s task may be seen as two-fold, as both *ex*egetical and *eis*egetical: it involves both drawing out the meaning implicit in Scripture, and reading meaning into Scripture. There is some evidence to suggest that the early Jewish commentators were not unaware of this distinction, but in general they give the impression that they are merely drawing out what is objectively present in Scripture. In practice it is difficult, if not impossible, to separate exegesis and eisegesis, since both processes are often going on simultaneously in the same act of interpretation. The *darshanim* are adept at exploiting real problems in the text as a way of reading their own ideas into Scripture. In any given instance it will probably be impossible to say whether the interpretation was suggested simply by meditation on Scripture, or devised deliberately as a way of attaching certain ideas to Scripture. The *darshanim* are so ingenious at finding points of contact for Tradition in Scripture, and argue their case with such verve and conviction, that it is very easy to suppose that their whole interpretation has simply emerged from pious meditation on Scripture. My strong suspicion is, however, that, despite appearances, the dynamo which drives midrash forward is located not in pure and disinterested meditation on Scripture, but in the need to validate the Tradition.

Perhaps I can give some substance to these remarks by citing the example of how Rashi handles the story of Creation in Genesis 1–2. Rashi is, of course, far removed in time from the period with which we are concerned, but at this point he is typical, I believe, of the earlier scholars, and the illustration is so neat that I find it hard to resist. Even a casual reader of Genesis 1–2 must be struck by the fact that there appear to be *two* accounts of Creation—one in Gen. 1.1–2.3, the other in Gen. 2.4-25. A more attentive reader may also note that there is a variation in the divine names corresponding to these two accounts: the first uses *Elohim*, the second *YHWH Elohim*. Modern Bible scholars, of course, explain these facts by means of the documentary hypothesis: Genesis 1–2 combines two originally distinct sources (P and J-E). Rashi equally notes the facts, but his assumptions about the nature of Scripture will not allow him to reach the same conclusions as the modern scholar. He starts from an early Rabbinic idea that there is a correlation between the divine name *Elohim* and God's attribute of justice, and between the name *YHWH* and his attribute of mercy.[7] He argues that God first intended to create the world on the basis of strict justice, but realizing that if he were to do so the world could not endure, he decided to temper justice with mercy, and, indeed, since the name *YHWH* in the second account of Creation precedes *Elohim*, to give mercy precedence over justice:

> *God (Elohim) created* (Gen. 1:1). The text does not say 'The Lord (*YHWH*) created', because at first God intended to create the world on the principle of strict justice, but he saw that if he were to do so the world could not endure, and so he gave precedence to the principle of mercy and joined it to that of justice, and this is why it is written, 'In the day that the Lord God (*YHWH Elohim*) made earth and heaven' (Gen. 2:4).

In that Rashi observes and tries to explain the problem of the two accounts and the variation of the divine names he is behaving as a true exegete. Any interpreter, whether ancient or modern, should tackle this problem. But the objective problem offers him the opportunity of reading into the text certain Rabbinic ideas about the tension between the divine attributes of mercy and justice which can hardly have been in the mind of the original redactor of the Pentateuch.

So far I have spoken of the function of midrash, and its aims. What now of the means by which it achieves its aims? The *darshanim* had at their disposal a whole array of techniques—Scripture could be interpreted by Scripture, word-play exploited, names etymologized, and even the numerical value of words and phrases computed (a device known as *gematria*). It is not possible to list and discuss all their methods here, and, indeed, it is less important to do so than we might at first suppose, because the individual exegetical techniques are less decisive in the definition of midrash than the general manner in which the interpretation is presented. I must stress that the so-called 7 *middot* (hermeneutical rules) of Hillel, the 13 of Ishmael, and the 32 of Eliezer ben Yose Ha-Gelili do *not*, as many suppose, provide a ready-made answer to the question of the methods of the *darshanim*. These obscure lists are beset by a host of historical and literary problems, and suffer from the fundamental drawback that they do not correspond all that closely to the actual practice of the *darshanim*. If midrash is a game and the various lists of *middot* are the rules, then it must be said that the rule-books bear little relationship to the game as actually played.[8] As with cricket or baseball, the rules of the 'game' of midrash are better grasped by watching the experts playing it, than by studying the rule-books.

In concluding this attempt to define midrash I shall highlight four general characteristics of early Rabbinic Bible exegesis.

First, midrash is in no sense a substitute for Scripture, or a re-writing of it. Scripture remains intact and it is presupposed that the reader will have it in front of him, or have it in his mind, as he reads the midrash. This is obviously true of midrashim such as Bere'shit Rabbah, or the Mekhilta of Rabbi Ishmael, but it is sometimes forgotten that it is equally true of the Targum. The actual liturgical setting of the Targum is important. Targum was recited in synagogue in conjunction with the reading of the Scriptures in their original Hebrew. Each verse of the Hebrew lesson was followed directly by the Targum in Aramaic till the end of the lesson was reached. The

Rabbinic rules for the delivery of the Targum in synagogue graphically illustrate the practical implications of the Rabbinic doctrine of the two Torahs. On the one hand Targum (which as interpretation lies on the side of Oral Law) is brought into the closest proximity to the text of Scripture; on the other hand every effort is made to prevent it from being confused with Scripture. Scripture was in Hebrew, the Targum was in Aramaic; Scripture was *read* from a scroll, the Targum was *recited* from memory; the Scripture reader could not at the same time deliver the Targum, nor vice versa, but two different people had to perform the two different functions.[9] Midrash, then, is laid side by side with Scripture. It has no independent life of its own.

Second, midrash is argumentative. On the whole it does not lay down the law or offer cut-and-dried statements. It frequently sets out a number of different opinions and debates their merits. In midrash the bones of the exegetical reasoning show through. This feature marks off Rabbinic midrash from other strands of early Jewish Bible interpretation (e.g. Qumran *Pesher*) in which the exegetical logic is often far from clear. Midrash as a style of exegesis is particularly useful to the modern scholar simply because it does not leave him in the dark as to how its conclusions were reached: it takes him step by step through the argument. New Testament scholars sometimes speak of 'crypto-midrash'.[10] If by this they mean that, contrary to appearances, a given text is an interpretation of some *unquoted* verse of Scripture, or that some piece of Bible exegesis depends, in fact, on an *unquoted* Biblical verse, then the notion is decidedly odd in the context of Rabbinic midrash. I cannot believe that the Rabbis would have seen any advantage in this sort of obliqueness and subtlety. They strove to make things as explicit as possible.

Third, midrash normally has a point of contact, a 'peg' in the text on which it hangs. It is a disciplined pursuit, not a fantasia on the text of Scripture. The game of midrash is demanding, its rules complex and strict. That the *darshanim* achieved such varied and exuberant results does not mean that they were not under restraint; rather it shows their immense skill and ingenuity in trancending the difficult conditions in which they chose to play. Certain New Testament scholars who believe that the infancy narratives in Luke are loosely modelled on Old Testament stories such as the birth of Samuel, apparently want to call such free adaptation of Bible midrash.[11] I am convinced they are mistaken, for in so doing they seem to be denying the tightly controlled and closely argued character of midrash. Some imaginative borrowings from Old Testament may, perhaps, be found in certain folkloristic *aggadot*, but it gets us nowhere to label this phenomenon 'midrash'.[12]

Finally, it is evident that the *darshanim* felt they were working within a very definite, on-going tradition of scholarship. They seemed to regard themselves primarily as the transmitters of the tradition. In passing on the traditions which they received, of course, they modified and 'improved' them, but such modifications are often external and intended, with the minimum of change, to adapt the tradition to its new context. They did not set any great store by originality: they took from others whatever they wanted (usually without acknowledgment) and adapted it as they saw fit. They sank their individuality and adopted a general, anonymous midrashic style. I doubt very much whether it is possible to identify the individual approach or style of a single early Rabbinic exegete.[13] The *darshanim* were engaged in a collective enterprise: they lent generously, borrowed freely, and lived with their hands in each other's pockets.

This must suffice for my brief definition of midrash. In the light of this definition is it possible to identify midrash outside Rabbinic literature? I am inclined to say, No: midrash is best confined to early Rabbinic Bible exegesis. The differences which I perceive between the Rabbinic and the non-Rabbinic texts are more important than their similarities. I am not, of course, denying that other Jewish scholars besides the Rabbis expounded Scripture, or that their exegetical methods, if not their literary forms, are sometimes similar to those of the Rabbis. But to call these other, non-Rabbinic interpretations of the Bible midrash is, to my mind, highly tendentious. A rather similar problem arises with regard to the term *halakhah*. Other early Jewish groups, as well as the Rabbis, interpreted and codified the law—one thinks immediately of the section on Sabbath law in the Damascus Document—but to talk of *halakhah* at Qumran, or in any of the other non-Rabbinic traditions, raises a host of misleading and question-begging associations. *Halakhah* is a distinctively Rabbinic phenomenon. So I am not impressed when I see scholars lumping together as 'midrash' texts as diverse as Chronicles, the Testaments of the XII Patriarchs, Enoch, Jubilees, Philo, Josephus, the LXX and the Targumim, the Qumran *Pesharim*, the Genesis Apocryphon, and the Mekhilta of Rabbi Ishmael. The only effect of such total lack of discrimination is to evacuate midrash of any real meaning: midrash becomes simply a fancy word for 'Bible interpretation'.

Such an indiscriminate use of the term is not entirely innocuous: it involves a bit of a 'swindle'. Labelling a piece of Bible exegesis 'midrash' appears to set it in a definite historical and cultural context, to hint at well-known, technical parallels. But all this may be entirely bogus. If our definition of midrash becomes too attenuated, then in using the term we may not, in fact, be saying anything new: we may simply be telling the reader that what lies before him is a specimen of early Jewish Bible interpretation—which may be crashingly self-evident! If midrash means no more than 'Bible interpretation', then it would be advisable to drop the term. And if we insist on using it so broadly then we shall have to consider subdividing the category, and speaking of Rabbinic midrash, Qumranic midrash, Philonic midrash, apocalyptic midrash and so on. The study of the subject can only be advanced through refinement. I certainly perceive important differences between Rabbinic Bible exegesis and that of Philo, or of the Dead Sea Sect. The way forward lies in trying to define these distinctive styles of Bible interpretation, rather than in treating them as an undifferentiated mass.

Having now outlined my position on the nature and function of midrash, I turn in the concluding part of this paper to consider the relevance of midrash to Gospel criticism. Midrash has been invoked in two quite different ways in the study of the Gospels. First, it has been used to illustrate the general approach of the Gospel writers to the Old Testament, or to elucidate the specific content of their Bible exegesis. This is an eminently sensible and uncontroversial procedure, especially if the Rabbinic texts are introduced, not to demonstrate 'borrowings' or 'influences', but to act as a foil to bring out the character of early Christian exegesis. Such a simple, heuristic use of the Rabbinic material skirts neatly round all the complex problems of the relative dating of the Rabbinic and early Christian sources.[14]

Second, midrash has become an issue in the study of the synoptic problem. The main advocate of its relevance there is Michael Goulder, who has argued the case at length and ingeniously in *Midrash and Lection in the Gospel of Matthew*. As I understand it, Goulder's thesis can be stated quite simply. The Gospel of Matthew is basically a midrash on the Gospel of Mark: Matthew took Mark and reworked him in a midrashic manner. If we discount some minor traditions which he may have independently received, then the only

Gospel material which we need suppose lay before Matthew was a copy of Mark: we can dispense with Q and all other hypothetical non-Markan sources. As a provincial scribe Matthew would have been well acquainted with midrashic method, and so his use of it would be perfectly natural and need cause us no surprise.

This appeal to midrash I find highly questionable. I think it should be very clear that the relationship between Matthew and Mark which Goulder envisages does not fall easily into the category of midrash as I defined it earlier, either in respect of form, or of method. I would identify three main areas of difficulty in Goulder's theory.

1. If Matthew is a midrash on Mark, then his attitude to the authority of Mark is surely puzzling. Midrash is normally performed on a canonic text. Did, then, Matthew regard Mark as canonic, as having the status of Holy Writ? Goulder seems to think that he did but he offers no real proof of this important premiss. He points to the fact that Matthew incorporates most of Mark into his own Gospel as evidence of his *respect* for Mark, but Matthew also freely changes Mark, and this could just as plausibly be seen as evidence of his disrespect: Mark is deficient—he needs improving! As I argued earlier, midrash was meant to stand *beside* Scripture: it left Scripture intact. In fact this was true not only of Rabbinic midrash, but of other forms of early Jewish Bible-exegesis as well: the Qumran *Pesharim* were laid side by side with Scripture, and even such works as the Genesis Apocryphon, Jubilees and Pseudo-Philo's *Biblical Antiquities*, which extensively incorporate and rewrite Scripture, were surely not meant to replace Scripture. All these works were composed at a time when the canon of Torah was firmly established and no longer a matter of dispute among the sects of Judaism. They were no more intended as a 'second edition' of Torah than Josephus's retelling of the Biblical story in his *Antiquities*. Are we to suppose, then, that Matthew wanted his Gospel to be read alongside Mark? Surely not. It is much more likely that he aimed to replace Mark. He has done his best to make the original Mark redundant. He has taken over into his own text whatever he thought was 'good' and 'useful', and added to it his own 'improvements', but he has woven together his Markan and non-Markan materials so smoothly that it is only by diligent use of a modern critical *Synopsis* such as Aland or Huck, and detailed comparison with the original Mark, that the Matthean plusses can be separated from the basic Markan source. Matthew had no desire to leave Mark an independent identity.

2. Goulder seems keen to show that Matthew himself is responsible for the greater part of his additions to Mark: his plusses are not based on independent tradition, he simply made them up. He appears to be under the impression that midrash provides him with a clear-cut model for such creative rewriting of a source, but this is not the case: he is ignoring the disciplined, rule-bound character of midrash which we noted earlier. To be sure, midrash is creative. Each *derashah* must have originated somewhere, in that someone must have thought of it for the first time; and since the midrashim contain many hundreds of individual *derashot*, it is fair to say that the tradition as a whole is intensely creative. But we must not ignore the countervalent conservative tendency of midrash: the *darshanim* received and passed on many interpretations which were not their own. Moreover, it is probably true to say that the role of the final editor of a collection of *derashot* was unlikely to be creative: his activity would have been confined mainly to collecting the material and accommodating it (often superficially) to its place within the collection. Goulder may or may not be right in arguing that Matthew invented his non-Marken material, but he is certainly wrong to suppose that such a conclusion automatically follows from his categorization of Matthew as a midrash on Mark. As a *darshan* Matthew could well have made up the non-Markan material, but it would be equally possible that he drew on independent tradition. Midrash as a genre is neutral on this point. And if the Gospel of Matthew is to be characterized as a collection of *derashot*, then Goulder is attributing to its final editor, Matthew, a degree of originality which cannot be easily paralleled in the Rabbinic midrashim.

3. Finally, the way Goulder 'homes in' on midrash as a model for the relationship between Matthew and Mark, to the neglect of other, more obvious Rabbinic parallels, strikes me as highly arbitrary. Rabbinic literature has also a synoptic problem. This exists at the level of short, individual *aggadot* (cf. the four versions of Rabbi Eleazar's Merkavah sermon[15]), and at the level of extensive 'literary' compositions (cf. the problem of the relationship between Mishnah and Tosefta, between the Gemarot of the Bavli and the Yerushalmi, between the various recensions of the Palestinian Targum[16]). Why does Goulder say nothing about the Rabbinic synoptic problem? Since most of Matthew's 'alterations' of Mark can be paralleled just as easily in the synoptic Rabbinic texts as in midrash, it is surely fair to ask him why he talks only about midrash. Perhaps he will now tell

us that the *Rabbinic* synoptic problem can be solved by an appeal to midrash! A case for this might just be made out, but it would be a very desperate one and would carry little conviction. There is a host of questions regarding the Rabbinic material which Goulder has simply not considered. Since his conclusions do not rest on a survey of all the relevant evidence, they are bound to be questionable. Bringing in this other Rabbinic material does not, alas, take us any closer to a solution of the synoptic problem, since the Rabbinic texts are bedevilled by exactly the same difficulties as have proved so intractable in the study of the Gospels. The only effect of introducing all these fresh parallels is to re-affirm the complexity of the problem. And so we find ourselves right back where we started, before Goulder's misguided attempt to cut through the Gordian knot by invoking the concept of midrash.

NOTES

*This paper originally included a preamble in which I drew attention to what I believe are common errors and misapprehensions in the use of Rabbinic sources by New Testament scholars. A number of colleagues urged me to publish these methodological observations separately. They have now appeared under the title 'Rabbinic Judaism and the New Testament' in ZNW 74 (1983), pp. 237-46.

1. Raymond Brown, *The Birth of the Messiah* (New York, 1977), p. 557; Michael Goulder, *Midrash and Lection in Matthew* (London, 1974), p. 28.

2. The pre-Rabbinic occurrences of the term midrash are: 2 Chron. 13.22; 24.27; Sirach 51.23; 1QS VI.23; VIII.15, 26; CD XX.6; 4QFlor I.14.

3. I feel that Le Déaut rather underplays the significance of literary form in his valuable article, 'A propos d'une définition du midrash', *Biblica* 50 (1969), pp. 395-413, in which he reviews at length A.G. Wright, *The Literary Genre Midrash* (New York, 1967). I would defend Wright's emphasis on form. However, he in turn underplays the significance of midrashic *method*, and in general his knowledge of Rabbinic literature is not all that sound. The bibliography on midrash is now enormous. The basic references may be culled from Gary Porten, 'Midrash: Palestinian Jews and the Hebrew Bible in the Greco-Roman Period', in H. Temporini and W. Haase (eds.), *Aufstieg und Niedergang der Römischen Welt*, II, Principat 19.2 (Berlin/New York, 1979), pp. 103-38. If I were asked to name only one study of the subject, then it would be Geza Vermes's brilliant essay, 'Bible and Midrash: Early Old Testament Exegesis', in P.R. Ackroyd and C.F. Evans (eds.), *The Cambridge History of the Bible*, I (Cambridge, 1970), pp. 199-232; reprinted in Vermes,

Post-Biblical Jewish Studies (Leiden, 1975), pp. 59-91. See also J. Neusner, *Midrash in Context* (Philadelphia, 1983).

4. One might compare the function of *pesher ha-davar* and *pishro* as 'spacers' between the text of Scripture and the comment with the use of 'and now' or 'now' (*ukhe'enet/ke'an*, etc.) in Aramaic letters to mark the transition from the opening to the body of the letter. See P.S. Alexander, 'Remarks on Aramaic Epistolography in the Persian Period', *JSS* 23 (1978), p. 164.

5. B.M. Bokser makes important observations on the character of Gemara as commentary on Mishnah in his two studies, *Samuel's Commentary on the Mishnah: its Nature, Forms and Content* (Leiden, 1975); *Post-Mishnaic Judaism in Transition: Samuel on Berakhot and the Beginnings of Gemara*, (Chico, 1980).

6. E.E. Urbach, *The Sages* (Jerusalem, 1975), I, pp. 286-314, gives a useful synthesis of early Rabbinic ideas about the Oral Torah. However, I feel he pre-dates the full blown doctrine of the two Torahs by a considerable margin. See further the Introduction to my sourcebook *Judaism* in the series Textual Sources for the Study of Religion, ed. J.R. Hinnells (Manchester University Press, 1984). In this work will be found representative specimens of midrash, and concrete examples of the Rabbinic hermeneutical *middot*, on which see below (esp. note 8).

7. See G.F. Moore, *Judaism* (Cambridge, Mass., 1927), I, p. 387; P.S. Alexander, 'The Targumim and Early Exegesis of the "Sons of God" in Genesis 6', *JJS* 23 (1972), pp. 65-66.

8. In Ishmael's list rules 5-11, dealing with the various possible relationships between general (*kelal*) and specific (*perat*) terms, appear to be an exercise in formal logic. They are not easy to instantiate from actual midrashic literature. On the literary and historical problems of the various lists of *middot* see my article 'Rabbinic Judaism and the New Testament', *ZNW* 74 (1983), pp. 242-44.

9. Unfortunately the standard introductions to the Targum do not say much about these rules. They are brilliantly summarized by Maimonides in his *Mishneh Torah*: see *Hilkhot Tefillah* XII.10-14. For an analysis of the rules see P.S. Alexander, 'The Rabbinic Lists of Forbidden Targumim', *JSS* 27 (1976), pp. 177-91; Alexander, 'The Targumim and the Rabbinic Rules for the Delivery of the Targum', *Supplements to Vetus Testamentum: Salamanca (1983) Congress Volume* (forthcoming).

10. I am not sure who first started this 'hare' running. It may have been the Jewish scholar Meir Gertner in his article, 'Midrashim in the New Testament', *JSS* 7 (1962), pp. 267-92. Gertner speaks of 'covert' or 'invisible' midrashim in the New Testament. He does not, however, provide convincing examples of this supposed phenomenon in Rabbinic texts. One sometimes finds *piyyut* cited as a Rabbinic example of highly allusive, or even 'crypto', midrash. However, there may be special reasons for the obliqueness of

piyyut, and it should be borne in mind that *piyyut* is bound to the Torah lectionary and has a liturgical setting. In that setting the Scripture to which it relates is clearly present.

11. See e.g. John Drury, *Tradition and Design in Luke's Gospel* (London, 1976), pp. 46-66.

12. It is often forgotten that not all *aggadah* is midrash. There is a vast body of Rabbinic tradition, much of it collected in Ginzberg's *Legends of the Jews*, which bears little or no relation to the Biblical text, even though it is about Biblical personages and events: it is 'lifted off' from the Bible, has its own, independent life, and develops with its own inner logic, which is *not* midrashic. In its nature and development it is akin to the hagiographical tales about the great Sages, such as Akiva and Yohanan ben Zakkai. There is much to be said for the view that folklore studies provide the key to the evolution of this non-midrashic *aggadah*. See Dan Ben-Amos, *Narrative Forms in the Haggadah: Structural Analysis*, Ph.D. Dissertation, Indiana University, 1966; J. Heinemann and D. Noy (eds.), *Studies in Aggadah and Folk-Literature = Scripta Hierosolymitana* 22 (1971), especially Z. Kagan's article, 'Divergent Tendencies and their Literary Moulding in the Aggadah', on pp. 151-70 of this volume. The body of non-midrashic *aggadah* can function in a manner similar to the body of non-Biblical religious custom. The *darshanim* can take elements from it and try to read them back midrashically into Scripture.

13. I am well aware that there have been attempts to establish the existence of different schools of midrash, most notably the rival schools of Ishmael and Akiva. The idea of the contrasting approaches of Ishmael and Akiva has dominated the history of early midrash, but I am not sure it is all that well founded. Its accuracy has been rightly questioned by Gary Porten, *The Traditions of Rabbi Ishmael II* (Leiden, 1977), pp. 2-7. On the general style of Rabbinic literature Neusner's judgment is pertinent: 'I postulate that we deal with a "collective literature", which, while perhaps in many elements beginning with a single author, was publicly transmitted, and rapidly made the property of the community of the schools. Whatever the role of individuals, it was rapidly obliterated and therefore does not matter. This seems to me important, for it must mean that the literary requirements of the materials before us are different from those of poetry or narrative such as are attributed to individual Jewish writers of antiquity. The impact on style is clear: nothing could be idiosyncratic, in the end relying upon the taste, judgment or sensibility of a single man. Everything had to be acceptable to the wider circle of authorities. This must mean that conventionality takes precedence over style, formulaic routine over unusual expression, the public consensus over the private insight' (*The Rabbinic Traditions about the Pharisees before 70* [Leiden, 1971], III, p. 3).

14. I must, however, repeat my protest against the notion of 'crypto-midrash'. The idea that an unspoken midrashic relationship exists between

some passage in the Gospels and an unquoted verse of Old Testament is not, to my mind, either 'sensible' or 'uncontroversial'. See further footnote 10 above.

15. M.Hagigah 2.1; Mekhilta of Rabbi Simeon ben Yohai, *Mishpatim* 21.1; TB Hagigah 14b; PT Hagigah II, 77a. On this see my article 'Rabbinic Biography and the Biography of Jesus', printed elsewhere in this volume.

16. D.J. Halperin, *The Merkabah in Rabbinic Literature* (New Haven, 1980), provides a detailed synoptic analysis of a fairly extensive piece of Gemara.

RABBINIC BIOGRAPHY AND THE BIOGRAPHY OF JESUS: A SURVEY OF THE EVIDENCE

Philip S. Alexander

Department of Near Eastern Studies, The University of Manchester
Manchester M13 9PL, England

I. *Introduction*

Three brief comments will suffice to set the present paper in context.

First, my purpose in this study is unashamedly descriptive and didactic. I shall try to survey the contents and problems of the Rabbinic biographical tradition and effectively leave it to the Gospel critic to draw his own conclusions as to the relevance of my material to his own discipline. What follows is a piece of *haute vulgarisation*. I take it for granted that New Testament scholars no longer have to be convinced that a knowledge of the Jewish milieu of early Christianity forms a necessary part of their academic competence.

Second, I must make it clear at the outset that I am not interested at the moment in reconstructing first-century Palestinian Judaism as a way of discovering the historical conditions in which early Christianity came into being. I regard such a project as intensely problematic, and perhaps over-ambitious. In the present paper it does not concern me in the least who 'borrowed' from whom, or who 'influenced' whom. My aim is simply to set the Rabbinic biographical tradition side by side with the Gospels, so that it can act as a foil to the Gospels and sharpen our perceptions of what is distinctive and important *both* in the Gospels *and* in the Rabbinic tradition.

Third, those used to the rich and subtle fare of New Testament scholarship may accuse me of a certain naiveté in my approach. *That* is quite deliberate, though I would prefer to speak not of 'naiveté' but of 'primitivism', in the sense in which art critics use that term. Paul Klee once said that he wanted to be 'as though newborn, knowing absolutely nothing about Europe'. I think he was expressing the feeling that European art had reached an impasse; it was over-ripe; it was dying from a surfeit of its own riches. The way forward was to be 'as though newborn, knowing absolutely nothing about Europe'. There is a sense in which I too would like to be newborn—knowing nothing of Gospel criticism! I want to look at the Rabbinic texts with clear eyes; to start from first principles; to ask very direct, very hard-headed questions. In the event, of course, Klee did not escape from his European past. No more can I escape from Gospel criticism which has been the forging house for so many of the basic tools needed in the analysis of the sort of texts that I study. It will be evident throughout this paper that I have an eye cocked at Gospel criticism. However, like Klee, I have striven for simplicity, and I hope this simplicity will be properly understood, and may even prove an inspiration to colleagues in the New Testament field.

II. *Classification of Rabbinic Anecdotes*

There is an abundance of material in classic Rabbinic literature which can broadly be designated as 'biographical' in that it purports to describe events in the lives of the Sages. This material is very diverse in character: it ranges from single sentences to elaborate anecdotes; it occurs in both aggadic and halakhic contexts; it includes stories in which the Rabbis are the protagonists and stories in which they figure only on the fringes of the action.

There is no single principle of classification which will enable us to divide this biographical material into neat categories. As far as the anecdotes are concerned (and they will be the subject of this study), three ways of classifying suggest themselves. First, we could classify according to form. The problem with this approach is that too few of the forms recur: we would find ourselves with a very large number of classes with only one or two members. *Aggadah* is much less narrowly formulaic and structurally repetitive than *halakhah*, and such similarities as do exist between anecdotes are often a matter of loose patterns, motifs and stock phrases. Second, we could classify according to point. This will work to some extent, but as a general method it breaks down because some stories do not have any obvious point, while others seem to have several points. Moreover, the process of deciding the point of a story can be highly arbitrary and subjective. Third, we could classify according to content. There are, indeed, certain themes which recur with reasonable frequency, and the comparison of thematically related anecdotes can be instructive; but a general classification along these lines runs into the difficulty that the contents of the anecdotes are extremely varied and once again we would end up with a multitude of single-member classes.

For our present purposes it will suffice to isolate a number of types of material by applying all three of these methods eclectically. Our types are rather rough and ready and do not by any means exhaust the material. However, they will serve to illustrate the nature of the evidence and lay down a basis for discussion.

1. *Precedents*.[1] Stories which recount actions of halakhic significance. These stories are introduced as an element in a halakhic discussion. They are usually short and unadorned, and quite frequently begin with *ma'aseh*.[2] The story is sometimes cited in lieu of a general ruling. Thus in TB Avodah Zarah 43a, in the course of a discussion on whether it is permissible to make a representation of the sun or the moon, a baraita is quoted to the effect that Rabban Gamliel had a chart with lunar diagrams which he used when questioning witnesses of the new moon (cf. M Rosh Ha-Shanah 2.8). Though no general ruling of Gamliel on the subject of images appears to exist, the story is taken to show that he permitted at least representations of the heavenly bodies. At other times, however (as in the account of Gamliel, Eleazar ben Azariah, Joshua and Akiva on the ship sailing from Brundisium—M Eruvin 4.1), the story stands side by side with its corresponding ruling. When this happens there are two obvious possibilities to be considered: either (a) the ruling has been derived from the story; or (b) the story is meant simply to illustrate and clarify the ruling, and may, in fact, be derived from it.

2. *Exempla*. Stories aimed at commending certain virtues. In terms of form and content two main types may be distinguished here: (a) stories which illustrate moral sayings; and (b) stories which describe how certain virtuous actions were rewarded. In the former type, which is particlarly common in the Avot deRabbi Natan, the anecdote is rounded off by a quotation of the saying: see e.g. the story about Hillel and the donkey-driver in Avot deRabbi Natan B 27 (ed. Schechter 55-56), which illustrates the maxim, 'According to the painstaking is the reward'. In the latter type, however, the moral is not explicitly drawn. For an example see PT Horayot III, 48a.39-55 (ed. Venice): Abba Judah, a man renowned for his liberality, lost all his goods and was in despair when R. Eliezer, R. Joshua and R. Akiva came to make a collection on behalf of the Sages. He sold half his one remaining field and gave the proceeds to the Rabbis. Then he went down to plough the half-field that was left. His ox fell and broke its

leg. When he bent down to raise up the ox, 'the Holy One enlightened his eyes and he found a treasure'. And so his fortunes were restored. Exempla are usually artfully constructed and every effort is made to engage and hold the attention.

3. *Responsa.* Stories in which a Rabbi answers a question posed by a pupil or by some other inquirer. The narrative framework is usually minimal: 'X asked Rabbi Y... Rabbi Y replied...' The broad structure of the anecdote is thus simply question followed by answer. The question may be about some difficulty in Scripture (e.g. T Bava Kamma 7.2: 'His disciples asked Rabban Yohanan b. Zakkai, 'For what reason does the Torah treat the thief more severely than the robber?'); or about a more general problem of religious practice (e.g. TB Menahot 99b: 'Ben Damah, the son of Rabbi Ishmael's sister, once asked R. Ishmael, "May one such as I who has studied the whole Torah learn Greek wisdom"?'). The answer normally involves the quotation of Scripture.

In some anecdotes a question or difficulty is put to the Sage with the obvious intention of embarrassing or confounding him. It often concerns a fundamental tenet of faith, and is posed by an 'outsider'— a heretic (*min*), the emperor, a philosopher, a pagan.[3] A difficulty may be raised from Scripture, or there may be an allegation that certain beliefs or practices involve illogicality, or impossibility, or inconsistency. When the difficulty is based on Scripture the refutation is from Scripture; in the other cases the refutation is often through a *mashal* and/or counter-question. The anecdote commonly consists simply of an objection and a refutation (e.g. TB Sanhedrin 91a: R. Ammi's answer to a heretic *re* resurrection of the dead), but there are several developed forms of this basic type worth noting: (a) in some stories the exchange is prolonged into a debate with several arguments and counter-arguments (e.g. TB Sanhedrin 38b: R. Idi's refutation of a heretic *re* Exod. 24.1); (b) the difficulty is not answered by the Rabbi who is asked but by some third party (e.g. TB Sanhedrin 38b: the heretic who questions R. Ishmael b. R. Yose *re* Gen. 19.24 is refuted not by Ishmael but by a fuller who happens to be present); (c) the Rabbi answers the difficulty, but when the objector leaves the Rabbi's disciples complain that he (the objector) has been 'knocked down with a straw'; the Rabbi then offers a second explanation to satisfy the disciples (e.g. Pesikta deRav Kahana IV 7, ed. Mandelbaum 74: Yohanan b. Zakkai's answer to a pagan *re* the red heifer).

4. *Scholastic Debates.* Stories which recount disputes between

authorities on matters of *halakhah*. It is very common to find divergent opinions of legal authorities simply juxtaposed, as in the form: 'If *p* is the case, Rabbi X says ... Rabbi Y says ... ' E.g. M Arakhin 6.1: 'If a man had dedicated his goods to the Temple and he was still liable for the payment of his wife's *Ketubbah*, R. Eliezer says: When he divorces her he must vow to derive no further benefit from her; R. Joshua says: He need not'. But we also find cases where the Sages are portrayed as being in direct dispute with each other. Thus the form just quoted is sometimes extended into a debate in which each of the named authorities advances arguments to support his position (see e.g. M Pesahim 6.5: R. Eliezer v. R. Joshua *re* the slaughtering of the Passover-offering on Sabbath). While the legal positions are stated in the opening formula in the present tense ('Rabbi X *says* / Rabbi Y *says*'), the debate is cast in the past ('Rabbi X *said* / Rabbi Y *said* to him'). As with responsa, the narrative framework of scholastic debates is usually minimal.

5. *Encomia*. Stories which aim to praise a certain master. These may involve a word of praise from the master's teacher, as in the story of how Eleazar b. Arakh expounded the mysteries of the merkavah before Yohanan b. Zakkai and was eulogized by him (see below). Some encomia involve a favourable contrast between the master who is praised and other scholars. E.g. TB Sukkah 28a: Hillel had eighty disciples ... the greatest of them was Jonathan b. Uzziel and the least of them was Yohanan b. Zakkai. They said of Yohanan b. Zakkai that he did not leave unstudied Scripture, Mishnah, Gemara, *Halakhah*, *Aggadah*, etc., and if the least of them was so great, how much more so was the greatest. Certain other types of story, such as accounts of miracles and martyrdoms, and disputes in which the master displays his cleverness in defeating an opponent, may also be partly encomiastic.

6. *Miracle-stories*. Rabbinic Judaism has a rather ambivalent attitude towards miracles: according to one tradition the age of miracles is past (TB Berakhot 20a); according to another a miracle has no probative force in a legal dispute (TB Bava Mezia 59a-b, see below). Miracle-stories are, however, reasonably common, though they tend to be related of the earlier masters. The explanation of the 'mechanism' of the miracle is normally simple and unmagical: the Sage stands in a privileged relationship to God; God, therefore, hears his prayer and performs the miracle at his request. Rabbinic miracles follow closely the Biblical repertory of miracles: the commonest

wonder is rain-making (see e.g. the story of Honi the Circle-Drawer in M Ta'anit 3.8).

7. *Death stories*. Rabbinic literature does not seem to be interested in investing the great masters with wonderful birth-stories, or in depicting them as having been infant prodigies. However, it does show a steady interest in how the Sages died. In a typical story the Sage's disciples gather round his death-bed and he gives them a final word of wisdom, as a sort of ethical last will and testament (see e.g. the account of Yohanan b. Zakkai's death in TB Berakhot 28b). There are antecedents to this kind of death-bed scene in the Bible (e.g. Gen. 49). Cf. also the Testaments of the XII Patriarchs. As a sub-group within this category may be included tales of martyrdom, such as the account of the martyrdom of Akiva in TB Berakhot 61b. The tales of martyrdom also have clear antecedents, e.g. in the story of Hananiah, Mishael and Azariah in Dan. 3 (cf. TB Pesahim 53b). It is also clear that stories of the Maccabean martyrs were known in some form to the Rabbis (cf. 2 Macc. 7.1-42 and 4 Macc. with TB Gittin 57b and Lam.R. I 16, 50, ed. Buber 42b). There was considerable discussion in rabbinic circles as to how far one should go 'to sanctify the Name'.[4] The martyr-stories illustrate and commend the ideas put forward in the rabbinic theology of martyrdom. They are similar in purpose to exempla, and like exempla are fully articulated narratives with an abundance of circumstantial detail.

III. *Development of the Anecdotes*

Several considerations suggest that many of the anecdotes existed prior to their incorporation into their present contexts. In the first place it is striking that many of the stories are cast in a closed, bounded form which makes it possible to detach them from their present settings: they are, on the whole, self-contained blocks of material which can be moved around and built into different contexts. There are a fair number of cases where we find the same story actually used in diverse settings: see e.g. the account of Yohanan b. Zakkai's escape from Jerusalem in TB Gittin 56a-b; Lam.R. I 5,31, ed. Buber 33a; Avot deRabbi Natan A 4, ed. Schechter 19; Avot deRabbi Natan B 6, ed. Schechter 19; or the story of how Eliezer b. Hyrcanus came to study Torah in Gen.R. 41(42):1, ed. Theodor–Albeck 397; Avot deRabbi Natan A 6, ed. Schechter 30; Pirkei deRabbi Eliezer I-II. Even assuming that the anecdote is original to one of the contexts where it now occurs, and that in the other instances it was borrowed from there, we still have clear proof that in those other instances the story existed prior to its present use.

Again, some of the anecdotes contain within themselves evidence of having been redacted out of different forms of the tradition. Thus in the tale of Rav Huna and the barrels of wine in TB Berakhot 5b we find variant traditions as to the *dramatis personae* and the ending of the story: the variants are introduced by the formula, 'There are some who say . . . (איכא דאמרי)'. The implication is that the redactor responsible for introducing the story into its present context knew at least two previously-existing forms of it. Finally, in a number of cases close analysis will disclose that an anecdote does not precisely fit the context where it is now found. E.g. in M Berakhot 5.5 we read: 'If he who says the *Tefillah* falls into error it is a bad omen for him'. Then we are offered an illustration: 'They tell of R. Hanina b. Dosa that he used to pray over the sick and say, "This one will live", or, "This one will die". They said to him, "How do you know?" He replied, "If my prayer is fluent in my mouth (אם שגורה תפלתי בפי) I know that he is accepted"'. On reflection the illustration is rather far-fetched and awkward: the point illustrated speaks of making a *mistake* in reciting a prayer, but the illustration is concerned with *fluency* in prayer. In the point illustrated it is stated that if a man makes a mistake in prayer it is a bad omen for *himself*; in the story a man prays and if his prayer is not fluent it is a bad omen for *someone else*. If we were to take the story by itself we would suppose that it refers to a spontaneous prayer of intercession for a sick person and not to the recitation of a fixed prayer such as the *Amidah*. It would appear, then, that the Hanina story existed prior to its being included here and that it is being made to serve a purpose for which it was not originally intended.[5]

In the course of being transmitted and re-used the anecdotes developed and changed. This is evident from a synoptic comparison of those stories which exist in a number of different forms. The laws governing this development are very complex and imperfectly understood. However, some can be isolated with tolerable certainty.

1.   Many of the anecdotes are cited to illustrate sayings, whether legal or moral. It is probable that in some cases the saying has, in effect, generated the illustration. Frequently all the ingredients of the illustration are contained within the saying, and it would have required little imagination to have worked them into a tale. For

instance, in M Berakhot 5.1 we read: 'The ancient *hasidim* used to wait an hour before reciting the *Tefillah*, that they might direct their hearts toward God. Even if the king salutes him he may not return the greeting, and even if a snake is wound round his heel he may not interrupt his prayer.' Here we have all the elements of a dramatic story: ancient *hasidim*—recitation of the *Amidah*—snake wound round the heel—not interrupting prayer. It comes as no surprise that in the corresponding passage of the Tosefta (T Berakhot 3.20; cf. PT Berakhot V, 9a.48-51, ed. Venice) there is a story about how a famous *hasid*, Hanina b. Dosa, was bitten by a snake while reciting the *Amidah* but did not interrupt his prayer. It would not be beyond the bounds of possibility for a saying to generate totally its illustration, but in some instances it may merely have imposed structure on antecedent materials. Thus the story just quoted did not arise totally from the saying: Hanina is no invention but a real historical figure, and there may have existed already a story about his encounter with a snake (TB Berakhot 33a).

2.   When we conclude that many of the anecdotes existed prior to their incorporation into their present contexts we must be careful not to picture this situation simplistically: it would be wrong to suppose that at the earlier stage the anecdotes existed in total isolation. An anecdote is formulated for some purpose, even if only for entertainment, and so presumably there never is a stage in its development when it does not have some kind of setting. So when we speak of using a pre-existing anecdote we are really speaking of its transfer from one context to another. It is very difficult to assess the impact of this transference on the form and content of an anecdote. If the new context is very different from the old it might lead to an extensive reworking of the story. On the whole, however, systematic recasting of anecdotes does not seem to have been practised: adaptation to a new setting was achieved largely by external glossing. We may have an example of this in TB Berakhot 5b: R. Eliezer (variant: R. Eleazar) fell ill; R. Yohanan went to visit him and found him weeping. He asked why he wept. R. Eliezer replied: 'On account of this beauty (i.e. the beauty of Yohanan) that is going to rot in the earth'. R. Yohanan said: 'On that account you have surely reason to weep'; and they both wept. The story is in all respects complete, but we find that it runs on: 'In the meanwhile (אדהכי והכי) he said to him: "Are your sufferings welcome to you?" He replied: "Neither they nor their reward". He said to him: "Give me your hand"; and he gave

him his hand and he raised him.' These closing words are surely a
gloss used to link the anecdote to its present context which deals with
the value of suffering.

3. In a number of instances we find encomiastic anecdotes have
been subjected to denigratory glossing. The gloss may be a simple
derogatory statement, such as R. Aha's comment on the story of how
Hanina b. Dosa saved the daughter of Nehuniah the ditch-digger
when she fell into a hole: 'Nevertheless Nehuniah's daughter died of
thirst' (TB Bava Kamma 50a).[6] Or the gloss may be in the form of a
further anecdote. Thus in Avot deRabbi Natan A 14 (ed. Schechter
59), after a series of stories in which Yohanan b. Zakkai praises
Eleazar b. Arakh above the rest of his disciples, we read the
following:

> When they [i.e. Yohanan's disciples] left his presence, R. Eleazar
> said: I shall go to Emmaus, a beautiful place with beautiful and
> delightful waters. But they said: We shall go to Yavneh where there
> are scholars in abundance who love the Torah. Because he went to
> Emmaus—a beautiful place with beautiful and delightful waters—
> his name was made least in Torah. Because they went to Yavneh—
> where there are scholars in abundance who love the Torah—their
> names were magnified in the Torah.

It can happen that a denigratory gloss is countered by a re-
affirmation of the praises of the Sage. E.g. in PT Berakhot V, 9a.48-
51 (ed. Venice), the story of Hanina and the snake is glossed with the
remark: 'If the man reaches the water first, the snake dies; but if the
snake reaches the water first, the man dies'. The comment is
disparaging, since, as Vermes observes, 'Hanina's survival is attributed
not to his holiness but to his speed'.[7] But then a further gloss is added
which re-asserts Hanina's privileged relationship to God: 'R. Isaac b.
Eleazar said: The Holy One, blessed be He, created for him (Hanina)
a spring of water under the soles of his feet, to fulfil that which is
written: He fulfils the desire of those who fear him, he hears their cry
and saves them (Ps. 145.19)'.

4. When various anecdotes about a master are brought together
it is sometimes observed that they conflict with each other. Such
conflicts may be resolved by constructing another anecdote. E.g. in
TB Ta'anit 25a there is a series of stories which stress the extreme
poverty of Hanina b. Dosa. Then there is a story about some goats
which were supposed to have belonged to him. This leads to the
objection: 'Whence did R. Hanina b. Dosa acquire goats, seeing that

he was so poor?' The objection is met by the following tale:

> R. Pinhas said: Once (מעשה ו') a man passed the door of R. Hanina's house and left there some hens, and the wife of R. Hanina b. Dosa found them. Hanina said to her: Do not eat their eggs. But as the eggs and the hens increased they proved to be a nuisance, and so Hanina and his wife sold them and bought goats with the proceeds. One day the man who had lost the hens passed by and said to his companion: I left my hens here. R. Hanina b. Dosa overheard this and said to him: Did you mark them? Yes, said he, and he described the mark and took away the goats. These were the goats that brought back the bears on their horns [i.e. the goats mentioned in the previous story].

It is possible that originally this anecdote was framed to illustrate the honesty and reliability of Hanina,[8] but in its present context it is used to harmonize the tradition that Hanina was indigent with the tradition that he owned goats.

5. A small motif occuring earlier in the tradition about a master may provide the basis or the inspiration for a motif in a later anecdote. E.g. the statement at T Sotah 15.3, 'When R. Eliezer died the Scroll of the Torah ceased to exist', may lie behind a vivid image in Eliezer's death-bed scene: 'Rabbi Eliezer raised his two arms and laid them on his breast and cried, "Woe unto me! For my two arms that are like two Torah Scrolls depart from the world"' (Avot deRabbi Natan 25, ed. Schechter 81; cf. TB Sanhedrin 68a).[9]

6. An anecdote about one master may serve as a model for an anecdote about another. Thus in TB Hagigah 14b (cf. PT Hagigah II, 77a.57-60, ed. Venice) the account of R. Eleazar's Merkavah sermon is followed by a story in which R. Joshua and R. Yosi the priest also expound Ma'aseh Merkavah and are eulogized by Yohanan b. Zakkai. The structure and contents of the two anecdotes are by no means identical, but they do share a general likeness and they are explicitly linked; the second opens: 'Now when these things (about R. Eleazar's sermon) were told to R. Joshua, he and R. Yosi the priest were going on a journey'. The Joshua/Yosi story is found appended to the account of Eleazar's Merkavah sermon only in the later sources. It is probably, therefore, a late imitation of the Eleazar anecdote. (For Eleazar's Merkavah sermon, see below.) Imitation may also be a matter of detail. Thus we find a rather similar motif in the death-scenes of Akiva and Eliezer. Of Akiva it says that when he recited the *Shema* under torture, 'he prolonged the word *ehad* until

he expired while saying it—'יהיה מאריך באחד עד שיצתה נשמתו באחד'
(TB Berakhot 61b); and of R. Eliezer we read that he discoursed to
his disciples on the clean and the unclean, 'until he expired while
pronouncing "clean"—והיה משיב על טמא טמא ועל טהור טהור עד שיצתה
נשמתו בטהרה' (Avot deRabbi Natan A 25, ed. Schechter 81; the
wording of the parallels—PT Shabbat II, 5b.57-8, ed. Venice, and TB
Sanhedrin 68a—is slightly different). Without entering into the
problem of which of these anecdotes has the priority, it would seem
reasonable to suggest that one has inspired the other at this point.

7.   Some scholars are inclined to assume that the stories develop
in the direction of greater complexity and dramatic force. They see
the evolution of biographical aggadot as being broadly similar to that
of aggadic midrash: ambiguities and difficulties are puzzled over and
resolved in new versions of the story. There are, indeed, cases where
we can be well-nigh certain that the longer and more complex
version of a tale is also the later. The tradition as a whole does seem
to be acquisitive: it adds but does not discard, and if contradictions
arise they are resolved by a process of harmonization which allows
both the conflicting elements to be retained. However, it would be
quite wrong to make it a rule that the longer and more complex
version must be later. Evolutionary models have an insidious
fascination for the modern academic mind, but they often conceal
subjectivity. Each case must be tried on its own merits. There is no
reason to rule out *a priori* the possibility that a late recension of an
anecdote has arisen through deliberate abbreviation and simplification.
In a number of instances it has been successfully demonstrated that
shortening actually has taken place.

These points can be illustrated by a synoptic comparison of the
different versions of the story of Eleazar b. Arakh's Merkavah
sermon.[10]

Synoptic Studies

	Mekhilta deRashbi	Tosefta	Bavli
A.	I	The story is told of Rabban Yohanan ben Zakkai that he was riding on an ass, and Rabbi Eleazar ben Arakh was driving the ass from behind.	The story is told of Rabban Yohanan ben Zakkai that he was riding on an ass while going on a journey, and Rabbi Eleazar ben Arakh was driving the ass from behind.
B.	Text missing.	He said to him: 'Teach me a chapter from the Work of the Chariot'.	He said to him: 'Master, teach me a chapter from the Work of the Chariot'.
C.		He said to him: 'Have I not said to you (sing.) from the beginning: One may not teach about the Chariot in the presence of one, unless he is a Sage and understands of his own knowledge?'	He said to him: 'Have I not taught you (plur.) thus: Nor the Chariot in the presence of one, unless he is a Sage and understands of his own knowledge?'
D.	He said: / 'If not, give me permission that I may speak before you'.	He said to him: 'Then I will lecture before you!'	He said to him: 'Master, permit me to say before you something you have taught me'.
E.	(See I below)	He said to him: 'Say on!'	He said to him: 'Say on!'
		Rabbi Eleazar ben Arakh began his exposition of the work of the Chariot.	(See I below)

F. Rabban Yohanan ben Zakkai descended from the ass, wrapped himself up, and sat on a stone under an olive tree.

G. He said to him: 'Master, why did you descend from the ass?'

H. He answered: 'Is it proper that while you are expounding the Work of the Chariot, and the Divine Presence is with us, and the ministering angels accompany us, I should ride on an ass?'

I. Rabbi Eleazar ben Arakh was expounding until fire was flickering all around him.

and he lectured before him.

Forthwith Rabbi Eleazar ben Arakh began his exposition of the Work of the Chariot, and fire came down from heaven, and encompassed all the trees in the field; and they all began to utter song.

J. What was the song they uttered? – 'Praise the Lord from the earth, you sea-monsters, and all deeps . . . fruitful trees and all cedars . . . Hallelujah' (Ps. 148.7, 9, 14).

K.			An angel answered from the fire and said: 'This is indeed the Work of the Chariot!'
L.	When Rabban Yohanan ben Zakkai saw that fire was flickering all around him, he descended from his ass,	He stood up, (See F above)	Rabban Yohanan ben Zakkai stood up, (See F above)
M.	and kissed him, and said to him: 'Rabbi Eleazar ben Arakh, happy is she who bore you.	and kissed him on his head and said: 'Blessed be the Lord God of Israel, who has given to Abraham our father a son who knows how to expound the glory of his father who is in heaven.	and kissed him on his head and said: 'Blessed be the Lord God of Israel, who has given to Abraham our father a son who knows how to understand, to investigate and to expound the Work of the Chariot.
N.		There are some who expound well but do not act well; others who act well but do not expound well; but Eleazar ben Arakh expounds well and acts well.	There are some who expound well but do not act well; others who act well but do not expound well; but you expound well and act well.
O.	Happy are you, Abraham our father, that such a one has come forth from your loins.'	Happy are you, Abraham our father, that Eleazar ben Arakh has come forth from your loins, who knows how to understand and to expound the glory of our father in heaven.'	Happy are you, Abraham our father, that Rabbi Eleazar ben Arakh has come forth from your loins.'

The four recensions of this anecdote cannot be set out neatly on a synoptic table because the corresponding elements and phrases do not always occur in the same order. To simplify the argument a little I have presented on the accompanying table only three of the recensions—those in the Mekhilta deRabbi Simeon b. Yohai, *Mishpatim* 21.1 (ed. Epstein–Melamed 158-59), T Hagigah (ed. Lieberman 380), and TB Hagigah 14b. The fourth, unquoted, recension may be found in PT Hagigah II, 77a.41-56 (ed. Venice). Now at first reading of the table I am tempted to say that the Bavli version of this tale is the latest of the three, and that its form of the story represents a development of the tradition beyond that found in the Tosefta and the Mekhilta. If asked to justify this view I would argue that the Bavli clearly strives to maximize the splendour of the occasion by introducing a series of dramatic motifs (see H-K); it develops the Tosefta tradition about Yohanan descending from his ass to listen to Eleazar (F) by means of question and answer as to his reasons for so doing (G-H); and (along with the Tosefta, but in contrast to the Mekhilta) it expatiates on the praises of Eleazar (N). But what are such arguments really worth? I wonder to what extent I may have been drawn to this conclusion because of latent assumptions as to the relative dates of the three Rabbinic sources where the anecdote is found—the Bavli, the Tosefta and the Mekhilta deRashbi. It is even possible I may have been influenced subconsciously by the way I have chosen to construct my synoptic table, with the Mekhilta on the left, the Tosefta in the middle, and the Bavli on the right. On deeper reflection I can find no objective evidence in the recensions themselves as to which of them is later and which earlier. Scholars who have found such evidence are, I feel, simply deluding themselves.

There is another caveat to be borne in mind in synoptic study of the Rabbinic anecdotes. It is important not to over-interpret the variations. Not every variant need have a subtle point; some may have arisen simply because the tradents were unable to reproduce the tradition precisely in the words in which they received it.[11] It is all too easy, having established to one's own satisfaction the chronological order of the recensions, to suppose that the later versions have changed the earlier for such-and-such reasons. Redaction-criticism should be applied with great caution to the Rabbinic texts—even where chronology is certain. It can lead us once again into subjective and circular argument. The literary relationships between the recensions are acutely problematic, and we must view with scepticism any attempt to derive one form of an anecdote directly from another. The key to the development of the tradition may lie in versions of the story no longer extant. The problem can be illustrated from the three forms of the Eleazar anecdote given on the table. The Tosefta and the Mekhilta differ on three main points: (a) the Mekhilta states that Yohanan b. Zakkai descended from his ass only after the sermon was over (L), whereas in the Tosefta he dismounts at the beginning of the sermon (F). (Zuckermandel's edition of the Tosefta, p. 234,1, makes the contrast even sharper by omitting E.); (b) the Tosefta does not have the item about fire coming down (I); (c) the two recensions disagree as to the wording of the first part of Yohanan's eulogy (M). It is not easy to account for these differences on the theory that the Tosefta is directly descended from the Mekhilta, or vice versa. And, I believe, it is a waste of time to try and find ingenious reasons for all these changes. It should be noted that the picture here is even further complicated by the fact that of the three variations mentioned the Bavli sides with the Tosefta on the first and on the third, but with the Mekhilta on the second!

IV. *Literary Aspects of the Anecdotes*

Though there is some evidence that collections of *aggadot* circulated in written form (cf. TB Temurah 14b), it is probable that our stories were normally transmitted orally. On the whole they are short. Occasionally we do come across longer sequences (as, e.g., in the account of Yohanan b. Zakkai's escape from Jerusalem in Lam.R. I 5,31, ed. Buber 33a), but on closer inspection these longer narratives usually break down into smaller and originally independent units of material.

There is a strong tendency to stereotype both characters and situations, and the language is heavily formulaic. Many of the motifs of the Rabbinic *aggadot* are commonplaces of folk-literature (e.g. the story of finding a pearl hidden in a fish—TB Shabbat 119a).[12] Some of the motifs have parallels in wisdom literature (e.g. the riddle, which is exemplified by the questions to Hillel—TB Shabbat 31a; or the theme of social *savoir faire*, as in the story of the philosopher faced with the problem of how to greet four of the Sages at once—Kallah Rabbati 7.4, ed. Higger 316-17). There is a striving to be dramatic. This is perhaps best seen in the fact that a very high proportion of the anecdotes is taken up with dialogue, and the dialogue is fast-moving, abrupt and allusive. Description is minimal.

The linkage between the various statements in *oratio recta* is usually a bare 'he said'. In reading this can give rise to ambiguity; it was presumably left to the reciter to make clear by tone and gesture who was supposed to be speaking at any given point. The use of repetition and of series is very common (see e.g. M Avot 2.8-9, the five disciples of Yohanan b. Zakkai). These devices can be very effectively deployed to delay the dénouement and build a climax (see e.g. the story of Eliezer, Joshua and Zadok at the wedding-feast of Gamliel's son— Sifre Deut. 38, ed. Finkelstein 74-75).

The artistic merit of the tales naturally varies with the abilities of their composers and transmitters. The famous story of the dispute between the Sages and Rabbi Eliezer about the oven of Akhnai (TB Bava Mezia 59a-b) will serve to illustrate some of their characteristics. More or less literally translated this runs as follows:

A.   1.   We learnt elsewhere: If it was cut up into rings and sand put between each ring, then Rabbi Eliezer declared it clean, but the Sages declared it unclean.

        2.   This was the oven of Akhnai.

        3.   Why of Akhnai?

        4.   Rav Judah said in Samuel's name: 'Because they surrounded it with arguments like a snake (*akhna*) and proved it unclean'.

B.   It was taught: On that day Rabbi Eliezer brought forward all the answers in the world, but they refused to accept them.

C.   1.   He said to them: 'If the *halakhah* agrees with me, let this carob tree prove it'.

        2.   The carob tree was uprooted from its place a hundred cubits (some say: four hundred cubits).

        3.   They said to him: 'No proof can be brought from a carob tree'.

D.   1.   Again he said to them: 'If the *halakhah* agrees with me, let this stream of water prove it'.

        2.   The stream flowed backwards.

        3.   They said to him: 'No proof can be brought from a stream of water'.

E.   1.   Again he said to them: 'If the *halakhah* agrees with me, let the walls of the schoolhouse prove it'.

        2.   The walls started to lean as if about to fall.

        3.   Rabbi Joshua rebuked them. He said to them: 'If the pupils of the Sages are disputing about *halakhah* what business is it of yours?'

4. The walls did not fall, for the sake of Rabbi Joshua's honour, nor did they become upright, for the sake of Rabbi Eliezer's honour.
5. They are still standing in the inclined position.

F. 1. Again Rabbi Eliezer said: 'If the *halakhah* agrees with me, let it be proved from heaven'.
2. A Heavenly Voice (*bat kol*) went forth and said: 'Why do you dispute with Rabbi Eliezer, seeing that in every case the *halakhah* agrees with him?'
3. Rabbi Joshua stood to his feet and said: 'It is not in heaven!' (Deut. 30.12).
4. What did he mean by, 'It is not in heaven!'?
5. Rabbi Jeremiah said: 'He meant: The Torah has already been given from Mount Sinai, so we pay no attention to a Heavenly Voice, since You wrote long ago in the Torah at Mount Sinai: "After the majority you must incline" (Exod. 23.2)'.

G. 1. Rabbi Nathan met Elijah. He said to him: 'What did the Holy One blessed be He, do in that hour?'
2. He said to him: 'He laughed and said, "My sons have defeated me, my sons have defeated me!"'

This is an unusually long and artfully constructed tale which shows some signs of glossing (at G and A.3-4), and, perhaps, also of conflation (at C.2: 'Some say: four hundred cubits'). The speed of the narration, the abruptness of the transitions, the high proportion of dialogue, the lack of scene-setting and circumstantial detail, are noteworthy and highly typical. A is the lemma, B–G an extension of it. Originally B–G may have had nothing to do with A, since B–G has its own quite separate point. The formula, 'on that day' (באותו היום), is a common Rabbinic redactional device used to link together originally independent elements. The basic point of B–G is crystal clear: it builds up to the 'punchline' in F.5: 'After the majority you must incline'. *Halakhah* is to be decided by the majority opinion of the Sages; the mind of God is to be discovered by debate, not by miracle, or even by a Heavenly Voice. The impact of the punchline is enhanced by delay. This delay is achieved by the use of the series: carob tree—stream of water—walls of the schoolhouse—heavenly voice. The actual point could have been made much more briefly and philosophically (*mutatis mutandis* through F alone), but it would have been much less memorable. The series is dramatic and arouses the reader's curiosity: it is a sort of *captatio benevolentiae*. The skilful use of both repetition and variation should also be noted. The pattern laid down in C and repeated in D is not carried through to the end of the series, though it probably could have been. E and F are longer and more varied. This helps to avoid monotony and establish the climactic character of F. The story is told with wit and humour, though its fundamental point is a very serious one. This light touch comes out clearly at E. The aetiology offered at E.5 is surely humorous. We are not supposed seriously to ask where this schoolhouse with its tilting walls is to be found, so that we can satisfy ourselves as to the truth of the tale. I also suspect that the variant quoted at C.2 ('Some say: four hundred cubits') is not to be taken seriously either. It is a piece of learned wit, a case of mock *doctrina*. There are several possible folklore elements in the story. The use of repetitive series is very common in folktales, though by no means confined to them. The atmosphere conjured up especially by G is remarkable. The intensely anthropomorphic picture of God, and the way in which God, the famous dead (Elijah), and the Rabbis live together in a timeless world of 'faerie' has a folkloristic ring about it.

V. *The Function of the Anecdotes*

Why were these biographical stories composed in the first place, and why were they preserved? The answer to these questions lies first and foremost in the position of the Rabbi in Rabbinic society. The Rabbi was a teacher who gathered round him a circle of pupils. Naturally the pupils told stories which would tend to glorify their teacher. They may occasionally have invented tales to play down the merits of rival scholars. Moreover, the conduct of a competent halakhic authority, even when he was not consciously deciding a point of law, came to be regarded as an important source of law.[13] Pupils not only listened to what the master said, but also closely analysed his actions (see e.g. the story about Eleazar Ha-Kappar and the annulling of the signet ring in TB Avodah Zarah 43a). A quantity of biographical material originated, therefore, with the disciples of the Sages and was passed down through the schools: it underscored the authority of the Sages (and, indirectly, of their pupils), and it provided a valuable source of *halakhah*.

The Rabbi also played a role outside the academies, in society at large, as a judge: he had a position of prestige and was an important locus of spiritual authority within the community. He was a holy

man, and not surprisingly some of the tales told about him cast him
in the role of a typical folk-hero. We must not, however, overstress
the veneration of the great Sages in classic Rabbinic Judaism. The
cult of heroes was widespread in the Greek world, but there were
strong restraints on 'heroification' in Rabbinic culture. There is no
solid evidence even for the practice of visiting the tombs of leading
scholars in the Talmudic period—a custom attested later. Some
Sages' names were commemorated in liturgical compositions, but
this was probably the highest accolade ever conferred.[14]

A large number of the anecdotes have an obviously edifying
character: they urge upon people certain virtuous or pious courses of
action; they hold up the conduct of the Rabbis for emulation. The
primary setting for these tales is to be found in preaching in the
synagogue; they provided *darshanim* with effective sermon-illustrations.
This type of anecdote is really a 'proverb' (*mashal*): by introducing a
named master into the *mashal*, instead of leaving it generalized, the
darshan achieved two ends: he made his illustration more concrete,
and he strengthened his point by associating the action he wished to
commend with a person of prestige and authority. Transmission of
these tales through synagogue preaching would have popularized
them and made them part of Jewish folk-tradition.

Disputes with heretics and pagans form a group of anecdotes on
their own. Judaism in the ancient world was involved in controversy
both with paganism and with Christianity. It would be natural,
consequently, to find a setting for these dispute-stories neither in the
academy nor the synagogue but in the forum where Jew and non-Jew
rubbed shoulders. It is tempting to suppose that the dispute-stories
functioned as an aide-mémoire for apologists. However, although
disputes and arguments undoubtedly took place, we cannot be sure
that the dispute-stories reflect the genuine substance of the debates.
In some cases it would be natural to identify the 'heretics' (*minim*)
with whom the Rabbis argued as Christians, but the texts of
Scripture cited by the *minim* do not appear to have been much used
by Christian apologists, or to have figured centrally in the Jewish-
Christian debate.[15] It is possible that in some cases the point of the
anecdote may not be to offer a refutation of 'the other side', but
simply to display for public approbation the cleverness of some Sage.
Or else the anecdote may put in the mouth of a heretic some
difficulty which the author of the anecdote was reluctant to raise in
his own name.

VI. *The Historicity of the Anecdotes*

As sources of historical information about the Sages the biographical anecdotes must be treated with caution. We are clearly not dealing with documentary or archival material but with orally transmitted tales, many of which are put in the mouths of tradents who lived generations after the time to which the narratives refer. The tradents of these stories were not interested in them for historical reasons. In general the Rabbis were not concerned with historiography—either in the modern sense, or even in the sense of a work such as 1 Maccabees. A lack of historiographical interest does not *ipso facto* condemn as unhistorical the information contained in the *aggadot*, but it does warn us not to assume that the people who shaped and transmitted these stories felt themselves under the same constraints of accuracy as the historian. For the most part the stories serve as homiletic or halakhic illustrations, and so the tradents may have considered themselves at liberty to mould their material as would best serve this end. Examination of the tales suggests that they have treated their material freely.

The strong tendency to stereotype also diminishes the historical worth of the traditions. Events are commonly described in terms of stock-situations, and characters in terms of types; speeches are full of formulaic expressions and the over-all structure of the anecdotes follows recurrent patterns. If genuine historical events are being described, then we must recognize that the particularity of those events has largely been lost, along with the individuality of the protagonists. It is also highly improbable that *ipsissima verba* are ever reported.

Another feature which must make the historian sceptical is the way the traditions grow and accumulate. This tendency was discussed earlier in the synoptic comparison of R. Eleazar b. Arakh's Merkavah sermon. Where the later forms of the anecdote are fuller it is perfectly obvious that the additional information they contain is not derived from independent, external sources, but has arisen under pressure of inner developmental laws. The situation is similar to that of aggadic midrash: there is no reason seriously to regard the Rabbinic embellishments of Biblical stories as an historical source for the Biblical period. We should be equally cautious about regarding later versions of Rabbinic biographical *aggadot* as containing genuine additional facts.

The problem is even more complicated with the biographical *aggadot* than with aggadic midrash. At least in the case of aggadic midrash we have in the Bible the first state of the tradition clearly demarcated from its later embellishments; but this is not so with the *aggadot*. We cannot simply assume that the earliest attested form of a story is the actual beginning of the tradition. The shape of the tradition at its inception is frequently lost from view, and it is hard to reconstruct how it evolved, even when there are a number of versions of the story. There are, presumably, genuine biographical details within the traditions. The generative model I have used to illustrate the development of the traditions rather presupposes an irreducible factual starting-point. But it is extremely difficult to determine in an objective way what those facts are: the facts, as it were, are carried in the traditions 'in solution', and there appears to be no way of getting them to 'precipitate'.[16]

VII. *Rabbinic Biography and the Gospels*

1. If we define a gospel as a collection of pericopae arranged within a chronological framework and manifesting a more or less definite theological *Tendenz*, then there are no Rabbinic parallels to the Gospels as such. This is by far the most important single conclusion to emerge from this paper. But the curious thing is this: what strikes me as odd is not that there are *Gospels* (such collections of anecdotal pericopae are surely eminently natural), but that such collections are totally absent from Rabbinic literature. There is not a trace of an ancient biography of any of the Sages. There is no reason to suppose that the scattered *aggadot* concerning any given master once formed part of some lost unified collection of tales or biographical account. Nor can we detect late in the tradition any movement towards combining the separate stories about a Sage into a 'life'.

This is a profound enigma. Many of the Rabbinic Sages were powerful, colourful personalities who made a deep impression on their contemporaries and fundamentally affected the development of Judaism. There were precedents for such biography in the Bible. We have, for example, a tolerably full account of the life of David, and much of the Pentateuch (as Philo saw) can be read as a *Vita Mosis*. The personal details about the Biblical figures were freely expanded in the *aggadah*, so the early Rabbis were apparently not devoid of biographical interest. Materials for a life of at least a few of the Sages were lying to hand at the later stages of the tradition. A case in point is Eliezer b. Hyrcanus. There is extant an account of how he came to study Torah (a story which includes significant hints about his family background). We have a tradition about his death. We have a number of vivid anecdotes about events in his life, and there is a large body of his sayings and legal rulings. It would surely not have been too difficult, with a little editorial ingenuity, to have woven this data together into a biography. After all, modern scholars from the nineteenth century onwards have strung together and embellished such material to produce lives of the Sages!

Such a 'life' would not, of course, conform to the canons of modern biography, but it would not have looked out of place in the ancient world. Contemporary Greek and Roman biographers did not insist on strictly chronological order, nor were they much interested in treating their subjects against the history and society of their times. They tended to be encomiastic. They were unconcerned with their subjects' psychological development, but presented them as types, rather than as individuals. A number of the Rabbinic *aggadot* can be paralleled in Greek and Roman biographical material, and as a connected narrative our projected 'life' of Eliezer could have looked something like Lucian's *Life of Demonax*, or the Gospel of Mark. Why, then, did no one think of producing a Rabbinic 'Gospel' of Eliezer b. Hyrcanus?

The obvious answer is that neither Eliezer nor any other Sage held in Rabbinic Judaism the central position that Jesus held in early Christianity. The centre of Rabbinic Judaism was Torah; the centre of Christianity was the person of Jesus, and the existence of the Gospels is, in itself, a testimony to this fact. This is undoubtedly true, but can it be the whole explanation? After all Christianity began rapidly to produce 'lives' of lesser figures—apostles and others. Paul's biography was being written as early as Acts. And why did the Rabbis not follow Biblical precedent, or contemporary Graeco-Roman practice? The enigma remains. However—and this I must stres—it is an enigma for the student of Rabbinic literature. The Gospel critic can simply note that there are no parallels to the Gospels as such in Rabbinic literature. If he is concerned with the origin of the over-all form of the Gospels then he must look elsewhere—to the Old Testament, or, probably more fruitfully, to the Graeco-Roman world.

2. Though there are no parallels to the Gospels as such in the

Rabbinic corpus, there are parallels to the individual pericopae, and at this level similarities are very strong. In terms of form, function, setting and motif, the Rabbinic anecdotes are very close to the Gospel pericopae, and there can be little doubt that both belong to the same broad Palestinian Jewish tradition of story-telling. The parallels to the Gospels provided by Rabbinic literature are often as good, if not better, than any drawn from the Old Testament, intertestamental texts, or Greek and Latin literature. This Rabbinic material confirms in broad outline the view that the Gospel pericopae circulated originally as separate stories about Jesus among the first Christians. Yet here too there are nuances to be noted. These come down in the end to one major factor: in the Rabbinic anecdotes we have 'oral literature', in the Gospels 'written literature'. I am struck by the intensely 'oral' character of the Rabbinic material, as against the more prosy 'written' style of the Gospels. The Rabbinic anecdotes are extremely compressed, allusive, witty, dramatic and learned: they read like bits out of a play, or (the analogy is surely apt) like scripts for a radio-programme. Like a radio-script they can be confusing to read. All becomes clear only in performance. The reason for this is not far to seek: the Rabbinic stories are more or less direct transcripts of the oral form. Their oral character has been preserved because of the peculiar and rather artificial emphasis in the Rabbinic academies on oral transmission—even when written texts were available.[17] By way of contrast the Gospel stories appear to me more ponderous and prosy: they were meant to circulate in written form. To be sure, it is possible to make distinctions within the Gospels: on the whole Mark is stylistically simpler than the other Gospels and predictably comes closest to the Rabbinic anecdotes. But even the Markan versions of the pericopae are often more literary in character than the Rabbinic stories. If the Gospel pericopae had an oral prehistory, then they can hardly have been in precisely the form in which we now find them— even in Mark. It is all too easy to forget that speech and writing are very different modes of communication, and transposing a story from one to the other can involve important stylistic changes. The Rabbinic anecdotes give us some idea of the early Jewish oral style of story-telling. A detailed comparison of the style of the Rabbinic tales and of the Gospels is a clear desideratum.

3. Since the Rabbinic anecdotes are so close to the Gospel pericopae, they provide an ideal test-bed on which Gospel critics can try out their analytical techniques and consider objectively the issues

and problems of their own field of study. Hypotheses can only be verified by showing that they apply to new, untried data. The following points which emerge from the study of the Rabbinic anecdotes raise interesting questions for the study of the Gospels.

(a) In the Rabbinic anecdotes there appears to be little interest in history for its own sake. Circumstantial detail is kept to the bare minimum, and where it does come in, it is usually absolutely necessary for the tale, or is a rather obvious dramatic embellishment. Query: Is this also true of the Gospels?

(b) In the case of the Rabbinic anecdotes form-criticism in any strict sense breaks down: it is impossible to classify the anecdotes purely and simply according to form, and to relate each form to a specific *Sitz im Leben*—this, despite the fact that the Rabbis were very form-conscious, and had a penchant for casting their material into a limited number of formulaic structures. Query: Does form-criticism really work all that well in the Gospels, or are similar problems encountered?

(c) The Rabbinic anecdotes have been redacted to fit their present contexts only minimally and externally—on the whole. They are largely left in the form in which they were received and 'glossed' into their present setting. Query: What is the extent of redaction in the Gospels? My impression is that the Gospel pericopae have been much more thoroughly redacted and integrated into the narrative framework than have the Rabbinic anecdotes, but if that is so, then it will be much more difficult to discover their prehistory.

(d) Where the Rabbinic anecdotes are extant in several versions it is difficult, if not impossible, to tell simply by synoptic comparison which is the earlier and which the later form of the story. Moreover, because of the oral character of Rabbinic tradition the possibility arises that the extant forms of a given anecdote are not related to each other *directly*, but *indirectly*, through intermediate forms no longer extant. In other words one extant form may originally have evolved imperceptibly into the other, the later form not being posited directly on the earlier. The tradition would then be rather like a film from which only four or five frames, from different parts of the roll, now survive. Originally those frozen frames flowed into each other imperceptibly through a series of intermediate frames now lost. This model has important implications for redaction criticism, and, if correct, makes the application of redaction criticism to the Rabbinic anecdotes a hazardous business. Query: Has Gospel synoptic criticism been any more successful than Rabbinic synoptic criticism in separating the earlier from the later forms of the tradition? Could the 'frozen frame' model have any relevance to Gospel criticism, or must we simply accept the common assumption that there is a more or less exclusive and direct literary relationship between the extant Gospels?

APPENDIX: BIBLIOGRAPHICAL NOTE

There are many anthologies of Rabbinic *aggadot*: see e.g., H.N. Bialik and Y.H. Rawnitzki, *Sefer ha-Aggadah: Mivhar ha-Aggadot shebeTalmud u-veMidrashim* (1st edn 1908-11; repr. Tel Aviv, 1947), Part II, *Ma'asei Hakhamim*; M. Gaster, *The Exempla of the Rabbis* (1924; repr. with a new Prolegomenon by W.G. Braude, New York, 1968); P. Fiebig, *Rabbinische Wundergeschichten des neutestamentlichen Zeitalters* (2nd edn, Berlin, 1933), on which see Morton Smith, *Tannaitic Parallels to the Gospels* (Philadelphia, 1951), pp. 81-84. My book *Judaism* in the series Textual Sources for the Study of Religion, ed. J.R. Hinnells (Manchester University Press, 1984), contains a small but representative collection of *aggadot*. There is no substitute, however, for studying the anecdotes in their original literary setting.

The central issue in the study of the *aggadot* has been the question of their historicity. Up until quite recently scholars simply gathered together all the stories of a given master, ran them through a sort of 'rationalist filter' to extract their miraculous and legendary elements, and then harmonized whatever remained into a 'life'. Many of the 'biographies' of the Tannaim and Amoraim in the *Encyclopaedia Judaica* (1971) are constructed on this principle. A classic example of this method in operation is L. Finkelstein's *Akiba, Scholar Saint and Martyr* (New York, 1936). Jacob Neusner was the first to subject this approach to radical and devastating criticism. The first edition of his *Life of Yohanan ben Zakkai* (Leiden, 1962), was rather in the traditional mould, but he quickly saw the need to analyse the sources in proper literary and form-critical fashion: see especially his *Development of a Legend: Studies on the Traditions concerning Yohanan b. Zakkai* (Leiden, 1970); *The Rabbinic Traditions about the Pharisees before 70*, 3 vols. (Leiden, 1971); *Eliezer b. Hyrcanus: The Tradition and the Man*, 2 vols. (Leiden, 1973). Two programmatic pieces by Neusner set his work in perspective: 'The Rabbinic Traditions about the Pharisees before 70 in Modern Historiography' in: Neusner, *Method and Meaning in Ancient Judaism*, III (Chico, 1981), pp. 185-

213; 'Story and Tradition in Judaism', in: Neusner, *Judaism: The Evidence of the Mishnah* (Chicago and London, 1981), pp. 307-28. The latter contains some fine literary analysis of two interesting *aggadot*. Note also W.S. Green, 'What's in a Name?—The Problematic of Rabbinic "Biography"', in: Green (ed.), *Approaches to Ancient Judaism: Theory and Practice* (Missoula, 1978), pp. 77-96; R. Goldenberg, 'The Deposition of Rabban Gamaliel II: An Examination of the Sources', *JJS* 23 (1972), pp. 167-90; Tz. Zahavy, *The Traditions of Eleazar b. Azariah* (Missoula, 1977). More traditional in their approach to the historicity of the *aggadot* are: M.D. Herr, 'The Historical Significance of the Dialogues between Jewish Sages and Roman Dignitaries', *Scripta Hierosolymitana* 22 (1971), pp. 123-50; S. Safrai, 'Tales of the Sages in the Palestinian Tradition and in the Babylonian Talmud', *Scripta Hierosolymitana* 22 (1971), pp. 209-32.

G. Vermes has shown the importance of stories about the early masters (e.g. Hanina ben Dosa and Honi the Circle-Drawer) for the study of the Gospels. See his excellent essay: 'Hanina b. Dosa', *JJS* 23 (1972), pp. 28-50; *JJS* 24 (1973), pp. 51-64; reprinted in Vermes, *Post-Biblical Jewish Studies* (Leiden, 1975), pp. 178-214; Vermes, *Jesus the Jew* (Glasgow, 1976), pp. 69-78. See further: A. Büchler, *Types of Palestinian Jewish Piety from 70 BCE to 70 CE* (London 1928; reprinted New York, 1968); G. Sarfatti, 'Pious Men, Men of Deeds, and the Early Prophets', *Tarbiz* 26 (1956/7), pp. 126-53 [Hebrew]; S. Safrai, 'The Teaching of the Pietists in Mishnaic Literature', *JJS* 16 (1965), pp. 15-33; W.S. Green, 'Palestinian Holy Men: Charismatic Leadership and Rabbinic Tradition', in: H. Temporini and W. Haase (eds.), *Aufstieg und Niedergang der Römischen Welt* II, Principat, 19.2 (Berlin/New York, 1979), pp. 619-47.

Literary and folklore analysis is a very fruitful approach to the *aggadot*. See: Dov Neuman [Noy], *Motif-Index to the Talmudic-Midrashic Literature*, Indiana University Ph.D. thesis, 1954; D. Ben-Amos, *Narrative Forms in the Haggadah: Structural Analysis*, Indiana University Ph.D. thesis, 1966; Ben-Amos, 'A Structural and Formal Study of Talmudic-Midrashic Legends', in *Fourth World Congress of Jewish Studies, Papers II*, pp. 357-59 (Jerusalem, 1968) [Hebrew]; Z. Kagan, 'Divergent Tendencies and their Literary Moulding in the Aggadah', *Scripta Hierosolymitana* 22 (1971), pp. 151-70; Dov Noy, 'The Jewish Versions of the "Animal Languages" Folktale (AT 670)—A Typological-Structural Study', *Scripta Hierosolymitana* 22 (1971), pp. 171-208.

On the 'sociology' of the Rabbinate see: E.E. Urbach, 'The Talmudic Sage—Character and Authority', *Cahiers d'Histoire Mondiale* 11 (1968), pp. 116-47; Urbach, 'Class-Status and Leadership in the World of the Palestinian Sages', *Proceedings of the Israel Academy of Sciences and Humanities*, II (Jerusalem, 1968), pp. 38-74; Urbach, *The Sages: Their Concepts and Beliefs*, trans. I. Abrahams (Magnes Press: Jerusalem, 1975), I, pp. 525-648; J. Neusner, *A History of the Jews in Babylonia*, III (Leiden, 1968), pp. 95-338; IV (Leiden, 1969), pp. 125-402; cf. Neusner, *There We Sat Down* (New York, 1972), passim; Neusner, *Talmudic Judaism in Sasanian Babylonia* (Leiden, 1976), pp. 46-135.; Neusner, *Judaism in Society: The Evidence of the Yerushalmi* (Chicago, 1983), pp. 115-253.

The following selection of studies deals with (1) Graeco-Roman biography; (2) the genre of the Gospels and their relationship to Graeco-Roman and to Rabbinic biography; (3) the relationship between the Rabbinic biographical *aggadot* and Graeco-Roman biography: A. Lumpe, 'Exemplum', *Reallexikon für Antike und Christentum*, VI (1966), 1229-67; A. Ronconi, 'Exitus illustrium virorum', *Reallexikon für Antike und Christentum*, VI, 1258-67; A.D. Momigliano, *Development of Greek Biography* (Cambridge, Mass., 1971); P. Brown, 'The Rise and Function of the Holy Man in Late Antiquity', *JRS* 61 (1971), pp. 80-101; E.L. Bowie, 'Apollonius of Tyana: Tradition and Reality', in: Temporini and Haase (eds.), *Aufstieg und Niedergang der Römischen Welt*, II, 16.2 (1978), pp. 1652-99; Morton Smith, 'Prolegomena to a Discussion of Aretalogies, Divine Men, the Gospels and Jesus', *JBL* 90 (1971), pp. 174-99; D.L. Tiede, *The Charismatic Figure as Miracle Worker* (Missoula, 1972); G.N. Stanton, *Jesus of Nazareth in New Testament Preaching* (Cambridge, 1974)—thin both on the Greek and on the Rabbinic parallels; J.Z. Smith, 'Good News is No News: Aretalogy and Gospel', in: J. Neusner (ed.), *Christianity, Judaism and other Greco-Roman Cults: Studies for Morton Smith at Sixty* (Leiden, 1975), Part I, pp. 21-38; C.H. Talbert, 'Biographies of Philosophers and Rulers as Instruments of Religious Propaganda in Mediterranean Antiquity', in: Temporini and Haase (eds.), *Aufstieg und Niedergang der Römischen Welt*, II, 16.2 (1978), pp. 1619-51; P.L. Shuler, *A Genre for the Gospels* (Philadelphia, 1982); A. Kaminka, 'Hillel's Life and Work', *JQR* n.s. 30 (1939), pp. 107-22; repr. in H.A. Fischel (ed.), *Essays in Greco-Roman and Related Talmudic Literature* (New York, 1977), pp. 78-93; L. Wallach, 'The Colloquy of Marcus Aurelius with the Patriarch Judah I', *Monatsschrift für Geschichte und Wissenschaft des Judentums* 31 (1941), pp. 259-86; H.A. Fischel, 'Studies in Cynicism in the Ancient Near East: The Transformation of the *chria*', in: J. Neusner (ed.), *Religions in Antiquity: Essays in Memory of E.R. Goodenough* (Leiden, 1968), pp. 372-411; Fischel, 'Story and History: Observations on Greco-Roman Rhetoric and Pharisaism', first published 1969; repr. in Fischel (ed.), *Essays in Greco-Roman and Related Talmudic Literature*, pp. 443-72; Fischel, *Rabbinic Literature and Greco-Roman Philosophy* (Leiden, 1973); E.E. Halevi [Hallewy], *Olamah shel ha-Aggadah* (Tel Aviv, 1972); Halevi, *Parashiyyot ba-Aggadah* (Tel Aviv, 1973); Halevi, *Ha-Aggadah ha-historit-biografit le-or mekorot yevaniyyim ve-latiniyyim* I-II (Tel Aviv, 1975–77). The classic studies of Rudolf Bultmann, *Die Geschichte der synoptischen Tradition* (Göttingen, 1965[5]), and Martin Dibelius, *Die Formgeschichte des Evangeliums* (5th edn by G. Bornkamm; Tübingen, 1966), both contain many references to Rabbinic *aggadot*. These should now be treated with great caution.

NOTES

1. A satisfactory nomenclature for the classification of the Rabbinic anecdotes is an obvious desideratum. My terminology is strictly practical. I have reservations about applying to the Rabbinic material terms such as 'sermon', 'Novelle', 'legend', and 'paradigm', which Dibelius, Bultmann and other New Testament form-critics use.

2. *Ma'aseh* at the beginning of biographical anecdotes occurs in a variety of constructions: (1) 'מעשה ש: e.g. M Berakhot 1.1, מעשה שבניו באו מבית; (2) 'מעשה ב' ... ש'; e.g. M Berakhot 2.5, מעשה ברבן גמליאל שקרא; (3) 'מעשה ו': e.g. M Sukkah 2.5, מעשה והביאו לרבן יוחנן בלילה הראשון שנשא. Other openings are: (4) וכבר: e.g. Sifre Deut. 38 בן זכאי לטעום את התבשיל (ed. Finkelstein 74,9), וכבר היו רבי אליעזר ורבי יהושע ורבי צדוק מסובים; (the parallel in TB Kiddushin 32b begins, בבית משתה בנו של רבן גמליאל); (5) 'פעם אחת: e.g. T Berakhot 1.2 (ed. Lieberman 2), 'מעשה ב' ... ש'; (6)... אמרו עליו על: e.g. אמ' ר' יהוד' פעם אחת הייתי מהלך אחר ר' עקיבא; M Berakhot 5.5, אמרו עליו על רבי חנינא בן דוסא, כשהיה מתפלל וגו'. However, many anecdotes plunge *in medias res*, without any stereotyped opening.

3. For a discussion of these stories see M.D. Herr, 'The Historical Significance of the Dialogues between Jewish Sages and Roman Dignitaries', *Scripta Hierosolymitana* 22 (1971), pp. 123-50.

4. See TB Sanhedrin 74a-b; TB Avodah Zarah 27b.

5. See further G. Vermes, *Post-Biblical Jewish Studies* (Leiden, 1975),

p. 179. Strictly speaking the pass. ptcp. qal of שגר is used of something recited without hesitation, and so it can apply to the recitation of a fixed prayer. See M Berakhot 4.3, ר' עקיבא אומר אם שגורה תפלתו בפיו, יתפלל שמונה; עשרה, ואם לאו, מעין שמונה עשרה; T Berakhot 3.3 (ed. Lieberman 12): ר' עקיבא או' אם שגורה תפלתו בפיו סימן יפה לו, ואם לאו סימן רע לו. Note also Exod. R. 9.1, שגר. כיון ששיגרו כל הלילה בפיהם נטלו אותו סימן hif., and Aram. שגר af., mean 'to improvise in prayer', 'to depart from the wording of a standard prayer': see Jastrow, *Dictionary*, 1522b.

6. אף על פי כן מתה בתו בצמא. So Goldschmidt reads (presumably following Bomberg). This is defended by Vermes, *Post-Biblical Jewish Studies*, p. 183 note 14. However, Vilna gives אף על פי כן מת בנו בצמא, 'Nevertheless his son died of thirst'. This appears to be a better attested reading: it is supported by the Munich and Florence codices, and by the parallel in TB Yevamot 121b. But why should Nehuniah's son be so suddenly introduced? The gloss may still be derogatory: Hanina may have saved Nehuniah's daughter, but he could not save Nehuniah's son. On the other hand it could be read as a neutral statement of fact: Nehuniah's daughter was saved, but his son died. The original context of the statement about Nehuniah's son is probably to be found in PT Shekalim V, 48d.30 (ed. Venice): Nehuniah used to dig ditches and cisterns, and he knew which rock would yield water . . . R. Aha said: And his son died of thirst.

7. *Post-Biblical Jewish Studies*, p. 185.

8. So Vermes, *Post-Biblical Jewish Studies*, p. 193.

9. See J. Neusner, *Eliezer b. Hyrcanus*, I (Leiden, 1973), p. 395; further Tz. Zahavy, *Eleazar b. Azariah* (Missoula, 1977), pp. 323-27.

10. The Mekhilta text is taken from a Genizah fragment in the University Library, Cambridge, which was first published by S. Schechter in *JQR*, o.s. 16 (1904), p. 443. The ms is now listed as Add. 3365 according to J. Bowker, *JSS* 16 (1971), p. 159 note 3. For further analysis see J. Neusner, *Development of a Legend: Studies on the Traditions concerning Yohanan b. Zakkai* (Leiden, 1970), pp. 247-51, with Morton Smith's comments in Neusner, *Eliezer b. Hyrcanus*, II, p. 442; also Neusner, 'The Development of the *Merkavah* Tradition', *JSJ* 2 (1971), pp. 149-60; J. Bowker, '"Merkabah" Visions and the Visions of Paul', *JSS* 16 (1971), pp. 157-73; D.J. Halperin, *The Merkabah in Rabbinic Literature* (New Haven, 1980), pp. 108-40. For other synoptic studies of Rabbinic *aggadot* see Neusner, *Development of a Legend*, pp. 187-264; R. Goldenberg, 'The Deposition of Rabban Gamaliel II: An Examination of the Sources', *JJS* 23 (1972), pp. 167-90; S. Safrai, 'Tales of the Sages in the Palestinian Tradition and the Babylonian Talmud', *Scripta Hierosolymitana* 22 (1971), pp. 209-32; P. Schäfer, 'Die Flucht Johanan b. Zakkais aus Jerusalem und die Gründung des "Lehrhauses" in Jabne', in: H. Temporini and W. Haase (eds.), *Aufstieg und Niedergang der Römischen Welt*, II, Principat 19.2 (Berlin/New York, 1979), pp. 43-101; P.S. Alexander, 'Three Enoch and the Talmud', forthcoming in *JSJ*.

11. It is also necessary to take into account manuscript-variants. These are often substantial. In the case of anecdotes which are extant in several recensions it is not always easy, because of conflate readings, to establish the original text of any single recension.

12. See Stith Thompson, *Motif Index of Folk-Literature*, V (Copenhagen, 1957), p. 113, N529.2; cf. pp. 87-88, N211.1 and the cross-references cited there; M. Gaster, *The Exempla of the Rabbis* (1924; repr. New York, 1968), p. 210, no. 118; cf. Matt. 25.27.

13. See M. Elon, 'Ma'aseh', *Encyclopaedia Judaica*, XI (1971), cols. 641-49; H. Albeck, *Mavo la-Mishnah* (3rd edn, Jerusalem/Tel Aviv, 1967), p. 92; Y.N. Epstein, *Mavo le-Nosah ha-Mishnah* (Tel Aviv, 1964), pp. 598-608.

14. However, there is evidence that the supposed tombs of the Maccabean martyrs at Antioch were visited by Jews and the martyrs venerated. See M. Hadas, *The Third and Fourth Books of Maccabees* (New York, 1953), pp. 103-109; E. Bammel, 'Zum jüdischen Märtyrerkult', *TLZ* 78 (1953), cols. 119-26; G. Downey, *A History of Antioch in Syria* (Princeton, 1961), pp. 109-11, 448.

15. It is possible to form some idea of the texts which figured in the Jewish-Christian debate from works such as Cyprian's *Testimonia* (ed. G. Hartel, *Corpus Scriptorum Ecclesiasticorum Latinorum*, [1868], III/1, pp. 35-184). See further J. Neusner, *Aphrahat and Judaism* (Leiden, 1971), pp. 150-244.

16. Safrai takes a more positive and optimistic view of the historicity of the anecdotes. He writes (*Scripta Hierosolymitana* 22 [1971], p. 210): 'The common feature of all such Aggadot is their genuine historical core. Even where conspicuously legendary descriptions are used, it is possible to determine what constitutes the historical element in the narrative, and this can be confirmed by reference to other well grounded accounts appearing in the aggadic tradition or else in the Halakhah. Almost without exception, the deeds ascribed to the Sages have not been severed altogether from authentic traditions and historical fact. It is possible, in most instances, to verify the main element by reference to the Halakhah or else to dicta uttered by the very same person who has happened to become the hero of the story or to statements made by their own immediate circle of disciples. All these items fit in well with the background of the historical reality of the particular generation in which the incident is reputed to have occurred. Generally, too, the names of the Sages of the various generations are not confused in these narratives handed down by tradition, nor are the relations between them inconsistent with respect to their times.' Safrai simply fails to justify his brave assertion that he can separate legend from fact. He must have privileged access to historical reality which the rest of us are denied. The futility of this position has been exposed for all time by the work of Jacob Neusner and his pupils.

17.   I make this as a considered statement, after much reflection. I am fully aware that it is controversial, but my defence of it must wait till another occasion. It would, of course, be absurd to assume that all Rabbinic literature is 'a direct transcript of the oral form'. This is a mistake made by those students of the *petihah* who suppose that the extant *petihot* give us direct access to the synagogue sermon. There can be no doubt that there is literary artifice in the Rabbinic texts—in some more obviously than in others. The memnotechnic formulae of the Mishnaic *halakhot*, which were designed *inter alia* to aid oral transmission, can hardly be typical of early Jewish oral communication: they surely represent a private Rabbinic style. However, I believe that there are elements in Rabbinic literature (principally in certain *meshalim* and *aggadot*) which do illustrate the early Palestinian Jewish oral style of story-telling. The style of early Rabbinic discourse is largely unexplored territory. See J. Neusner, 'Form and Meaning: Mishnah's System and Mishnah's Language', in: Neusner, *Method and Meaning in Ancient Judaism* [I] (Missoula, 1979), pp. 155-81.

CONTEMPORARY ANALOGIES TO THE GOSPELS AND ACTS: 'GENRES' OR 'MOTIFS'?

F. Gerald Downing

Northern Ordination Course
Brighton Grove, Manchester M14 5JP

For half a century, from the early 1920s to the late 1960s, the gospels seem to have been treated as *sui generis*. In the last ten or twelve years *'genre* studies' have increased, perhaps as a by-product of redaction criticism. As C.H. Talbert has pointed out, looking at the gospels as literary 'wholes' is very likely to encourage us to ask questions about the kind of whole they represent, the frame or frames of reference in which they may have been produced and used.[1]

A convenient starting point for the present essay is P.L. Shuler's *A Genre for the Gospels*.[2] I have not read for myself all the secondary literature that he cites (and so any omissions of his are even more so omissions of mine). But I have recently read quite a wide range of writing from around the first Christian century, rather more than Shuler actually refers to. I intend to argue against him (and so also against others with whom he is broadly in agreement) that the attempt to discern importantly distinctive *genres*, *Gattungen*, such as *bios* over against *historia*, or *encomium* as a species over against other kinds of *bios*, is mistaken and misleading. There are, however, I shall suggest, still very important other analogies between various pieces of contemporary narrative literature on the one hand, and our gospels and Acts on the other. I shall also suggest that these analogies imply some negative conclusions for theories of the literary inter-relationships of the synoptic gospels which dispense with 'Q'. More positively I shall suggest that these analogies may encourage and help us in attempts to enable an understanding of the gospels in our own century.

I

First, then, I would agree with Shuler that Talbert has shown K.L. Schmidt, R. Bultmann and others wrong in claiming the synoptic gospels to have been *sui generis*.[3] By demonstrating that there are important *features* in common between these gospels and some examples of contemporary hellenistic literature, Talbert has made it clear that the former are in no general sense 'unique'. However, this does not in itself entail that the gospels exhibit any distinct contemporary 'form'. This latter question remains open. Shuler is also right, I think, in arguing that Talbert has produced sets of *ad hoc* analogies for each of the gospels and Acts in turn, without showing that these sets ever constituted a *genre* recognized as such at the time.[4]

My response to Shuler himself, however, is that though his own attempt to pick out a form that was acknowledged in theoretical discussion at the time is rather more plausible, yet *in practice* there is still no such distinctive form to be found. On the other hand, there are far more common *motifs* to be found than either he or Talbert allow, and these are common motifs that are to be found widely distributed throughout the literature that may appear distinctive or even be theoretically distinguished by writers at that time.

To give Shuler his due, he clearly allows for a degree of fluidity in his chosen *genre* (of *encomium*, laudatory biography).[5] But he hopes nonetheless to demonstrate a 'system of shared conventions', a 'distinctive pattern'. And, still to give him his due, he is able to quote some very apposite and apparently definitive theoretical discussions of the *genre* he proposes for our attention: for instance, Polybius:

> . . . the former work, being in the form of an encomium, demanded a summary and somewhat exaggerated account of [Philopoemen]'s achievements, so the present history, which distributes praise and blame impartially, demands a strictly true account . . .[6]

On the basis of a number of similar references Shuler would seem fully justified, then, in his conclusion:

> As a genre [laudatory biography, encomium] most certainly had at its axis the techniques of amplification and comparison, in addition to those rules of praise codified in the formal encomium. It may be said, therefore, that the genre was concerned with a portrait of the individual, the presentation of the *bios* pattern from birth to death (according to the designs of the author) and that the particular contents of the pattern usually included praiseworthy actions,

deeds, accomplishments, sayings, and so forth, either in toto or in part.[7]

Yet the question must be asked whether many or indeed any first-century hellenistic writers once out of school paid more than lip-service to such ideal recipes and theoretical distinctions.

For instance, Shuler quotes Plutarch, and again, seemingly appositely, in the latter's preface to his Alexander, '... it is not histories that I am writing, but lives...'[8] But, interestingly, Plutarch himself raises the question of history in others of his prefaces (Theseus, Romulus, Lycurgus, Numa, Demosthenes, Marcellus) without making any such distinctions or contrast. In these cases, then, *bios* is assumed to be at least a form of *historia*, even if selection and emphasis may differ (but see further below on even that qualification). And we are able to go further than noting this kind of formal introductory discussion, if we look in detail at the results in Plutarch's (and others') actual writing. How does the treatment of any given character differ between a life by Plutarch and a history by someone else?

As a preface to attempting to answer this question from research of my own, may I point out that Talbert, for instance, drew quite a lot of his evidence for biographical procedures from Josephus's historical works;[9] and that Shuler himself uses Livy as an example of biographical procedure.[10]

It is also worth noting the practice of other historians. Josephus in his *Antiquities* models himself on Dionysius of Halicarnassus's *Roman Antiquities* which in turn are very similar in many respects to Livy's *History of Rome*. Josephus and Dionysius in their histories both include little encomiastic summaries of favourite characters, often including comparisons with others in general or in particular. Josephus (*Vita* 413) tells us we can find the rest of his *bios* in his *Jewish Wars*—that is, there is no call to re-write history as biography, as self-encomium. Though he may feel he needs to apologize for his Greek style, he shows no sign of any need to excuse assimilating biography and history. Further, we find much in common between the respective accounts of Moses and of Joseph as presented by Josephus in history and by Philo in biography (and both sets are as readily milked for examples by Talbert and by Shuler). In just the same way the treatment of Romulus, Numa, Publicola and Camillus in Dionysius's history are very closely reproduced in Plutarch's *Lives*, and that even when Dionysius is not Plutarch's main source.

History and *bios*—whether plain, encomiastic, comparative or whatever—cannot in practice be at all readily distinguished.

I have examined some thirty-three documents (Plutarch, Dionysius, Lucian, Josephus, Philo, Livy, Diogenes Laertius, Quintilian) alongside the four gospels, Acts, and Paul's letters (excluding the Pastorals), and in them have found some 38 recurrent motifs. Obviously some might distinguish or combine what I have discerned (e.g., perils in youth as opposed to perils in following chosen adult path). They are in fact by and large *topoi* that Quintilian picks out in and around the passage Shuler quotes from him in illustration.[11] The only items not in Quintilian on judicial pleading and other public addresses nonetheless also occur very frequently in history-writing, in superficially distinctive auto-/biographical material, in the gospels, Acts and Paul.[12]

If one were wanting to give an account of some fellow-human in these varying contexts, one would be likely to make extensive use of items from this common narrative 'vocabulary' of motifs. I list the proportions that I find, from among the largely pagan sources surveyed (33) and the Christian (6). Historical value of the sources (17:2); family background (27:6); birth (referred to) (11:4); baby-and-childhood (3:2); precocity, beauty—something exceptional in childhood (19:3); trouble in the family (17:4); danger in youth (13:1); concern for ancestral tradition (22:5); perils in full career (25:6); travels (18:6); deliberate risking of death (26:6); self-discipline (22:6); non-miraculous great deeds (16:6); omens, prodigies, miracles (26:6); overt divine guidance (27:6); quality of thought—of a thinker (10:6); effectiveness as teacher, leader (16:6); acknowledged authority (14:6); extent of following (21:6); care for followers (8:6); care for the poor, the underprivileged (21:6); for complete outsiders (12:6); concern for integrity of marriage, sexual purity (22:6); forgiving, reconciling (24:6); superiority to wealth (22:6); concern for law, justice, community (29:6); humility and gentleness (27:6); had some faults, weaknesses (17:6); religious piety (33:6); showed real emotion (23:6); looked to own death (16:6); death and burial (23:5); perhaps alive after death (9:6); influence after death (9:5); and explanations of obscure customs, etc. (22:5). The number of these motifs that occur at least once in each piece is given below in footnote 12. The smallest totals do come in the histories: but they are anyway shorter. Livy's Romulus has as many as Plutarch's (23).

The full weight—or lack of it—of these examples cannot really be judged from such a list. Perhaps some day a fuller study with more examples might be published; but even that could only be substantiated by a careful reading of the sources. It is only a list such as this that Quintilian offers for Shuler to quote.

(It also seems to me that a similar result is forthcoming if you examine one motif in detail—for instance, the death of the hero. Common minor motifs again appear in pagan, Jewish and Christian writing. I hope to display this sometime in a discussion of the final chapters of Mark.)

In preparation for a large collection of excerpts that I have gathered and classified and tabulated to illustrate the first-century world[13] I include ten motifs for the life of the hero, two sets from pagan sources, two from hellenistic Jewish Greek, two from hellenistic Jewish Aramaic/Hebrew, and two Christian. I do not suppose any of them are particularly novel discoveries; but it is very easy to illustrate from such sources the wondrous birth, precocity, calling, signs, trials, followers, death, apotheosis and continuing power of the admired leader—accounts that resemble one another and present problems of selection more than of discovery.

That the use of such motifs is not restricted to particular categories of material should really cause no surprise, even if one starts with a theoretical account such as that in Quintilian. He makes it clear (*Institutes* 3.4.15) that his three genera were further subdivided by others (e.g., Cicero). When he describes his aims—to praise, blame, advise, dissuade, drive home or rebut a charge—they are also the aims of Dionysius in writing history (*R.A.* 1); 'while conciliation, narration, proof, exaggeration, extenuation, and the moulding of the minds of the audience by exciting or allaying their passions are common to all three kinds of oratory' (*ibid.*, as also noted by Shuler); yet not only are these common to all kinds of oratory, they are also aspects of historiography as understood by Dionysius (*ibid.*)

Against the validity of the kind of comparison I am making between early Christian and contemporary hellenistic literature it has been argued, following K.L. Schmidt, that the former is 'obviously' *Kleinliteratur*, and so, as obviously distinct from the latter, aristocratic and highbrow writing. Yet writers like Quintilian are sure you must be able to adjust your material to a diverse audience; you must be able to appeal to the listening crowd as much as to the high-born judges or assessors; you must be able to write imaginary speeches in the style of ordinary people; you must be able to interrogate rustics

(*Institutes* 3.8). Another contemporary, Dio Chrysostom, could teach in Rome, and also scrape a living in exile as a sophist and then as a Cynic missionary to the uttermost parts of the earth. He makes it clear that there were others much more of the people than he, yet with a message and medium much over-lapping with his own (*Discourses* 32, 33, and 42 especially). Listening to speakers who directly or indirectly framed their utterances in these sorts of way was an important part of *popular* entertainment and culture. (H.D. Betz has shown, to my satisfaction at least, how naturally influenced Paul is by the kind of argumentative procedures discussed in Quintilian[14].) Mark writes somewhat lower down the cultural scale than do Plutarch or Quintilian, and more 'provincially' (wherever he was geographically when he wrote), and Luke is a little more 'up-market' than Mark. The 'pieces on the board' of Christian narrative might seem to some rather crudely carved and coloured; but clearly they would be seen as similar sets of similar pieces for a similar narrative 'game'. Read aloud, the Christian writings would have many readily recognizable narrative motifs.

The provisional conclusion to be suggested at this point, then, is that the discernment of contemporary narrative *genres* is of little use. Even if noted at the time they were probably school-room ideals, not researched descriptions of practice. A few parallels with such theoretical models in, say, Matthew tells us little of his likely intention or method in writing. A much more illuminating positive conclusion is that much of our early Christian narrative literature belongs to the ordinary everyday world of first-century narrative communication. It is commonplace, *not* peculiar, not in any way esoteric.

II

Parallels between Christian and other first-century literature are not however restricted to narrative. There are also common motifs in more discourse material. There is just one distinction that I (and others) have found between *bios* and *historia*: only in the latter, by and large, do we find the long consecutive arguments put as speeches on the lips of protagonists to tell the reader or hearer how events are moving or what their implications are for human living; thus when Plutarch uses Livy or Dionysius, the speeches disappear or are summarized; Josephus's Joseph and Moses both allow for speeches which do not occur in Philo (though there is a dialogue in the latter's *Moses*). For all the parallels between Luke's gospel and his Acts it is only in the latter that discursive speeches occur. Looking, however, for the moment, at this point where there does seem to be a 'generic' distinction, I hope that I have effectively shown elsewhere that Luke, Josephus and Dionysius share a very similar inventory of social, political and religious *ideas* from which to stock the more general speeches made by some actors in their histories. It would seem that a writer at the time might well select from the ideas of his group themes he might suppose would match popular educated mildly enlightened and fairly conformist attitudes that obtained among his intended audience, aiming at the common ground of urban culture, avoiding so far as possible local or sectarian idiom, or phrasing it so that the common core showed clearly through the local colouring.[15]

Again it is the motifs (here one could also say 'themes'), the kinds of beads you choose for stringing together, that is significant.

Now, although such speeches do not, or not nearly so often appear in *bios* material as in history, yet other kinds of discourse do. The supposed legislation of Romulus and of Numa occur both in Dionysius's and in Livy's accounts, and again in Plutarch; in fact Plutarch's *Publicola* has such material where it seems lacking in Dionysius's history. And, of course, where we have a portrait of a philosopher, we may have the shapeless (or at best thematic, but scarcely chronological or developmental) string of *chreiae*, pronouncement stories, as in Diogenes Laertius (*passim*) and in Lucian's *Demonax*. As appropriate, a great many of the philosophic hero's opinions may form a large proportion of an account of him. (Even so we may still find quite a large selection of standard narrative motifs here as well: 17 for Lucian's Demonax, 18 for Diogenes Laertius's Diogenes of Sinope, the Cynic.)

These two characters conveniently bring us to our next and for now final set of motifs (or, in this case, again, themes) shared by Christian and other hellenistic literature of the first century. In contrast with most of Luke and with Josephus, these are in the more radical area of contemporary Cynic preaching. Though we may take due note of A.J. Malherbe's protest against lumping Epictetus, Dio Chrysostom and others in a heap with the material in his collection of *Cynic Epistles*,[16] covering them with a catch-all term like 'stoic-cynic', yet there does seem to be at least a genuine continuum. The man from Sinope may appear a little tamed in Dio—though I'm not totally persuaded of that—and Dio's discourses certainly come from different periods of his life and circumstances. But Diogenes figures all through as a more important—more quoted—figure than even Socrates. And even Plutarch, as another instance, gives Socrates only twice the attention Diogenes receives, however conformist Plutarch appears; Plutarch does quote the radical and anti-monarchist *chreiae*. On the basis then of this widespread interest in Cynic radicalism (and in some contrast, as just noted, with Luke and Josephus), I would suggest that some early Christians selected from the common stock of Jesus tradition, stories and teaching, what would look like— and was perhaps meant to look like—a variant of Cynic radicalism. They presented a life-style, a world-view that would have been readily understood by those used to hearing Cynic preachers at street corners, in the markets, in the lecture-halls.[17]

In what now follows I note motifs in 'Q' that are paralleled by Cynic interests and concerns. (Anyone unpersuaded as to the existence of 'Q' can take it as a selection from Matthew which Luke found interesting and Mark did not; or that Matthew added to Mark, to Luke's approval.)

We begin by linking Jesus with a radical predecessor, John (whom Josephus presents as a representative of the 'fourth' philosophy[18]), standard practice in Diogenes Laertius. John is critical and abrasive. True blessedness is considered, poverty preferred. Retaliation is rebuked, as is judging others without self-awareness. Deeds are what matter. Strangers may well respond better than fellow-citizens. Royalty is despised. The preacher expects to be a disturbance. He makes adults consider children. He details the preacher's impoverished life-style. Whole communities are castigated. The disciple prays as son to divine father, and no one else rules him; the greatest peril is inner blindness; morality over-rides ritual concerns. Like the Cynic, the 'Q' disciple is expected to announce his truth fearlessly. He avoids this-worldly cares, and the dangers of wealth; he is ready to respond to any divine summons. As such he may split families; but the divine demands of the present far outweigh the securing of future ease. There are two ways, and the disciple chooses the hard one that is right.

If a group went round south Syria, say, preaching this kind of message, I do not see how their hearers could avoid at least asking, are these some new Cynics? Even their dress, as G. Theissen has pointed out, would raise the question.

It is further intriguing that 'special Matthew' (or, for some, those parts of Matthew that Luke preferred to forgo) actually seems to intensify the resemblance (or, again, it might be stated as 'the parts Luke chose to forgo are even closer in many respects to broadly Cynic teaching'). The links with Magi and Egypt, the request for instruction on 'the good', all point to a 'philosopher': the leader insists on initiation; he stresses 'interiority'; he refuses to return abuse; he cares about sexual mores, including the indulgence of lustful feelings; he refuses oaths; he demands perfection; he insists that God sees all; common human example is not good enough; religion should not be ostentatious; the day's ills are enough for the day; the golden rule is to be adopted; but help is to be given to those who need it, not those who can repay; mankind is a mixed lot, like tares among wheat; there is a responsibility to 'shepherd' others; there is the possibility of a special filial awareness of the divine purpose; as sons, the disciples are free; the divine presence is close; human response must be consistent (and forgiving); discipleship may involve celibacy; service to God and man is 'alike'; others must be made aware of their 'hypocrisy'; and disciples must avoid it.[19]

For much (or even all of this) there may well be rabbinic parallels. This is not an argument about provenance, but about selection and presentation. This sort of selection would, I suggest, have created many resonances for many pagans or ex-pagans who heard it. It would seem very unlikely that 'Matthew' could have remained unaware, even supposing the resemblances were originally coincidental. Luke, as I have suggested, seems determined to lessen them. Matthew must be supposed to have been at the very least happy to let them stand.

I have tried to show something of the extent to which these early Christian documents fit within the general public culture of the day—general, rather than merely provincial or merely sectarian (though of course provincial and sectarian traits remain strong).

III

If we accept on the basis of the evidence here referred to that at least the gospels and Acts constitute an integral part of the continuum of hellenistic literature of the time, then it would seem to follow that in considering how they were put together we should consider very carefully contemporary hellenistic redactional procedures. Fairly recently I published a two-part article comparing the redactional procedures of Luke in particular with those of Josephus.[20] Their stated aims are very similar, as are their redactional preferences. This seems to afford us our closest and fullest analogy, a Jewish hellenistic writer recasting a sacred text, and at times having to 'conflate' parallel narratives.

The picture I drew there of Josephus is supported by the standard understanding of the relationship between Dionysius of Halicarnassus and Livy[21] as depending on a 'common lost source'. There do not seem to be many detailed source-critical studies (I have yet to find many) in this Greco-Roman field. I do note an analysis of Plutarch's use of Dionysius's Coriolanus by D.A. Russell, which arrives at conclusions very similar to mine on Josephus—expansion, abridgment, occasional transposition.[22] I have myself attempted a comparison of Dionysius's Camillus (*R.A.* 12.8ff.) with that of Livy (5.13ff.) and of Plutarch (*Camillus* 2ff.). It would seem quite clear that whatever the relationship of the original pair, Plutarch, writing a century or so later, depends on both. He conflates a few details (the significance of the Alban lake, the description of the Roman kidnapper) and adds some further ideas not in either. He re-orders to make a more rational—and economic—narrative (the Veiian citizen does not blab about the crucial oracle before being taken to the Roman head-quarters for interrogation). Usually one factor is dealt with at a time—e.g., the failure to celebrate the Latin festival aright. It is perhaps relevant to note that when Plutarch explicitly cites Livy he misquotes him (on whether the statue of Juno was thought to have spoken, or only later said to have done).[23]

Plutarch thus produces his story in his own way, fairly arbitrarily, happily paraphrasing, re-writing, with no attempt to piece together bits of his parallel narrative sources. This is very similar to Josephus's use of the sacred text of scripture. It is also, as I suggested in the article referred to above, quite like the imagined use of Mark and 'Q' and other material by Matthew on his own, and again by Luke using Mark and 'Q' and other material of his own. Both writers would have to be seen to be quoting verbatim rather more than do self-conscious stylists such as Plutarch; Josephus quotes very little. But it is quite simple, following Josephus's procedure, to add teaching material ('Q' plus other sayings) into a largely distinct narrative framework (Mark). It is very rare (on this hypothesis) for Mark and 'Q' to overlap; where they do they can be conflated by simple addition for the most part (baptism, Beelzebul, mission charge, apocalypse). There is no long sequence of parallel but not always unanimous narrative to confuse the redactor.

Other hypotheses of synoptic origins ask us to imagine the third writer of the trio coping with precisely that kind of complexity: Luke conflating Mark and Matthew[24] or Mark conflating Matthew and Luke.[25] Every available analogy we have from the time suggests that neither starting point would have produced the result supposed. Either 'third' writer would have to be supposed to have carefully 'unpicked' the second's use of the first. For such a procedure there is no contemporary analogy at the time, nothing to suggest it was worth doing, no guidance on how to do it (difficult enough with printed synopses and coloured pens; extremely difficult with lengthy scrolls on small tables).[26]

It is not impossible to suggest plausible reasons for Mark wanting to conflate (even, conflate and condense) Matthew and Luke; or for Luke wanting to write his own version of Mark and Matthew. Intentions are easy to imagine. What cannot plausibly be imagined is our early Christian writers finding any reason to unpick before re-writing. Every contemporary analogy in the literature among which I hope I have shown they belong would have pressed in the other direction.

If this assertion that the two hypotheses being criticized involve such a procedure is doubted, I can only refer the reader to the discussions listed at note 25, but otherwise repeat some very general indications that can perhaps be checked in a synopsis. If Luke knew and used Matthew and Mark (including Matthew's version of Mark) why are there so *few* and such minimal agreements with Matthew's use of Mark? In sequences such as the Baptism, the Beelzebul controversy, and so on, where on this hypothesis Matthew has expanded an existing Markan passage with new material as well as quoting some of Mark closely, and has apparently adapted other parts, Luke omits any of the close quotations, re-adapts the adaptations, but often cites the unique additions word-for-word. This is clean contrary to *anything* our other first-century sources would lead us to expect. Twin sources in close agreement would be followed closely; here agreement is spurned. In disagreement a third version would be written, only loosely following either of the other; here it is disagreement which is closely followed. Not only is the material 'unpicked', then, and meticulously, but it is unpicked to allow an unprecedented and barely coherent choice.

Mark as conflater of Matthew and Luke is even odder; not only is he involved in a similar unpicking, but he refuses *even more* ready-made conflation, *all* the really close Matthew-Luke parallels in contexts he preserves, affording material with very similar import.

It must be emphasized again, at the risk of tedium, that there is here *no* argument to suggest that possible motives could not be found that *could* have led such a Luke or a Mark to want to convey a message in general and in detail such as we find, in preference to the other two used as sources. The discernment of 'intentions' always 'over-determines' any given literary product, anyway. Purposes can easily be imagined, and supported in detail. What is being argued is that it would have been *in each case* an illogical way of attaining such an end, a technically very difficult way, and a way for which there is no contemporary analogy. It is these factors that make a Griesbach or a Farrer hypothesis implausible.

The gospels do not at other points appear *sui generis*; it would be strange if the 'third' of any scheme of literary dependence were to have been nonetheless an innovator on this scale: if Luke, especially because he is even closer in his express intentions to contemporary writing; if Mark, because he is even odder in his procedures.

IV

There is a further corollary that perhaps deserves attention. A great deal of 'background', 'environment' or 'context' research that is done seems concerned to discover the 'origin' or the 'sources' of New Testament ideas, whether main-stream Jewish (if such there were), or sectarian or hellenistic; or pagan mystery ideas, local and specific or widespread and syncretistic; or gnostic; or popular philosophical; or something else vaguely 'religious'. It is 'source' or 'origin' that is sought.

The question of the *destination* of the writing, and the writer's or writers' awareness of their audience seems to get lost. Yet the consideration of links, parallels, analogies, whatever, from the 'audience' angle does make quite a difference: it makes a difference to selection, style, and expression. It is rather less likely that the audience affords the actual *content* of what you want to say, at all. Some audiences might want simply to receive their own current opinions clearly echoed back to them—perhaps that was the way with sophists. But even a sophist's hearers wanted some novelty. Luke might want to show the Christians held an entirely respectable variant of vaguely stoic theism; but it was their own version. Matthew's fellow Christians would not, I guess, after the cost of conversion, have simply wanted to have their original Judaism or original cynic paganism regurgitated. But the selection, style and expression may very well have been heavily influenced by a writer's understanding of his intended hearers.

A final point follows, I think, from this one. If the gospels and Acts do appear to be part of the general public culture of the time, then our evidence for early Christianity is for a faith from the start in process of interpretation and translation; and it is being translated for a diverse culture that could be sceptical as well as credulous, empiricist as well as theoretical and idealist, quotidian and secular as well as pious and prayerful. It is not 'relativized' to one provincial sect. And that ought to make translation and interpretation for our own century easier both in principle and in practice. We have many more clues from the first century than our more pessimistic 'cultural relativists' allow.[27]

NOTES

1. C.H. Talbert, *What is a Gospel?* (Philadelphia, 1977); compare also C.W. Votaw, *The Gospels and Contemporary Biographies in the Greco-Roman World* (Philadelphia, 1970[2]).

2. P.L. Shuler, *A Genre for the Gospels* (Philadelphia, 1982).

3. Shuler, *Genre*, ch. 1.

4. Shuler, *Genre*, pp. 21f.

5. Shuler, *Genre*, pp. 26f., 56; note recently the comments on genre by H.C. Kee, 'The Socio-cultural setting of *Joseph and Asenath*', *NTS* 29 (1983), p. 397: his own conclusions, and those cited from B.E. Perry.

6. Shuler, *Genre*, pp. 21, 29, and p. 38, top (from Polybius 10.21.8).

7. Shuler, *Genre*, pp. 56f.; cf. his very apposite quotation from Quintilian, *Institutes* 3.7.10-18, on pp. 53f.

8. Shuler, *Genre*, p. 40, quoting from Plutarch, *Alexander and Caesar* 1.1-3.

9. Talbert, *op. cit*, pp. 35, 36, 57, and nine notes.

10. Shuler, *Genre*, p. 91.

11. See n. 7 above.

12. The following are the 'characters' from the respective authors, with (in brackets) the number of motifs from my list below that I have detected in

each. Plutarch: Theseus (25), Romulus (23), Lycurgus (24), Numa (19), Demosthenes (25), Cicero (25), Solon (19), Publicola (11), Alexander (27), Caesar (20), Agesilaus (23), Pompey (22), Pelopidas (24), Camillus (20), Marcellus (18); Dionysius: Romulus (*R.A.* 1 and 2) (24), Numa (*R.A.* 2) (16), Publicola (*R.A.* 4,5) (18), Camillus (10); Livy: Romulus (Bk. 1) (23), Numa (Bk. 2) (6), Publicola (Bk. 4) (8), Camillus (Bk. 5) (15); Lucian: Demonax (17), Alexander (18), Peregrinus (26); Philo: *de Ios.* (27), *de Vit. Mos.* 1 and 2 (27); Josephus: Joseph (*Ant.* 2) (25); Moses (*Ant.* 2, 3, 4) (27); and Josephus himself (*Life*) (26); Diogenes Laertius, Diogenes of Sinope (VI) (18); Quintilian, *Institutes* 3.4-8 (25); Matthew (33); Mark (30); Luke (36); John (29); Acts (32); Paul in Galatians, 2 Corinthians and Philippians (30). The histories do on average have less (but still note both Dionysius's and Livy's Romulus, and Josephus's Joseph and Moses. Some reference to the character in youth is in most Lives—but missing from Plutarch's Publicola, and effectively from his Caesar; compare Mark and John . . .).

13. *Strangely Familiar*, forthcoming.

14. H.D. Betz, *Galatians* (Philadelphia, 1981).

15. Compare my 'Ethical Pagan Theism and the Speeches in Acts', *NTS* 27 (1981), p. 544.

16. A.J. Malherbe, *The Cynic Epistles* (Missoula, 1977), Introduction, p. 1.

17. Dio Chrysostom, *Discourses* 32.9-10; 33.3-6; 42.4, especially.

18. Josephus, *Ant.* 18.4-10, 23-25, 116-19. Luke's John is noticeably conformist by contrast. Though Luke includes this cynic—sounding material, the approval of Roman officials in Acts makes it respectable.

19. Sources for the lists (which I spell out at greater length in 'Cynics and Christians', *NTS*, forthcoming) include Dio Chrysostom, Epictetus, Diogenes Laertius, Seneca, and *Cynic Epistles* (see above n. 16) together with oddments from elsewhere. It is noted how content later Christians were to accept the resemblances (or some of them).

20. 'Redaction Criticism: Josephus' *Antiquities* and the Synoptic Gospels', *JSNT* 8 (1980), pp. 46-65; 9 (1980), pp. 29-48.

21. Compare the Introduction by E. Cary to the Loeb edition (Harvard, 1937).

22. D.A. Russell, 'Coriolanus', *JRS* 53 (1963), p. 1; also C.B.R. Pelling, 'Plutarch's Method of Work in the Roman Lives', *JHS* 19 (1979), pp. 74-96, and 'Plutarch's Adaptation of his Source Material', *JHS* 20 (1980), pp. 127-40. 'This biographical genre is an extremely flexible one' (p. 139).

23. I hope to publish this study in due course.

24. See M. Goulder, *Midrash and Lection in Matthew* (London, 1974), and various articles; J. Drury, *Tradition and Design in Luke's Gospel* (London, 1976).

25. Mark conflating Matthew and Luke, W.R. Farmer, *The Synoptic Problem* (New York, 1964); B. Orchard, *Matthew, Luke and Mark* (Manchester, 1976). For an analysis of the procedure involved, see the

careful study by C.M. Tuckett, *The Revival of the Griesbach Hypothesis* (Cambridge, 1983); see also my 'Towards the Rehabilitation of "Q"', *NTS* 11 (1965), pp. 169-81.

26. W. Sanday, 'The Conditions under which the Gospels were written', in W. Sanday (ed.), *Studies in the Synoptic Problem* (Oxford, 1911), pp. 16ff. C.B.R. Pelling, *opera citeriora*.

27. See again n. 13 above.

A GRIESBACHIAN PERSPECTIVE ON THE ARGUMENT FROM ORDER

David L. Dungan

Department of Religious Studies
University of Tennessee, Knoxville, Tennessee 37996

One of the critical areas of disagreement within current debate over the Synoptic Problem is the proper interpretation of the evidence dealing with the order of pericopes in the Synoptic Gospels. We are just beginning to glimpse the full significance of the warning uttered some years ago by E.P. Sanders, to wit:

> ... the facts of order as they are usually stated are misleading; the phenomenon of order has yet to be stated and explained adequately.[1]

In his subsequent article on the subject,[2] however, Sanders failed to deal squarely with the most important source of confusion: the fact that the two most widely used synopses today are very misleadingly arranged. He did note one very important fact, however. He showed how Tischendorf's synopsis did not reveal certain literary phenomena that Huck's did.[3] But he failed to press this discovery to the full extent it should be.

For example, I am convinced that part of the reason why Griesbach's statement of the literary facts regarding the phenomena of order of pericopes fails to convince anyone today is because of the simple fact that no one uses *his* synoptic chart to look at the evidence he saw. His statement is well known:

> Mark compiled his whole work (i.e., apart from about 24 verses . . .) from the works of Matthew and Luke in such a manner that (A) it can easily be shown what he took from the one and what he took from the other; (B) he retained the order preserved by Matthew in such a way that wherever he forsakes it he sticks to the path of Luke and follows him and the order of his narrative step by step, to such an extent that, (C) the verses and words where he passes from Matthew to Luke or returns from Luke to Matthew can not only be

pointed out, but also (D) the probable reason can generally be
given . . .[4]

and further:

> When Mark has closely adhered to either Matthew or Luke for a
> long stretch, he often passes with a sudden leap from one to the
> other, but soon returns to his former guide; and this could not have
> been done unless he had simultaneously seen and compared the
> works of each.[5]

Griesbach's reference to the 'sudden leap from one to the other' is
a 'fact' that can be seen or not seen depending upon the synopsis one
uses. Since the vast majority of scholars today use either Huck or
Aland, it is hardly surprising that they regard Griesbach's description
of Mark's behaviour with considerable skepticism, for the simple fact
is that Huck's arrangement is only partially suited to a demonstration
of this sort of evidence, while Aland has arranged his synopsis
according to no principle whatever except atomization into details.
In other words, to see what Griesbach saw, one should use the
synoptic chart he included with his discussion. Then what he
described is very easy to see.[6]

Indeed, in view of the naive and unselfcritical use of the synopses
now in print, I am not surprised at the incredible spectacle of Two
Document proponents (from Streeter down to our own times)
confusedly using the exact same, i.e., Griesbachian, statement of the
literary facts regarding order of pericopes as a prime support for the
priority of Mark. Recently, of course, this situation has been noticed
and a few Markan priorists have conceded that the use of Griesbach's
argument for Markan *priority* was 'logically fallacious' (Neirynck,
Tuckett). But the damage is visible all across the board. The most
egregious symptom is the wide-spread conviction among the majority
of our colleagues that this aspect of the Synoptic Problem is one of
many 'reversible' arguments, i.e., all that the argument from order
'proves' is that Mark is merely some sort of 'middle term'. We will
fight our way out of this morass only by means of a new generation of
synopses that are organised with much greater sophistication than is
the case today. A long step in the right direction is the new synopsis
by J.B. Orchard, *Greek Synopsis of the Four Gospels* (Edinburgh,
1983).[7]

Moving to the second notable feature of the current debate
regarding order of pericopes, and in light of what has just been noted

in the last paragraph, I wish to comment on a very recent development among the leading Markan priorists. If they have called for the relinquishment of Streeter's statement of the argument from order as any 'proof' for the priority of Mark, what do they propose to use instead? They must have *some* sort of position regarding this very important phenomenon.

To give us an answer to this question, we cannot do better than to consider Frans Neirynck's claim that it is not necessarily 'scientific' to begin by examining all *three* Gospels simultaneously. In his article on the 'Synoptic Problem' for the *Interpreter's Dictionary of the Bible, Supplementary Volume*, Neirynck has written:

> The relative order of sections in Mark is in general supported by both Matthew and Luke; where Matthew diverges from Mark, Mark's order is supported by Luke, and where Luke differs from Mark, Mark's order is supported by Matthew. From this statement of the absence of agreement in order between Matthew and Luke against Mark . . . proponents of the two-document hypothesis draw the conclusion that Mark is the common source, independently edited by Matthew and Luke.

This statement of the literary facts is well known. All that is missing is for Neirynck to have said on which synoptic arrangement it is possible for him to *see* the literary phenomena he here describes. Be that as it may, Neirynck pauses to give all Two Document proponents an historic warning: this argument will no longer serve as 'proof' for the priority of Mark:

> [As to the validity of this argument,] B.C. Butler has contended that there is a logical error in the traditional argument from order. A number of scholars, among them some who continue to espouse the two-document hypothesis on other grounds (Styler, Fuller), have in fact dismissed the argument as useless.

Neirynck himself clearly agrees with this dismissal. Then he continues with an equally historic proposal: the theory of the priority of Mark must be given a *new starting point* with regard to the phenomenon of order:

> However, some other observations need to be made.
> i. If the relative order of the gospel *episodes* [sic] is studied as a specific literary phenomenon, it becomes clear that there are virtually no places where Matthew and Luke agree against Mark . . .
> ii. The description of the evidence as 'alternating support' (i.e.,

when Matthew diverges from Mark, Mark's order is supported by
Luke, and when Luke diverges from Mark, Mark's order is
supported by Matthew) should be corrected by a more concrete
approach. In fact *the basic phenomenon to be reckoned with is the
common order between Mark and Matthew and between Mark and
Luke.*[8]

The suggestion put forward here by Neirynck is nothing else than
the approach originally pioneered by Lachmann in response to
Griesbach. In analogy with a carefully conceived opening in chess,
we might call this the 'Lachmann Gambit'. Neirynck considers it to
be 'the more concrete approach', not only here but also in other
writings. Correspondingly, he accuses the Neo-Griesbachians of
'abstract thinking', and urges them to take 'a more concrete approach'.
For example, he distributed at the Münster Griesbach Colloquium a
paper later printed under the title, 'The Griesbach Hypothesis: The
Phenomenon of Order', *ETL* 58 (1982), pp. 111-22. In it he complained
that the 'post-Butlerian era' (for Neirynck the modern fortunes of the
Two-Document Hypothesis fall into two 'eras'—before and after
Butler's book on Matthew) was hampered by too much 'abstract
thinking':

> In a previous study on the argument from order[9] I observed that
> for too long this discussion has been characterized by *abstract
> reasoning* [sic], which is still the case in the 'post-Butlerian' era. I
> noted with reference to Farmer's argument, 'the significance of the
> phenomenon [*sc.* the absence of agreement against Mark] becomes
> questionable with a more concrete approach. The basic statement
> remains the common order Mark-Matthew and Mark-Luke.[10]

Note that the complaint is directed at Farmer for emphasizing
something 'abstract', namely, the seeming importance of 'lack of
agreement against Mark'. Neirynck's objection appears to consist in
the claim that Farmer has over-emphasized a side issue, a minor
aspect of the total evidence. In place of this, he urges us to focus our
attention on something else, something more central and basic,
namely the *common order*—specifically (a) the common order between
Matthew and Mark on the one hand, and (b) the extensive common
order between Luke and Mark on the other. To Neirynck, this
approach is 'more concrete' presumably because it allegedly focusses
our attention on a phenomenon that is more basic, more numerous,
more widespread, etc. Of course, the whole battle to find the proper
starting point is precisely the task of finding what is most 'natural' or

least arbitrary. One begins with what is most basic and proceeds from there. But how is one to determine what is most basic in this case? Neirynck sheds further light on his thinking in the continuation of the paragraph quoted above:

> In Luke, the alternations of the Marcan order are limited in number, and the transpositions in Matthew are confined to Mt 4,23–11,1. Emphasis upon the alternating support seems to imply that agreements and disagreements with the relative order of Mark are treated as comparable quantities. In fact, disagreement against Mark is the exception and the absence of concurrence between Matthew and Luke is less surprising that the somewhat misleading formulation 'whenever the other departs' may suggest.[11]

As one reads this, two impressions arise. First of all, it does seem to be the case that Neirynck is at least in part thinking in *numerical* or quantitative terms. He appears to be thinking in terms of those phenomena that have the greater numerical preponderance. Secondly, and more importantly, one wonders what synoptic arrangement he was using. Since he had not told us, we might accidentally stumble into a trap by using a very differently arranged synopsis than the one he used to 'see' the evidence to begin with. To overstate matters a bit, his statements could be quite 'true' with one synopsis, and quite 'false' with another one. I have seen some arrangements that heighten the amount of disagreement among the Gospels, and others that conceal the divergences. If Neirynck was using a synopsis similar to Huck's, and I believe he was,[12] then he used a very misleading arrangement of the Gospel texts, and I would need to have much more explanation from him as to how he arrived at his generalizations about the common order. Third, and most important, from a Griesbachian point of view, Neirynck still misstates the Neo-Griesbachian approach with regard to the phenomena of order: we look at the *combination* of triple agreement in order *and* alternating support (especially the sudden Markan leaps from one side to the other) which *together* comprise the whole set of data to be accounted for.

Be this as it may, Neirynck himself must have felt dissatisfied with what he had just said, for he continued to argue the point in a footnote appended to the end of the last sentence. This was no 'mere footnote', however, for it contained the crux of the whole discussion, including the only admission I know of that his position in this respect is simply a repetition of Lachmann's:

This [approach I am taking] is only a return to the original Lachmann argument. [As such, I do not understand] what is meant [by Farmer's reference to] Lachmann's 'oversimplification', [nor why Farmer should say] that 'a great disservice has been done to gospel studies by Karl Lachmann's method of comparing Mark with Matthew and Luke with Mark *one by one* rather than *together*' [sic]. But is there any scientific basis for the assumption that all three Gospels should be 'viewed together at once', 'in a single, synthetic judgment'?[13]

A good question. Is there, indeed? I dare say we are at the heart of the matter. What really *is* the most 'scientific' starting point, no matter whether one wishes to work with the Two-Document Hypothesis, the Two-Gospel Hypothesis, or any of the other more complex theories involving multiple lost recensions of Ur-gospels? This much can safely be said. Neirynck and the Neo-Griesbachians do agree that the argument from order of pericopes is the most fundamental *issue*—the one which must be dealt with at the very outset.[14] But even then the question arises: how does one know when one has grasped it in its most fundamental aspects, in its essentials? I will say this: we are at this very moment looking at the *only* fundamental disagreement separating Neirynck and the Neo-Griesbachian School.

Having said that, we must therefore put the question to him: is it really more natural, less arbitrary, truly logical to *begin* by examining just Mark with Matthew and then Mark with Luke? To start off by looking at only two at a time? Why just those pairs? The proposal strikes me as rather a strange idea. Why should a theologically motivated ploy that arose in Lachmann's mind as a way of combatting the fearful scholarship emanating from the circle of Tübingen 'atheists' now claim to be, in *our* time, the most 'scientific' starting point possible? I should have thought that anyone would realize that one mustn't *begin* the comparison of the Gospels by hacking the set into two halves, and then examining each half piecemeal all by itself, i.e., without ever looking at the other half. An approach like that is bound to result in abstract reasoning; it isn't nearly concrete enough.

NOTES

1. *Tendencies of the Synoptic Tradition* (Cambridge, 1969), p. 277.

2. 'The Argument from Order and the Relationship between Matthew and Luke', *NTS* 15 (1969), pp. 249-61.

3. At one point, Sanders put his finger squarely on one of the little-understood but central problems: 'The usual statement . . . that either Matthew or Luke supports Mark's order except where both omit the passage entirely (see Streeter, *Four Gospels*, p. 161) . . . is true, however, only if one limits one's view to *complete pericopes as they are set forth in Tischendorf's synopsis*' (sic). Then he makes an extraordinarily important observation bearing directly upon the fundamental question of order: by what criterion does one decide *how much* to divide up the Gospels' narrative for purposes of comparison? Sanders notes, 'Such a limitation [of the size of pericopes in Tischendorf's synopsis] would be justifiable only if one wished to establish, by comparing our Gospels, the original order of *events* [sic] in the Ur-Gospel, and thus, it would be hoped, in Jesus' own life'. Although I do not agree that this is the *only* possible motivation, Sanders *has* touched on what I consider to be the main redactional consideration of our original authors, and hence the only logical criterion for division of the narrative in our modern synopses if, and only if, their chief use is intended to be redactional research. Neither Huck nor Aland nor Benoit–Boismard is so constructed. Sanders goes on: 'This limitation [to "events"] is completely unwarranted if one wishes to investigate the literary relations among our Gospels'. That is a blatant non-sequitur. But Sanders adds: '*When smaller units are brought into view* it is readily seen that there are places in which neither Matthew nor Luke follows Mark's order' (emphasis mine). What Sanders actually means by this last sentence is that if one wished to do *form-critical analysis* of the narratives, then the artificially small divisions (so typical of today's synopses) are quite appropriate, although both Greeven's revision of Huck and Aland have become *so* detailed, and oriented to such microscopic comparison, that it is clear they have been (consciously or unconsciously) prepared for the text critic and no one else.

4. Trans. J.B. Orchard and T.R.W. Longstaff (eds.), *J.J. Griesbach: Synoptic and Text-critical Studies 1776–1976* (Cambridge, 1978), p. 108.

5. *Ibid.*, p. 113.

6. See *ibid.*, pp. 78-79.

7. See especially the Introduction, pp. xi-xv. With regard to this very important reversal in basic position, I believe it was G.M. Styler who was the first of the Markan priorists to admit in print that it was 'illogical' to use Griesbach's argument from order to support the opposite conclusion, a view he now repeats in C.F.D. Moule's third edition of *The Birth of the New Testament* (London, 1982), p. 290. See also C.M. Tuckett, 'The Argument from Order and the Synoptic Problem', *TZ* 36 (1980), pp. 338-54. The article by Malcolm Lowe, 'The Demise of Arguments from Order for Markan Priority', *NovT* 24 (1982), pp. 27-36, on the other hand, is a glaring example of what Neirynck calls 'abstract reasoning'.

8. *Interpreter's Dictionary of the Bible, Supplementary Volume*, K. Crim et al. (eds.) (Nashville, 1976), pp. 845f.

9. 'The Argument from Order and St Luke's Transpositions', *ETL* 49 (1973), pp. 784-815, reprinted as an appendix in his *The Minor Agreements of Matthew and Luke Against Mark* (Louvain, 1974).

10. *Op. cit.*, p. 114.

11. *Loc. cit.*

12. He and Professor A. Denaux (Brugge) are about to publish a Dutch synopsis that differs from Huck in only a few major respects, principally the location of the Sermon on the Mount vis-à-vis the order of Mark. Instead of locating it after Mark 3.19 (with Tischendorf, Lagrange, Boismard, Aland, Orchard), or after Mark 1.39 (Huck and imitators), he locates it after Mark 1.20 (where Griesbach also put it in his Synopsis); see his 'The Sermon on the Mount in the Gospel Synopsis', *ETL* 52 (1976), pp. 350-57.

13. 'The Griesbach Hypothesis: The Phenomenon of Order', *ETL* 58 (1982), p. 115 n. 19.

14. Here also Neirynck provides an exceptionally important clarification, with which I am in total agreement—and, curiously, it brings us back to the first point made by E.P. Sanders. At the end of his consideration of the research of Sanders and Farmer in 'The Griesbach Hypothesis' Neirynck says: 'I would like to make here just one general remark: although the study of the location of individual sentences and phrases is undeniably most interesting, it should not be confused with the specific phenomenon of the relative order of the gospel sections (*ordo narrationum, Perikopenfolge*) which is more directly related to the composition of the gospel as a whole and remains particularly important in questions of literary relationship' (p. 121). Although Neirynck does not explain why this distinction is so important (and I do not intend to go into this in any length here), this much should be pointed out: the essential reason is because the *paragraph* divisions are related to *events* conceived of as wholes or 'meaning units', which is the way the Gospel writers tended to use their materials. Fragments like sentences or phrases, on the other hand, are a *modern* print-oriented invention, made possible by our synopses themselves. I would go further. Precisely because the most commonly used synopses are so misleadingly constructed, the view took root and grew up which says that the Gospel materials were passed on in small snippets of tradition (the theory known as 'Form Criticism'). Nothing could be further from the truth.

CERTAIN RESULTS REACHED
BY SIR JOHN C. HAWKINS AND C.F. BURNEY
WHICH MAKE MORE SENSE IF LUKE KNEW MATTHEW,
AND MARK KNEW MATTHEW AND LUKE

W.R. Farmer

Perkins School of Theology
Southern Methodist University, Dallas, Texas 75275

While the question of 'Q' may remain a viable one for many, I intend to proceed on the methodological assumption that most experts are now willing to grant that the case for 'Q' has been damaged by the work of Austin Farrer and others, and that it may be a useful exercise to turn back to the work of two earlier Oxford scholars and consider some of their conclusions from a 'post-Farrer' vantage point.

Sir John C. Hawkins

On pp. 168-72 of his book, *Horae Synopticae* (Oxford, 1909[2]), in a section entitled 'The Transference and Repetition of Formulas, Especially in Matthew', Hawkins sets forth evidence which leads him to ask: 'Do not such cases of repetition and transference of formulas point . . . to oral processes of preservation and transmission?' (p. 173). For our purposes, the few examples of what Hawkins calls 'transference' may be set aside (pp. 172-73). It is the 'repetition of formulas' listed on pp. 168-71 that interests us.

Hawkins defines what he has in mind by the use of the term 'formula' as follows: 'For want of a better word, I use the term "formula" to express the short sentences, or collocations of two or more words, which recur mainly or exclusively in one or other of the Synoptic Gospels, so that they appear to be favourite or habitual expressions of the writer of it' (p. 168).

Hawkins divides these 'formulas' into two categories. The first category consists of formulas 'confined exclusively to one Gospel'. He lists 15 such formulas peculiar to Matthew, 6 peculiar to Mark, and 12 peculiar to Luke. Hawkins notes that these lists of formulas 'are not intended to be exhaustive, but to give specimens of expressions or "formulas" peculiar to each Synoptist'. What is important to note is this: Even though these lists may not be complete, they nonetheless indicate that all three of the synoptic Gospels contain 'formulas' which appear to Hawkins to be 'favourite or habitual expressions' of the respective writers.

It is the second category of 'repeated' formulas that interests us most. Here, Hawkins makes no similar disclaimer that his lists may be incomplete. He writes as follows: 'But there is another class of them [repeated formulas] which is more important and interesting, because it is more likely to throw light upon the process of the formation of the Gospels. I mean those which are used once (or, in a few cases, twice) by a Synoptist in common with one or both of the others, and are *also* used by that Synoptist independently in other parts of his narrative'.

In the case of Matthew, Hawkins lists 19 'favourite and habitual expressions' of Matthew which are used once or twice by Matthew in common with one or both the other Synoptists, and are *also* used by Matthew 'independently in other parts of his narrative'.

How does this evidence weigh in testing the hypothesis that Matthew copied Mark and 'Q'? We cannot determine with accuracy the extent to which the hypothetical 'Q' contained formulas used in common with Matthew and Luke, but used by the author of 'Q' independently in other parts of that document, since we do not have the document and cannot check what that document may or may not have contained apart from what has been copied by Matthew and/or Luke. So, Hawkins's data affords us no proper test of 'Q'. But it would appear to be quite different in the case of the hypothesis that Matthew copied Mark. Here we might expect that Matthew would, in the process of copying Mark, inadvertently take over into his text some of the 'favourite or habitual expressions' of Mark. How could he avoid doing so, unless he studiously determined which formulas Mark used two or more times and decided to conveniently omit these formulas from the text of his Gospel? While this is not impossible, it appears to me to be unlikely.

But, is there anything in Hawkins's data that can be construed as positive evidence which will 'throw light upon the process of formation of the Gospels'? Hawkins certainly thought so, and he concluded: 'A careful examination of such cases [formulas of Matthew used in common with one or both the other synoptists, and *also* used by Matthew independently elsewhere in his Gospel] certainly [*sic*] leaves the impression that the mind of Matthew was so familiar with these collocations of words that he naturally reproduced them in other parts of his narrative, besides the places in which they occurred in his sources'. Hawkins continues: 'It is to be observed that these apparent reproductions often occur earlier in the Gospel [of Matthew] than do the apparently original occurrences of the formulas, which seems to indicate that Matthew drew them from his memory of his sources and not from documents before him. So far as it goes, then, the drift of this section is in favor of some considerable element of the oral theory' (pp. 171-72).

What is there in the linguistic data compiled by Hawkins that leads him to such an unusual and unexpected conclusion? I may be using the terms 'unexpected' and 'unusual' anachronistically. In any case, I think most experts on the Synoptic Gospels would be reluctant today to make use of the kind of appeal to 'oral theory' that Hawkins makes. In the England of 1898, however, the 'oral theory' was held in relatively high esteem, and it is possible that Hawkins's conclusions may not have appeared 'unusual' at that time. But, from a 'post-Farrer' vantage point, I think Hawkins's conclusions are indeed unexpected. For, Farrer has taught us that when we put ourselves in the place of the Evangelists and attempt to understand what, for example, Luke is doing, we not only do not need 'Q', we also do not need to make extensive use of the 'oral theory'. We can account for the Gospels, generally speaking, much better when we assume that they are written by authors who are free to compose their gospels, using such sources as they may have had, rather freely. This understanding radically reduces the need to appeal to any 'oral theory'.

Let us consider the data of Hawkins from a 'post-Farrer' vantage point. Hawkins lists 19 Matthean formulas which occur in common with one or both the other Synoptists, and are *also* used by Matthew independently in other parts of his Gospel. Hawkins found 11 of these 19 Matthean formulas in the text of Luke. This is confirmatory evidence of what Austin Farrer has taught us. If Luke knew and used Matthew in the composition of his Gospel, we would expect that, from time to time in copying Matthew, Luke would inadvertently copy into the text of his Gospel some of Matthew's 'favourite and habitual expressions'.

But wait, does it also go the other way? Is this evidence, like so much that is cited by experts on the Synoptic Problem, inconclusive, circular, or even reversible? Hawkins lists 7 'favourite and habitual' expressions of Luke which are used in common with one or both the other Synoptists, and are *also* used by Luke independently in other parts of his Gospel. Hawkins found 2 of these 7 Lucan formulas in the text of Matthew. This evidence tends to disconfirm Austin Farrer's position. For, this is more like the evidence we would expect if Matthew were copying Luke. From a 'post-Farrer' vantage point, one might argue either that this kind of evidence has no probative value, or, more reasonably, that its probative value is limited, and must be supplemented by other considerations. If this kind of evidence has any probative value at all, we would say that, on balance, it weighs in favor of Austin Farrer's view that Luke did know and copy Matthew, although clearly the evidence in at least 2 instances goes the other way. A critic convinced on other grounds that Luke did know and use Matthew would be constrained to explain these two instances, perhaps on redactional grounds. This probably would not be hard to do. Indeed, it probably would not be too difficult for someone convinced (on other grounds) of the existence of 'Q' and of the independence of Matthew and Luke, to explain the 11 instances where Hawkins has found Matthean formulas in the text of Luke. But, on the surface, it would appear that it probably would be less of a task to explain the 2 anomalies for the Austin Farrer hypotheses than it would be to explain the 11 anomalies for the 'Two-Document hypothesis'. That is why we say that, on balance, this particular category of Hawkins's linguistic evidence weighs in favor of Luke's use of Matthew, and supports Austin Farrer's hypothesis.

But what happens when we turn to Mark? Does this category of evidence weigh in balance one way or the other on the question of Marcan priority or posteriority? And if it does, does it weigh consistently on one side of the scale of evidence? Or, as in the case of Matthew and Luke, does the balance marker waver back and forth? If it wavers back and forth, does the balance marker finally come to rest neatly in the middle, with each side of the scale evenly balanced, or does the marker tip in one direction or the other?

Before we examine the evidence for Mark, which has helped Hawkins turn to the oral theory, it is only right to review the terms I have proposed for our discussion of this data. I have proposed that we start with the general recognition that a great deal has happened since 1898. In particular, we can no longer proceed as if the existence of 'Q' is an assured result of 19th century German criticism backed up by Sanday's 17-year Oxford seminar on the Synoptic Problem. This is where Streeter left the matter in 1924. But, as Farrer has shown, Streeter is probably wrong on 'Q'.

The question before us now is: Could Streeter also have been wrong on Marcan priority? I have proposed that we assume, for the sake of discussion, a 'post-Farrer' vantage point. What does this entail? Only that Luke used Matthew? Not at all. It entails much more than that. It entails the intellectual courage to reassess fundamental questions. Carrying forward Austin Farrer's exquisite use of irony, let me pose the question of Marcan priority as he posed the question of 'Q'.

Why should we dig up solid foundations? Why should we reopen questions long taken as settled? Much critical and expository work rests squarely on the hypothesis of Marcan priority, and if this hypothesis loses credit, the nuisance will be great. The books we rely upon to guide our thought about the history of Christ will need to be read with painful and unrelaxing reinterpretation. Nor is it only the effect on past studies that disquiets us. We want an accepted foundation for our present studies, and it seems a grievous thing that we cannot proceed with them until we have re-investigated what was unanimously settled by previous generations. Is there to be no progress in learning? Now that criticism is a science, are we not to hold any established positions as permanent conquests, from which a fresh generation can make a further advance? Have we always to fight old battles over again? Minds of high ability and scrupulous integrity were brought to bear on the question of Marcan priority in the great days of source-criticism. They sifted to the bottom, they counted every syllable, and they agreed on the priority of Mark. Is it likely that we, whose attention is distracted by the questions of our day, can profitably do their work again? And what reason have we to trust our judgment against theirs, if we find ourselves dissenting from their conclusions?

If we are not to follow Streeter and others who have held confidently to Marcan priority, it will not be because these scholars reason falsely, but because the premises from which they reasoned are no longer ours.

I take the situation to be this. Since Austin Farrer wrote 'On Dispensing with Q', those who have followed his counsel to read

Luke through carefully, to test whether there was any need to appeal to 'Q', have uniformly, so far as I know, come to the same conclusion: there is no need for 'Q'. This has fundamentally altered the state of the Synoptic Problem. This alteration has taken place so gradually, that we have not observed the extent of the alteration. Nevertheless, the change that has taken place removes the chief ground on which the credibility of the theory of Marcan priority has rested. For the theory of Marcan priority has been made plausible not only by appeal to the way in which belief in the existence of 'Q' can explain where Matthew and Luke got the material they have in common that is not in Mark, but also by appeal to the additional epicycle of an overlap between Mark and 'Q' to explain the text of Matthew when it appears to be more original than the parallel text in Mark. In these instances, so the argument goes, Matthew has not copied Mark, but 'Q'. And, of course, in these instances 'Q' has preserved the tradition in a more original form than has Mark. But, if there was no 'Q', what then? Ought we not, in the spirit of Austin Farrer, be prepared to think (having gotten by so well the past 27 years without really missing 'Q') that perhaps we can give up the other half of the 'Two-Document hypothesis', namely, belief in Marcan priority?

In any case, the evidence from Hawkins speaks for itself. Hawkins does not list a single 'favourite or habitual expression' of Mark which is also found in a parallel text of Matthew. On the other hand, he lists 'favourite or habitual expressions' of Matthew which are also found in one or more parallel texts of Mark. In other words, Hawkins's evidence, in this instance at least, weighs consistently against Matthew's use of Mark, and in favor of Mark's use of Matthew.

Similarly, Hawkins does not list a single 'favourite or habitual expression' of Mark which is also found in a parallel text of Luke. But on the other hand, he lists 7 'favourite or habitual expressions' of Luke which are also found in one or more parallel passages in Mark. Thus, this category of Hawkins's evidence weighs consistently against Luke's use of Mark, and in favor of Mark's use of Luke.

Had the alternate research paradigm we are now considering been a viable option for Hawkins, he would have had available for consideration a hypothesis that was more consistent with his data than was the Two-Document hypothesis. Thus, he might have been spared the fate of succumbing to that siren call of romanticism—the 'oral theory'.

In summary, this category of evidence, which Hawkins found both

interesting and important, makes more sense if Mark is posterior to
Matthew and Luke. Hawkins's lists are incomplete and can be
improved. In fact, a comprehensive analysis of the text of Mark
identifying the literary characteristics of that Gospel has just been
completed by David Peabody, in which the work of Hawkins has
been reviewed.[1] Peabody proposes that there are six phrases in Mark
which are used once by Mark in common with one or both the other
Synoptics, which are *also* used by Mark independently in other parts
of his narrative. These are (1) καὶ λέγουσιν αὐτῷ διδάσκαλε οὐ
μέλει σοι, (2) τις τῶν παρεστηκότων, (3) καὶ ἐκόπασεν ὁ ἄνεμος, (4)
εἴ τις θέλει, (5) πάντα δυνατά, (6) οἱ δώδεκα.

A note at the top of p. 171 of my copy of Hawkins reads: 'N.b.
Mark–1. καὶ ἐκόπασεν ὁ ἄνεμος 4.39; 6.51 // Matt. 14.32', indicating
that some years ago I had already noted one of Peabody's six phrases,
and had begun a list for Marcan phrases which appear in Matthew
and/or Luke. At the bottom of the same page, I have two additional
entries of different dates which read: (1) ἅψωνται τοῦ κρασπέδου
τοῦ ἱματίου αὐτοῦ Matt. 14.36 // Mark 6.56, also Matt. 9.20, and (2)
μήτι ἐγώ εἰμι (κύριε) Matt. 26.22 // Mark 14.21, also Matt. 26.25. I
have indicated that these two entries should be listed as items
number 20 and 21 in Hawkins's list of Matthean formulas which
appear in the text of Mark and/or Luke. (I do not know whether this
list will be extended when we have the completed work of Dennis
Tevis on Matthew in hand.[2])

All of this is to confirm my statement that Hawkins's lists are
incomplete and can be improved. But, until this has been done and
the results are published, Hawkins's lists remain standing as a part of
a classic work which is widely thought to support the Two-Document
hypothesis, but which, at least in the case of the lists on which we
have focused, actually support the view that Luke used Matthew, and
Mark used both Matthew and Luke.

I request that we reflect on this. Scholars are human. We see what
we want to see. And, if we find something we are not looking for and
it goes against our theory, we are inclined to discount it as unim-
portant. You may say no! Look at your note at the top of p. 171 of
your copy of Hawkins! You noted a phrase which goes against your
theory. You made a record of it. Your note indicates that you were
prepared to view it as the first of possibly other entries of the same
kind. True, but let me tell you of an incident that, in my view, is at
least equally telling in the opposite direction.

During the summer of 1961, E.P. Sanders, then a young research assistant, carried through some statistical studies on the Gospels. First, the total vocabulary common to Matthew and Mark was subjected to analysis, looking for evidence which would indicate the direction of literary dependence. In order to isolate what might be regarded as potentially significant data, Sanders set himself two criteria: (1) A word had to appear in one of the two Gospels at least 3 times as often as it did in the other. (2) In the Gospel in which the word appeared fewer times, it could appear *only* in passages where there was evidence of copying.

The results of this test confirmed what I had by then come to suspect, namely, that it was not, as I had once thought, Matthew who had copied Mark, but just the opposite; Mark had copied Matthew. Buoyed by these 'positive' results of scientific analysis, I asked Sanders to run the same test on the total vocabulary common to Mark and Luke. Since it was not disputed that Luke had copied Mark, I reasoned that if the same test indicated in corresponding proportions that Luke had copied Mark, it would serve to validate the method and increase confidence in the results of the test of the vocabulary common to Matthew and Mark.

In fact, the results went the other way. This was very disappointing to me. This was before I had any inkling that, in fact, Mark indeed could have used Luke. I say this, even though, at the time, I had already read in the history of the Synoptic Problem sufficiently to know that there had been some scholars in the 19th century who had held the 'odd' view that Mark had used both Matthew and Luke.

So, what did I do with these 'unwanted' results? I suppressed them. At least, as I look back now, I can see that that is what I did. Although at the time I rationalized my actions as follows: 'Since these results of our test on Mark and Luke are far less decisive than those obtained on the test of Matthew and Mark, you can regard these statistics as inconclusive, and continue to hold that the results of the test on Matthew and Mark indicate that Mark copied Matthew, but without the benefit of being able to say that the method has been verified by an independent test of the vocabulary common to Mark and Luke, and indeed, with a diminished confidence in the reliability of all such statistical studies'.

The results of Sanders's analysis of the vocabulary common to Matthew and Mark were typed up and circulated. No corresponding portion of our limited research funds was provided Sanders to type up the results of his test of the vocabulary common to Mark and Luke. Nor was he encouraged to save his notes. Unless he has done so on his own, the results of this test are lost and can only be recovered from memory. As I recall, the results were, indeed, statistically inconclusive, especially when the differing lengths of the two documents was factored in. However, the indication of the direction of dependence, slight as it may have been, definitely was in the direction of Mark's having copied Luke. That much is very clear in my mind.

I will not say that this is an egregious example of the suppression of evidence. Hardly grounds for my being voted out of S.N.T.S. But I do count it as an example of what happens—and happens in good conscience. As they say in the Black church, 'Do I have a witness?'

So, I repeat: we see what we want to see. And, having found what we are looking for, we tend to become intolerant with those dummies who do not see what we see. I am convinced that this is all too often our human predicament.

And what is the best cure for this? I think it is the goodly fellowship of independently-minded colleagues, and, above all, trusting relationships within that fellowship.

The 17-year-long Oxford seminar on the Synoptic Problem apparently was such a goodly fellowship. Certainly the diversity and high quality of the essays which members of that seminar contributed to the closing volume: *Oxford Studies in the Synoptic Problem* (ed. W. Sanday; Oxford, 1911), testify to the indendence and fair-mindedness of those who participated in that scholarly fellowship.

But, after the Great War, a different spirit came to prevail, one that remained unchallenged in synoptic studies at Oxford until a new generation began with Austin Farrer and the 'Q' parties. In defense of his 'Fundamental Solution' to the Synoptic Problem, Streeter wrote:

> The examples adduced above are merely a sample given to illustrate the general character of the argument. But it is an argument essentially cumulative in character. Its full force can only be realized by one who will take the trouble to go carefully through the immense mass of details which Sir John Hawkins has collected, analysed and tabulated; pp. 114-153 of his classic, *Horae Synopticae*. How anyone who has worked through these pages with a Synopsis of the Greek text can retain the slightest doubt [*sic*] of the original and primitive character of Mark, I am unable to comprehend. But since there are, from time to time, ingenious persons who rush into print with theories to the contrary, I can

only suppose, either that they have not been at pains to do this, or else that—like some of the highly cultivated people who think that Bacon wrote Shakespeare, or that the British are the Lost Ten Tribes—they have eccentric views of what constitutes evidence (*The Four Gospels*, p. 164).

This was in 1924. Fourteen years earlier both Streeter and Hawkins had contributed model essays to the classic collection: *Oxford Studies in the Synoptic Problem*. Hawkins's essay is entitled, 'The Disuse of the Marcan Source in St. Luke ix. 51–xviii.14'. Hawkins argued that the parallels between Mark and Luke in this central section of Luke are not 'sufficient to prove any *direct use* of one of these Gospels by the other' (p. 52). These parallels, which Hawkins admitted were difficult to explain on the Marcan hypothesis, are readily explained on the hypothesis that Luke used Matthew, and that thereafter, Mark used both Matthew and Luke.

Hawkins discussed three passages—Luke 10.25-28; 11.15, 17-23; 13.18, 19. In each case there is both a Marcan and Matthean parallel. And in each case the Marcan and Matthean passages are in the same relative order in the respective Gospels. In each case, Mark so carefully conflated the Lucan version with its Matthean parallel which he took up in Matthew's order, that the verbal agreements between Luke and Mark against Matthew, or Mark and Matthew against Luke, are rather slight. So slight indeed are they that they led Hawkins to conclude that there was in this section of Luke no clear evidence of direct literary dependence between Mark and Luke. Mark was able to conflate these sayings so carefully, mainly because he was working with sayings Luke had initially copied from Matthew.

Careful analysis of these three sayings dealt with by Hawkins indicates that Mark did make use of material from this great central section, but the circumstances under which he did so are notable. First, Mark took nothing from Luke in this great central section for which he did not have a Matthean parallel. Second, he conflated the material he used with the Matthean parallel. And, third, he tended to give the saying a place in his Gospel corresponding to its order in Matthew.

There are seven passages where the degree of verbal agreement between Luke and Mark is great enough to warrant these passages being considered in this connection.

1. Luke 10.25-28 // Matthew 22.34-40 // Mark 12.28-31;
2. Luke 11.14-23 // Matthew 12.22-30 // Mark 3.22-27;

3. Luke 12.10 // Matthew 12.32 // Mark 3.28-29;
4. Luke 13.18-19 // Matthew 13.31-32 // Mark 4.30-32;
5. Luke 14.34 // Matthew 5.13 // Mark 9.50;
6. Luke 16.18 // Matthew 19.9 // Mark 10.11-12;
7. Luke 17.2 // Matthew 18.6-7 // Mark 9.42.

In every case, except Luke 14.34 and 16.18, there are sufficient agreements between Mark and Luke against Matthew to warrant the judgment that Mark probably consulted the Lucan parallel to each passage in Matthew. Luke 14.34 is a saying which all three Evangelists have in a different order. In the other six cases, Mark and Matthew have the saying in the same relative order in their Gospels.

Under these circumstances, it is evident that Mark's redactional procedure with reference to Luke's great central section is intelligible on the Griesbach hypothesis. There was a great deal more sayings material which Luke had copied from Matthew in this section, some of which Mark probably could have conflated successfully. The question, therefore, remains: Why did Mark omit material he presumably could have incorporated into his Gospel? But this question of omissions is never completely answerable on any hypothesis. There are always certain unresolved questions as to why any particular Evangelist omitted the material he did. Streeter's words are a proper reminder of the attitude to be taken on this question in the light of the actual circumstances under which the modern critic works: 'Very often we can surmise reasons of an apologetic nature why the Evangelists may have thought some things less worthwhile reporting. But, even when we can detect no particular motive, we cannot assume that there was none; *for we cannot possibly know either all the circumstances of churches, or all the personal idiosyncrasies of writers so far removed from our own time*' (*The Four Gospels*, p. 169. My italics. See also William R. Farmer, *The Synoptic Problem, A Critical Analysis* [London & New York, 1964], pp. 250-53).

C.F. Burney

My teacher, James Muilenburg, once told me that he had wanted to study with C.F. Burney. Muilenburg made frequent reference to Burney's work on John, and always spoke well of it. Burney was a name I never heard mentioned at Cambridge (1947-49), or if I did, I have no memory of it. But at Union Theological Seminary, I was made aware through Muilenburg that, as time permitted, I would someday need to take account of Burney's work.

The occasion to read Burney did not arise until the fall of 1958. It happened this way. We had had a report on 'The "Q" Parties at Oxford' at our National SBL meetings in, I believe, 1956. During the 1957 meetings of SBL, I had been treated to the unbecoming spectacle of a notable scholar publicly 'slapping the wrist' of a younger scholar because he had read a paper casting doubt on the existence of 'Q'. I knew nothing about the matter myself. But I could tell that the points the younger scholar had made were not being answered by his critic. And, I made a mental note of this high-level breach of academic integrity.

It was during the summer of 1958 that I was in the study of Joachim Jeremias. He had been called to the telephone in another room. As I glanced at the books on the shelves around me, my eyes were drawn to a volume entitled: *Studies in the Gospels, Essays in Memory of R.H. Lightfoot*, edited by Nineham. I had met R.H. Lightfoot in his office in 1949 in connection with a paper I had prepared for C.H. Dodd's seminar on the fourth Gospel—which paper Lightfoot had subsequently published in *The Journal of Theological Studies* of which he was then editor. Naturally, I was interested to know what was in the volume.

But my interest turned to excitement when I discovered that this volume contained Austin Farrer's essay. I had heard enough about Farrer's work to anticipate that this essay would carry me to the font of the 'Q' Parties at Oxford. I do not recall how long Jeremias was out of his office. But it was long enough for me to make the mental resolution that, at the first opportunity, I would follow Farrer's advice and work through Luke to see whether one could dispense with 'Q'. Later that summer I worked out the time to complete this task, and I found that what Farrer had concluded was clearly the case. One can dispense with 'Q'. Or, so it seemed to me.

That fall on returning to Drew University, I set as the topic for the NT Graduate Seminar, the question of 'Q'. On the opening day of the seminar, I announced that we would be testing the 'Q' hypothesis and that we would assume as a methodological presupposition for our research that Matthew and Luke had copied Mark. At the following session of the seminar, one of the students asked whether I had read Butler's book, *The Originality of St. Matthew*. I answered that I had not, but that I had heard of it, and that I understood that it had been written by a Roman Catholic, and that I did not want the work of our seminar to get mixed up with the work of Roman Catholic scholars on an issue in which the Roman Catholic Church had a vested interest. At that time I was innocent of the vested interest Protestants have in Marcan priority. So, I self-confidently exercised my power as chairman of the seminar and moved on, expecting the students to respect my concern for keeping the work of our seminar independent of ecclesiastical interests.

Fortunately, however, the academic integrity of our seminar was saved by the syndics of the Cambridge University Press. For, the next day, the student who had asked me whether I had read Butler's book appeared at my office door with his copy in hand. I invited him in and we began to talk about the book. I asked whether I could look at it. I was surprised to see that it had been published by Cambridge University Press, and without any indication whether the author was, or was not, a Roman Catholic. I commented on this and the student asked whether I knew that C.H. Dodd had recommended that Cambridge University Press publish the book. I acknowledged that I did not know this and asked him how he knew it. He replied that Matthew Black had told him and other students studying NT at Edinburgh that this was the case, and added that Black had said that his students would have to take account of Butler's book.

Recognizing that there was no way that I could get out of forming a critical opinion of what Butler had written, I asked the student to leave the book with me and promised to report on the matter at our next seminar. As soon as I could find the time, I began reading the opening chapter of Butler's book. It was painful reading. I would keep going over what Butler had written without being able to follow or accept the logic of his reasoning. Once it became clear, however, that Burney's work in his book, *The Poetry of Our Lord*, was important for the case Butler was attempting to make, I knew what I wanted to do. I decided to make this the occasion to become acquainted with Burney. So, I put Butler down and walked over to the library and checked out Burney's book. I returned to my office and began to read. As I recall, this is what happened.

Against the background of my exposure to the form-critical work of Gunkel on the Psalms, and Muilenburg's adaptation of Gunkel's method in his seminar on Isaiah, I had no difficulty in following and appreciating at least Burney's appeal to parallelism in clarifying the formal structure of the sayings attributed to Jesus in the Gospels. It made sense to me. For one thing, on Burney's analysis, the Matthean forms of Jesus' sayings generally turned out to be more original than the Lucan parallels. Since I had come to the conclusion that Luke had used and modified Matthew, Burney's findings were supportive of what I had already come to see by my own redactional and form-critical analysis of Luke, made only a month or so earlier. So, as I read on, my confidence in the reliability of the method Burney was following gradually built up, until I came to a passage where, on Burney's analysis, Matthew's form of Jesus' saying was adjudged more original than the Marcan parallel. Obviously, this was an anomaly for which I was, at that time, mentally unprepared. Nor was Burney's footnote of any help. For, believing in Marcan priority, and recognizing the problem his find had created for that hypothesis, Burney turned to the more developed theory of an overlap between Mark and 'Q' as an explanation for his disruptive data. Does not this indicate, he asks, that Matthew has not copied Mark here, but rather, the saying source 'Q' which in this instance has preserved the saying of Jesus in a form more original than the form it has in Mark? Since I had come to doubt the existence of 'Q' and, since I was quite sure of Marcan priority, the effect of this unexpected turn of events was to shake my confidence in Burney's method. But, as I read on in Burney's book, my confidence in his method gradually built up again, until, for the second time, I ran into the same problem. Once again on Burney's analysis the Matthean form of Jesus' saying was more original than the parallel in Mark. And, once again, there was the same kind of footnote offering the same explanation of the anomaly. This time there was for the first time a brief moment of doubt. 'What if', I asked myself, 'it was the other way around? If there was no 'Q' source, is not the simplest explanation for Burney's data Mark's dependence on Matthew?' But I very quickly pushed this dissenting, if not heretical, thought out of my mind. My doubt of the validity of Burney's method returned. It did not occur to me then to ask the question which I ask today. Having so readily entertained the possibility that 'Q' never existed, why was I so unready to reflect seriously on the possibility that Marcan priority could be equally dubious? What is there about the idea of 'Marcan priority' that evokes such devotion, not unlike that given in other theological schools to the idea of 'The Virgin Birth'? Could these ideas be 'watchwords'? Could they be standards or banners around which, in the not-too-distant past, the Children of Light would rally as they set forth to do battle against the Children of Darkness? What kind of divine inspiration was once drawn from these mere symbols—these words—these theologumena? But at that time, so long ago, when I was still in the prime of my innocence, I just did what I could. I read on. And, once again, my confidence in the dependability of Burney's method returned, so that when, a few pages later, I came to a passage where, again on Burney's analysis the Matthean form was more original than the Marcan, I put Burney down and, for the first time in my life, I seriously entertained the question: 'What if Mark was not first? What if Mark copied Matthew?' Obviously, I needed a test.

Where was the best evidence for Marcan priority to be found? Surely, in the passion narrative—for I had been assured by C.H. Dodd and the French Dominican New Testament expert, Benoit, that it was in the passion narrative of Mark that we had the earliest and most reliable tradition about Jesus.

After supper I returned to my office and, with the evening before me, I sat down with a synopsis, fully expecting that, within a couple of hours, I would be able to identify several passages where anyone could see that Mark was clearly the more primitive Gospel. I expected that with these passages in hand I would be able to appear before my seminar, vindicated in my judgment that I had been right in discounting the significance of Butler's book, if not in suggesting that it represented special pleading for the Roman Catholic Church.

But, this was not to be. I was unable to find a single passage where it seemed clear to me that Matthew had copied Mark. There were many passages where one could see that relationship as a possibility, but none where I thought I could argue that this was probably the case. On the other hand, I found some passages where I thought it would be possible to argue for Mark having copied Matthew. The vast majority of passages I perceived as neutral on the question. I was really surprised by this turn of events. But, by this time, I had become somewhat stoical about the whole matter. The next day, when I had the opportunity to do so, I returned to Butler's book. This time I did not encounter the same difficulty in following Butler's reasoning.

When I met my seminar later in the week, I recounted what I had done. One week later I announced that we would need to suspend judgment on Mark's priority to Matthew. But we would continue to presume, as a methodological presupposition for our research, Luke's use of Mark. Of that we could be sure.

Burney's results, in general, fit the Griesbach hypothesis well; both at the point of Luke's use of Matthew and at the point of Mark's use of Matthew. But what about Mark's use of Luke *and* Matthew? This is the heart of the matter for the Griesbach hypothesis. It is the *sine qua non* for that theory. Does Burney come to any important result which makes more sense on a theory assuming Luke's use of Matthew and Mark's use of Matthew *and* Luke? Yes, he does.

In the preface of his book, on pp. 8-9, Burney writes as follows:

> While referring to the footnotes on pp. 74, 75, the writer would point in particular to his separation (p. 118) of the passage Mark 13.9-13 out of Mark's 'little apocalypse' solely on the ground of its rhythmical form, before he was aware of the fact that precisely this passage stands in Matthew 10.17-22 in a wholly different context; and, to his rejection of Mk 13.10 ('And to all nations first must the gospel be preached') in this passage as a gloss, on rhythmical grounds, before noticing that the verse was actually absent from the parallel passage Luke 21.12-19, and from Matt. 10.17-22. The natural inference, based on the rhythmical distinction of Mark 13.9-13 from its context, and upon the fact that the passage occurs in a different context in Matthew, is that it is a discourse, not eschatological in original intent, which Mark has borrowed from Q and set in the midst of an eschatological discourse; and which Matthew has likewise embodied from Q and placed (or retained) in a more appropriate position, viz. in connection with other discourses bearing on the commission of the disciples. Matthew has also adopted the same passage from Mark in Ch. 24.9-14, i.e., the chapter which gives his version of the 'little apocalypse'; and here, we see how the process of giving an eschatological character and setting to the passage, begun by Mark, has been carried still further.

Leaving aside the question of the validity of Burney's appeal to the phenomenon of rhythm, a point on which I am not competent to judge, his method has led him to recognize what other scholars have noted on independent grounds, namely that Mark 13.9-13 has its true parallel in Matt. 10.17-22, and that Matthew has, indeed, preserved this tradition as Burney puts it, 'in a more appropriate position'. Bo Reicke simply refers to its (i.e. Matt. 10.17-22 // Mark 13.9-13) more original setting. Here again, Burney appeals to the existence of 'Q' to explain the results of his work. From our post-Farrer vantage point we are led to seek some other way to explain the data. I think that Burney's results in this instance make more sense on the research paradigm where Luke uses Matthew, and Mark uses both Matthew and Luke. Of course, one first has to understand what Luke does with Matthew—*leaving Mark out of view*. For, on the Griesbach hypothesis, contra Austin Farrer, when Luke used Matthew, Mark had not yet been written. Once we see how Luke has used Matthew it then becomes clear, it seems to me, what it is that Mark has done in composing his version of the 'little apocalypse' (see pp. 275-78 of my *The Synoptic Problem*).

1. *How Luke used Matthew's Apocalyptic Discourse*

At 21.5 Luke began following Matthew 24.1ff., utilizing Matthew 24.1-7, 15-19, 29-35. Luke thus utilized a considerable portion of the material in Matthew 24, and always in Matthew's order. However, there are significant omissions and one major insertion which require explanation. Luke 21.11b marks a transitional point in Luke's text. Up to this point Luke had been following Matthew 24.1-7. But the next literary unit in Matthew contains the words: 'but he who endures to the end will be saved' (Matt. 24.13). These words constitute a doublet to the identical phrase in Matthew 10.22b. At this point Luke evidently turned back to Matthew 10 to compare the material there with what he found in Matthew 24. For some reason Luke preferred Matthew 10.17-22 to its parallel, Matthew 24.9-14. Perhaps Luke preferred the reference to Christians 'being hated by all' in Matthew 10.22a to their 'being hated by *all the Gentiles*' in Matthew 24.9b. In any case, Luke 21.12-19 is parallel to Matthew 10.17-22, and since Luke in 12.11-12 had already copied Matthew 10.19-20, he is led to paraphrase those words at this point (Luke 21.14-15)—presumably in order to avoid creating a doublet, which would leave the appearance of redundancy in his work. It is to be noted in this connection that he did the same thing in 21.22, where he was dependent on Matthew 24.16-17, part of which he had used previously in Luke 17.31. This is a perfectly comprehensible literary device, and lends support to the hypothesis that Luke was using Matthew as his source (or a source similar to Matthew which has material in the same order as does Matthew). For it is the natural practice of a writer making use of a narrative source to move in general in a forward direction through the source. And when a writer using a narrative source skips forward in the source to copy material out of order for some special reason, then later, when moving forward through the source he reaches material he has previously used, it is natural that he either skip that material or utilize it in the light of the fact that he had already made some previous use of it.

After substituting Matthew 10.17-22 for Matthew 24.8-14, Luke returned to Matthew 24, and began copying at verse 15 (Luke 21.20-. 24 // Matt. 24.15-22). The difference between Luke and Matthew can be explained as follows: (a) Luke 21.20, 23b-24, are Lucan modifications reflecting a post-70 AD situation where the readers of Luke's Gospel could be expected to be acquainted with historical accounts of the destruction of Jerusalem and the treatment of its captives by the Romans; (b) Luke 21.22, 24 contain Old Testament references which indicate that Luke may have been utilizing other tradition in his modification of Matthew in these verses; (c) Luke 21.21a is identical with Matthew 24.16. But Luke 21.21b is a paraphrase of Matthew 24.17-18. Luke had previously used these verses of Matthew in editing Luke 17.23-37. That section of Luke constitutes a special problem. In all probability Luke had access to a special source which contained apocalyptic material parallel to material in Matthew 24. Luke 17.26-30 exhibits synonymous parallelism and is probably in a more original form than its parallel in Matthew 24.37-39. But it is quite possible that Luke drew from Matthew 24 some or all of the other material in 17.23-37, which is paralleled in Matthew 24. In any case, in Luke 21, material in Matthew 24, which is paralleled in earlier sections of Luke, is either omitted or, as in the case of Matthew 24.17-18, paraphrased. There are no exceptions. There is no verbal overlap between apocalyptic material in Luke 21 and corresponding material elsewhere in Luke. In other words, apocalyptic material which is presented as a whole in Matthew 24 is found in Luke, neatly divided and presented in different parts of his Gospel. And whenever there is an overlap in content, as for example between Luke 17.31 and Luke 21.21b, the neatness of this redactional division is preserved through the literary artifice of paraphrase.

Luke 21.25-27 is parallel to Matthew 24.29-30. Luke had previously drawn from Matthew 24.23-28 in his editing of Luke 17.21-24, 37. Therefore, he omitted this portion of Matthew's text in his editing of Luke 21, and began working with Matthew 24.29ff. Luke 21.25-33 is parallel to Matthew 24.29-35. Luke had already incorporated material parallel to Matthew 24.36-42, back in Luke 17.26ff., and he therefore omitted this section from his account in ch. 21. Furthermore, in Luke 12, the Evangelist in editing material on the theme of 'the folly of postponing repentance' (Luke 12.35–13.9) took the material in

Matthew 24.43-51 and joined it with a parable from his special source material which enjoyed the common motif: 'Blessed be the servant who is ready when his master comes' (Luke 12.37 // Luke 12.43). Therefore, in Luke 21 the Evangelist also omitted this closing section of Matthew 24.

In the above manner, it is possible to explain all the significant redactional differences between Luke 21.5-33 and Matthew 24.1-51. All the Lucan parallels to material in Matthew 24, which are found outside Luke 21, occur in the great central section of Luke. It has been shown that Mark made no direct use of this section of Luke's Gospel. This explains the striking fact that the Marcan version of Matthew 24 in Mark 13.1-32 is limited to the sections of Matthew 24, which are found in Luke 21. There are instances where Mark, having been led to compare a Matthean parallel to a section in Luke 21.5-33, copied Matthew's text more closely and fully than had Luke. And in one instance, Mark continued to copy Matthew's text beyond the point where he might have stopped, had he slavishly limited himself to those passages in Matthew 24 which he found in Luke 21 (*compare* Mark 13.21-23 // Matt. 24.23-25). Nevertheless, it cannot be disputed that the literary units of Matthew 24, which are not found in Mark 13, are also not found in Luke 21, but are found in the great central section of Luke. These literary units are three in number: (1) Matthew 24.26-28 // Luke 17.23-24, 37; (2) Matthew 24.37-41 // Luke 17.26-37; (3) Matthew 24.43-51 // Luke 12.39-46.

These redactional phenomena are afforded a ready explanation on the Griesbach hypothesis. They constitute a difficulty for the Augustinian hypothesis, since there is no apparent reason why Mark should have omitted these three literary units from his Gospel, in view of the fact that he otherwise copied the text of Matthew 24 very closely indeed. Similarly on the Marcan hypothesis, since there are minor but significant agreements between Matthew and Luke against Mark in Matthew 24.1-7 and 24.30-35, which (on Streeterian terms, at least) require these verses, as well as 24.26-28; 24.37-41; and 24.43-51, to be attributed to 'Q', it is difficult to know why Mark would have omitted from 'Q' exactly those literary units which Luke does not have in common with Matthew 24, in Luke 21, but does include elsewhere. Since Mark would have no preknowledge of how Matthew and Luke would arrange material they independently drew from 'Q', it does not seem possible to explain why Mark's selection from 'Q' would have followed the pattern it does. Furthermore, one would be

expected on the terms above to imagine the following redactional
procedure on the part of Matthew: (1) In 24.1-7 Matthew conflated
Mark and Q; (2) In 24.8-25 he copied Mark, though he may have
conflated vv. 17-18 with a closely parallel passage from 'Q'; (3) In
24.26-28 he returned to 'Q' for three verses; (4) In 24.29-35 he
conflated Mark and 'Q'; in 24.36 he copied Mark; (5) But in
24.37-51 he copied 'Q' again. He furthermore probably interrupted
this use of Mark and 'Q' by inserting passages from M at 24.10 and
24.30.

It may not be possible to deny categorically that a writer would
have proceeded to edit material in this fashion. But it is incumbent
upon those who think that Matthew so proceeded to consider the
possibility that, instead of being added by the Evangelist to what he
found in Mark and 'Q', the following verses were an organic part of
the material available to him when he composed his Gospel: (1) 'And
then many will fall away, and betray one another, and hate one
another. And many false prophets will arise and lead many astray.
And because wickedness is multiplied, most men's love will go cold'
(24.10-12). (2) 'The sign of the Son of Man shall appear in heaven,
and then all the tribes of the earth will mourn' (24.30).

Even more likely to have been an original part of the apocalypse is
the Matthean text: 'Pray that your flight may not be in the winter or
on a sabbath' (24.20). The parallels in Luke and in Mark have no
reference to the Sabbath. It is difficult to dismiss the suggestion that
the reference to the Sabbath in Matthew's text is a sign of the original
Palestinian provenance of the materials in Matthew 24, and that the
absence of this reference in Luke and Mark is a sign that these
Gospels were written for churches in which the Sabbath had lost its
importance. Only on the hypothesis that Matthew copied Mark (by
which the critic is forced to make an Evangelist committed to the
universal mission to the Gentiles reponsible for Judaizing sections of
his Gospel), would one deny that this reference to the Sabbath was
an indication of the primitivity of the tradition in Matthew 24, taking
the critic back to the time when Christians had not yet consciously
disassociated themselves from Judaism and its practice. There is no
sound reason to doubt that most of the material incorporated by the
Evangelist into Matthew 24 is Jewish-Christian in origin and
Palestinian in provenance, nor that Matthew's version of this material
is closer to the original than Luke's or Mark's. It has been possible to
explain Luke's redactional use of this material from Matthew. It is

now necessary to show that it is possible to explain Mark 13.1-32 as a conflation of Matthew 24.1-36 with Luke 21.5-33.

2. How Mark Combined Matthew's Apocalyptic Discourse with Parallel Texts of Luke.

On the Griesbach hypothesis, Mark 13.1-8 is a conflation of Matthew 24.1-8 with Luke 21.5-11. The verbal agreement among all three is quite extensive. The agreement between Matthew and Mark against Luke is considerable. The agreements between Luke and Mark against Matthew are minimal and sporadic, being of the same order as the agreements of Matthew and Luke against Mark. This indicates that while Mark has rather carefully combined the closely related texts of Matthew and Luke, he had tended to follow the fuller text of Matthew.

All three Gospels agree in including the exhortation to be 'watchful' (Mark 13.5 // Matt. 24.4 // Luke 21.8). But in 13.9 (and 13.23) Mark heightens this motif of 'watchfulness', which is to climax in and dominate his ending of the apolyptic discourse in 13.33-37. A linguistic analysis of that ending indicates that it is a Marcan construction based upon the Lucan and Matthean endings to the discourse and related passages from Matthew 25 (Luke 21.34-36; Matt. 24.42-44; 25.13-15). Therefore, the agreement of Matthew and Luke against Mark in the omission of the exhortation to 'watch' found in Mark 13.9 (and 13.23 as well) is an indication of the secondary character of this feature of Mark's text, and also its probably Marcan origin.

At that point, Mark reached the place in the text of Luke where Luke had shifted back to Matthew 10.17-22, as a substitute for its parallel in Matthew 24. Mark evidently perceived that Luke had made this shift, and followed his redactional lead in doing the same. When Mark turned to Matthew 10.17-22, the true parallel to Luke 21.12-19, he not only conflated these two passages, but once again adhered more closely to the text of Matthew than to the text of Luke. For understandable reasons mentioned above, Luke had paraphrased Matthew 10.19-20 in Luke 21.14-15. Luke in 21.18 had also introduced into his version of Matthew 10.19-20 an idea from Matthew 10.30, 'But not a hair of your head will perish'. Luke's wording represents an interpretation of the exact words of Matthew's text: 'But even the hairs of your head are all numbered', which Luke copied rather closely while following Matthew 10.26-33 in Luke 12.2-9. In any case, Mark followed the text of Matthew closely at the point where Luke paraphrased and agreed with Matthew against Luke in omitting the saying from Matthew 10.30 which Luke had reworded and introduced into his text.

In that part of Luke's text which is paralleled in Mark 13, it is striking that at all three places where Luke's text indicates that he paraphrased sentences from Matthew which he had copied faithfully earlier in his Gospel, Mark adhered closely to the text of Matthew. These three places are Luke 21.14-15, 18, and 21. The point is that Mark was on perfectly safe ground in following closely the texts of Matthew in all these places, since Luke had testified against the originality of his text at these points by elsewhere in his Gospel having preserved the text which Mark found before him in Matthew. From this point of view, Mark's Gospel is superior to that of Luke at those points in this section where Luke makes positive deviations from the text of Matthew. Mark's Gospel in this section would not completely satisfy adherents of Matthew's Gospel. But it would especially commend itself to those adherents of Luke's Gospel who were sensitive to the charge that their Gospel had unnecessarily departed from a wording of the tradition to which Luke elsewhere testified. No one would want his Gospel to be inconsistent. This would have been especially true for adherents of Luke.

Mark was not produced for readers who would appreciate the literary finesse of Luke in avoiding redundancy. Mark wrote his Gospel for a church which knew more than one Gospel, and was tired of unnecessary bickering over the rival claims and counter-claims of the adherents of different Gospels; the chief rivals and contenders for general acceptance apparently being Matthew and Luke. Mark 13 is a revision of Luke 21, in which Mark recognized the superior claim of the parallel texts in Matthew 10 and 24 on the ground that Luke elsewhere in his Gospel supported the text of Matthew 10 and 24 against the Lucan parallel texts in Luke 21.

At the end of Mark 13.9, the reference to 'bearing witness' which he found in both Luke 21.13 and its parallel, Matthew 10.18, was associated by Mark with the reference to 'a witness to all the Gentiles' in Matthew 24.14, and Mark therefore incorporated the substance of that tradition in 13.10.

In 13.11-13, Mark conflated Luke 21.14-17 with Matthew 10.19-22 (Huck–Lietzmann is misleading in its arrangement of the parallel materials at this point), omitting Luke 21.18 and adhering more and more closely to the text of Matthew. Mark then returned with Luke to Matthew 24.15ff. From that point in the text of Matthew, Mark adhered so closely to the text of Matthew that Marsh could write: 'there is such a close verbal agreement for twenty verses together, with the parallel portion in Matthew's Gospel, that the texts of St. Matthew and St. Mark might pass for one and the same text, in which a multiplication of copies had produced a few trifling deviations. At least they do not differ more from each other than each differs from itself in different manuscripts.'[3]

What Marsh failed to note, however, was that although the differences between Mark's text and that of the *parallel* passages of Matthew seemed trifling, there were four significant passages in Matthew's apocalyptic discourse for which Mark had no parallel: (1) Matthew 24.10-12; (2) 24.26-28; (3) 24.30; and (4) 24.37-51. These same four passages are missing from Luke 21.5-33. These common omissions, together with the minor and sporadic agreements between Mark and Luke against Matthew in Mark 13.14-32, indicate that Mark was not only following the text of Matthew as closely as a copyist might, but that he was also shaping his version of the apocalyptic discourse in the light of the parallel version in Luke 21.5-33.

Wherever the text of Luke followed that of Matthew, Mark copied the common text so closely that the agreements between Matthew and Luke against Mark were reduced to insignificance. Likewise, whenever the text of Luke deviated from that of Matthew, Mark followed the text of Matthew so closely that the agreements between Mark and Luke against Matthew were reduced to insignificance. This is why it is possible to describe Mark's version of the apocalyptic discourse as a revision of Luke's, in which the general shape of Luke's version of the discourse was preserved, but in which the text was revised to bring it into accord with the text of Matthew, from which Luke's text was originally derived, and which Matthean text was significantly supported elsewhere in Luke's Gospel, even supported in some cases in such a way as to testify against the authenticity of the text of Luke's version of the discourse.

Mark's ending of the discourse affords further evidence of the secondary character of his Gospel in comparison with Matthew and Luke (see further my *The Synoptic Problem*, pp. 278-83).

Conclusion

In this paper I have shown how certain results of Sir John Hawkins and C.F. Burney would be explained on the research paradigm that Luke used Matthew and that Mark used Matthew and Luke. I am not presuming to question nor to affirm the scholarship or reasoning of these critics. My purpose is simply to point out that, had they had the viable alternative to the Two-Document hypothesis that we have, and had they been persuaded, as many of us are, that confidence in the 'Q' hypothesis is unwarranted, then they would have had reason from their own research to wish to join with us in giving serious consideration to the Owen–Griesbach hypothesis.

That Hawkins and Burney thought that they had good reasons for ruling out of consideration the research paradigm we are considering, I do not deny. No one questioned their integrity at the time, nor should we at this late date. But whether they had good reasons for ruling out of consideration the paradigm we are considering can only be settled by historical research in which we would undertake to read the scholarly literature available to them. There is not time to go into that subject in this paper. It is enough for us to ponder whether they would agree with us that (in the light of the work of Austin Farrer and others) in explaining anomalies for their research paradigm, these Oxford scholars made an unwarranted use of a very questionable theory, i.e., the 'Q' hypothesis.

NOTES

1. D.B. Peabody, *The Redactional Features of the Author of Mark: A Method Focussing on Recurrent Phraseology and Its Application* (Ph.D. dissertation: Southern Methodist University, 1983).

2. D.G. Tevis, *An Analysis of Words and Phrases Characteristic of the Gospel of Matthew* (Ph.D. dissertation: Southern Methodist University, 1983).

3. Herbert Marsh, *Introduction to the New Testament* (translated by Marsh from the 4th edition of J.D. Michaelis's *Einleitung in die göttlichen Schriften des Neuen Bundes* [Göttingen, 1778], augmented with notes, etc., by Marsh and including a dissertation on the origin and composition of the first three Gospels by Marsh), 4 vols. (Cambridge, 1793-1801), Vol. III, Part II, p. 170.

SOME OBSERVATIONS ON PROFESSOR FARMER'S 'CERTAIN RESULTS...'

Michael Goulder

University of Birmingham
P.O. Box 363, Birmingham 15

Bill Farmer is certainly right to draw our attention to the importance of errors of method in both Hawkins and Burney. Hawkins is wrong to infer an oral tradition from the evidence he adduces, and Burney is wrong to infer a Mark/Q overlap every time Matthew has a better rhythm than Mark. Not tens but hundreds of thousands of pages have been wasted by authors on the Synoptic Problem not paying attention to errors of method, which are extremely common. They arise particularly from the failure clearly to set out the steps and alternatives in the argument; and Hawkins and Burney are both guilty here of this. As Farmer says, we all tend to be blinkered by our own position, and material is often produced as evidence for that position without noticing that it is possible to see the identical material as supporting a counter-position. Arguments may thus be reversible.

Unfortunately Farmer's own paper is not exempt from these failings. It is in three sections, and the argument of the first two (on Hawkins and Burney) leaves crucial alternatives unconsidered. The third section is an exposition of Mark 13 and pars. on the Griesbach hypothesis, and seems to me coherent but not plausible; and to rest on the fallacies of sections (1) and (2).

(1) Hawkins lists a number of 'favourite or habitual' expressions of Mark, in fact six, each of which occurs twice only in his Gospel and nowhere else, e.g. 'he said in his teaching', or 'for he knew not what to answer'. Farmer says, 'we might expect that Matthew would, in the process of copying Mark, inadvertently take over into his text some of the "favourite or habitual" expressions of Mark'. He repeats this presumption later, noting that *per contra* Hawkins gives some fifteen 'favourite or habitual' expressions of Matthew which also occur once in Mark. 'In other words', he concludes, 'Hawkins's evidence, in this

instance at least, weighs consistently against Matthew's use of Mark, and in favor of Mark's use of Matthew'.

The argument is not stated, but is of the form: If document A (Mark) has favourite expressions not found in document B (Matthew), A is unlikely to be known by B; whereas if B has favourite expressions occurring once in A, it is likely that A has carried them over from B inadvertently. But this is a fallacy. A's favourite expressions may not have appealed to B; indeed they may be classified as favourite *because* they did not appeal to B. Sometimes later B may copy in expressions from earlier A inadvertently; and sometimes a casual expression of earlier A may appeal strongly to B so that he uses it often. I was Austin Farrer's pupil, and a great admirer of his style. Some 'favourite phrases' of his will not be found in my own writings: perhaps they are a bit high-Church for my taste. Some I take over 'inadvertently': I notice myself writing now and again 'very likely', or 'the inscrutable wisdom of God'. Others I think are just the thing. He might have used them only once or twice, but whenever I was in pious mood I used to work in 'our holy faith', or 'the divine providence' to good effect. But on Farmer's argument this last group of phrases would be evidence that Farrer was copying me! There is a second statement of the same false argument in the passage on Sanders's research project.

Farmer also seems to confute the argument himself. He refers to Hawkins, who cites fifteen favourite expressions of Matthew, which are peculiar to him, and fifteen others which have a parallel each in Mark. He also tells us that Hawkins lists six favourite expressions of Mark which are peculiar to him; and he gives us Peabody's list of six favourite expressions of Mark which also occur in Matthew or Luke—five of them in Matthew. So the phenomena are almost identical for the two Gospels, and no argument could be made from them in any case.

I do not wish to seem hard on Farmer, as I made virtually the same error of method myself in a paper to the SNTS seminar in 1981, where Farmer was present! Three of my instances of 'inadvertent' carrying over of a characteristic Matthaean phrase by Luke were on Hawkins's list on pp. 170f.: 'you generation of vipers!', 'there shall be weeping and gnashing of teeth', 'and it came to pass when Jesus finished these sayings'. They might just be Q phrases that Matthew liked very much; though there are other reasons in fact for preferring the inadvertence explanation, which I offered.

There is a ready explanation for most of the Marcan parallels on Hawkins's Matthew list, on the standard hypothesis: viz., Matthew is providing a second, similar incident to the one he is taking over from Mark. Thus, 'in whom I am well pleased', taken over in the Baptism, also seems suitable for the Transfiguration voice from heaven; 'The kingdom of heaven/God has drawn near' was Jesus' first message taken over from Mark, and commends itself both as the Baptist's message, and for the Apostles' preaching; 'Go behind me, Satan' is carried over from Mark 8.33, and it seems apt for Jesus to say to the devil at the Temptations, 'Go, Satan'. Three of Hawkins's instances (13, 14, 15) are in the Husbandmen parable and also in Matthew's Wedding Feast; but then Matthew has himself composed the Wedding Feast on the model of the Husbandmen, and set it immediately following the latter. 'Have mercy, son of David' is repeated from Mark's Bartimaeus, but is introduced into Matthew's similar Blind Men miracle in ch. 9, and the Canaanite Woman in ch. 15. In all these cases there is not the least embarrassment in explaining the phenomena on the hypothesis that Matthew knew Mark.

(2) There is a similar failure clearly to state the argument, and to consider the alternatives, with Burney—a failure which goes back to Burney himself. Burney retranslated the Synoptic logia into Aramaic, and he regularly 'awarded the palm to Matthew' for the best form; 'best' in balance of parallelism and antithesis, and 'best' also in alliteration and rhyme. But Burney's presupposition is given in the title of his book, *The Poetry of Our Lord*: whichever version of the logia gives the best Semitic poetry in retranslation will be the closest to what Jesus actually said. But this is only a presupposition, and Farmer himself challenges it by saying: 'We can account for the Gospels, generally speaking, much better when we assume that they are written by authors who are free to compose their gospels . . . rather freely'. In other words we have two alternatives. (i) Burney's view: Jesus taught in good Aramaic poetry, best preserved in Matthew, and somewhat marred in the later Lucan and Marcan versions. Farmer also opts for this position, but does not note the other possibility: (ii) Jesus taught in rough Aramaic poetry, rather as we have it in Mark, and this was later brushed up and improved by Matthew. Of course this second view would cover only improvements in Greek, which would be limited to the rhythm; but then the rhyme and alliteration are almost entirely the result of Semitic prefixes and suffixes. So the phenomena are ambiguous: Burney, unsurprisingly

for 1925, assumes (i); but Farmer sees through his presupposition on p. 77, only to assume it himself on pp. 87ff.!

As they stand, therefore, Burney's observations do not yield either conclusion, and certainly do not prove (i). (ii) is, however, the more attractive option. Jesus was brought up as a carpenter's son in a Galilaean village, and is likely to have had a limited education; Matthew was probably a trained *sopher* in a city church in Syria, and could cite the OT in Hebrew or Greek at will. He uses sophisticated Jewish methods of exegesis, and adapts the scriptures thereby, so he is likely to have felt free to treat the dominical tradition in the same way—as Farmer puts it, 'to compose his Gospel rather freely'. Option (ii) seems the only choice for those like Matthew Black who (a) note that Matthew is more Semitic than Mark in many small details (*An Aramaic Approach to the Gospels and Acts* [Oxford, 1967³], *passim*), and (b) retain Marcan priority; though they do not always take it! The appeal to superior rhythm as a sign of prior form is still widespread, but it is fallacious. If the superior rhythm occurs in the Matthaean form, it is probably a sign of Matthew's redaction.

(3) In the latter part of his paper, Farmer offers an account of the history of the Mark 13 discourse material on his hypothesis. An account of this kind has to pass three tests: (a) it must be coherent; (b) it must correspond plausibly with all the phenomena; and (c) it must do so better, and must explain more, than competing hypotheses. I do not think that Farmer's hypothesis is incoherent: I cannot see why there should be any contradiction in the idea of Mark checking through his copies of Matthew and Luke in the way described by Farmer—in rough terms, leaving out those pieces of Matthew which Luke does not have in Luke 21. Luke similarly might have treated Matthew in the way Farmer describes.

Plausibility, however, is another matter. A test for the Griesbach theory comes with Luke 21.12-19, the persecution section, since Matthew has the Mark 13.9-13 section at 10.17-22, and a different, but similar version at 24.9-14: but 'for some reason' (p. 91) he has moved over to Matt. 10.17-22. The motive suggested is weak: Luke could have dropped 'the Gentiles' from Matt. 24.9b if he did not like it. A second difficulty arises with Luke 21.21b (p. 92), since there is a parallel to this at Luke 17.31, and Luke is supposed to be leaving out of his version of Matthew all that he has inserted earler. 'In all probability Luke had access to a special source'—but this is just what Farmer has properly criticized Burney for arguing, and it is just the kind of adhoc-ery-pokery which Popper so properly lampooned. Would *any* evidence, Popper would ask, persuade Farmer that his theory was mistaken? There is a further major difficulty over Luke 17.21-37 which is not discussed at all. On the standard view, Luke is following Mark here and Q there; on Farrer's view, Luke is following Mark here, and (most of) the Matthaean additions to Mark there. But Farmer is 'leaving Mark out of view'; and he does not tell us on what basis Luke divided Matt. 24 up. Did he have a fuller special source, perhaps?

Farmer quite properly sees that Luke has amended the earlier tradition to bring it into line with the Church's post-70 experience. We seem to have reference to the Jewish War in detail in Luke 21.20-4, and the ἀκαταστασίαι of 21.9 may be the same; the 'great earthquakes' of 21.11 are likely to refer to the Vesuvius eruption of 79, and Luke allows a period after the fall of Jerusalem 'till the times of the Gentiles are fulfilled', omitting the 'immediately/in those days' from the following verse. Mark, however, is very unspecific about the fall of Jerusalem. The abomination of desolation, the flight of the Judaeans to the hills, and the great Tribulation leading into the End-events are all fused together, with an eager 'let the reader understand'. So the apparent relative dating of the two documents makes Griesbach implausible: Mark (by general consent) should be written about 70, Luke around 90.

Often Farmer seems not to take competing hypotheses very seriously. Burney is cited (p. 90) for the Mark 13.9-13 pericope being 'in a more appropriate position' in Matt. 10; but it is not considered whether Matthew might have transferred it thither for this very reason. Farmer says 'it is difficult to dismiss the suggestion that ... the sabbath in Matthew's text (24.20) is a sign of the original Palestinian provenance' (p. 94); but he does not treat seriously the alternative (and normal) view that Matthew is rejudaizing Mark. It is a *non sequitur* to suppose that a Jewish Christian like Matthew would be against a universal mission to the Gentiles: Galatians and Colossians show Jewish Christians evangelizing Gentiles, but—like Matthew—they insist on the Law being kept. On p. 95 Farmer suggests that Mark has telescoped material from Matt. 24.42–25.15 into his Doorkeeper ending to the discourse; this seems possible, but not so likely as the alternative view, that Matthew expands the parabolic element 'rather freely'. Farmer's Mark seems to remain a shadowy figure. We are told what he is doing, but no clear motive for such action seems to emerge: whereas, on the standard/Farrer hypotheses, the pastoral concern of Jewish Matthew in the 70s, and of Gentile Luke in the 80s, seem clear and convincing. Farmer is faced with the problem of massive omissions by his Mark, and says, 'This question of omissions is never completely answerable on any hypothesis' (p. 85); but on the standard hypothesis Matthew has omitted practically nothing.

In the last resort conviction depends on a lot of little points, and I give half a dozen trivial points of difference between Mark 13 and Matt. 24 where it seems easier to explain the Matthaean form as a clarification of Mark than to offer reasons for Mark's supposed changes to Matthew. Mark 13.6, 'Many will come saying . . . "I am"'; Matt. 24.5,' . . . "I am the Christ"'. Mark 13.14 τὸ βδέλυγμα . . . ἐστηκότα; Matt. 24.15 . . . ἐστός. Mark 13.18, 'Pray that it be not in the winter . . . '; Matt. 24.20, 'Pray that your flight be not . . . '. Mark 13.26, 'And then shall they see the Son of Man coming . . . '; Matt. 24.30, 'And then shall appear the sign of the Son of Man in heaven, and all the tribes of the earth shall mourn, and they will see the Son of Man . . . '. Mark 13.27, 'He will send the angels'; Matt. 24.31, 'He will send his angels with a great trumpet-blast'. Mark 13.32, ' . . . nor the Son, but the Father'; Matt. 24.36, ' . . . nor the Son, but the Father only'. We are looking for the hypothesis that will explain the most. In these (and hundreds of other) verses Matthew can be explained as improving, correcting, clarifying and amplifying Mark: a hypothesis by which Mark is making Matthew less clear, correct and full, seems inferior.

REPLY TO MICHAEL GOULDER

W.R. Farmer

1. *The argument from inadvertent taking-over of characteristics of a source*
Where there are two documents between which the verbatim agreement is close enough to suggest one has copied the other, when the favorite expressions of one are found in the other, it is not (*contra* Goulder) a fallacy to regard this as evidence that it is likely that the favorite expressions of the one have been carried over from the other inadvertently.

It is, of course, possible for one author to know and even make use of the work of another author and not incorporate his source's favorite expressions. But the closer he copies the text of his source, the more likely it is that he will inadvertently include such expressions *at least in a fragmentary form.*

Goulder misleads the reader when he writes: 'Sometimes later B may copy in expressions from earlier A inadvertently; and sometimes a casual expression of earlier A may appeal strongly to B so that he uses it often'. It is wrong to suggest that these two literary phenomenon are equally likely. The second literary phenomenon is known as 'hap-coinage'. Someone 'happens' to coin a 'happy' phrase that others regard, as Goulder says, as 'just the thing'. But this 'hap-coinage' explanation should not be appealed to in the first instance.[1]
It is a far less frequent phenomenon in copying. For a defense lawyer to plead that his client is innocent of the charge of plagiarism on the grounds that the favorite expressions of the plaintiff's written style are found in his client's book because the plaintiff thought some of his client's expressions 'just the thing' and made them into 'favorite expressions', would be making a very weak case for his client. No doubt, the judge would be more confident of his legally obliged decision against the accused, if the 'favorite expressions' of the plaintiff were found in the work of the accused in a 'fragmentary'

form. That would constitute even stronger evidence favoring literary dependence. For it is hardly possible to hold that the 'hap-coinage' phenomenon takes place unless the dependent author thinks a particular expression in his source is 'just the thing'. A fragmentary form of a 'favorite expression' would hardly be perceived as 'just the thing'. It would be a case of '*almost* "just the thing" and I know how to polish it up right'. But one would resort to this kind of explanation only in cases where one has reasons to exclude the phenomenon of 'inadvertent' copying. If one is certain on other grounds that author B is dependent on author A, the presence of the literary character-istics of author B in the work of author A must be explained in some other way than that of 'inadvertent copying'. In that situation, one does the best he can. But one does not elevate *ad hoc* explanations into literary criteria. To do so reduces criticism to specious 'special pleading'. In this instance, this (in my opinion) is what Goulder has done.

In working on the synoptic problem we should recognize the importance of the presence, *in a fragmentary form*, in the work of one synoptic author, of the favorite expressions or redactional character-istics of one or both the other synoptic authors. This phenomenon constitutes *prima facie* evidence for literary dependence. Any judge following the rules of evidence operative in an Anglo-Saxon court of law would be expected to so rule. For him to fail to do this would provide grounds for an appeal of the court's decision.

2. *The import of Burney's method*

If Burney's method of analyzing the poetic form of the sayings tradition in the synoptic Gospels is basically reliable, as I think it is, then Goulder's understanding of Matthew would need revision. Matthew is indeed at liberty to compose the text of his gospel 'rather freely'. But did Matthew take the 'rough Aramaic poetry' as we have it in Mark's version of Jesus' teaching and 'brush up and improve it'? Burney thought not and appealed to Matthew's use of 'Q'. If one gives up 'Q' as Goulder has done, and continues to hold that Matthew has copied Mark, as Goulder still does, he is imprisoned in a critical limbo where he finds himself having to resort to an unusual and unexpected conjecture: i.e., that the evangelist Matthew is responsible for the poetic structure of Jesus' teaching. We can test this conjecture on Goulder's own terms. What happens to the poetic form of Jesus' teaching at the hands of Luke when he is copying

Matthew? We know that Luke tends to destroy the phenomenon of synonymous parallelism. Why would Luke do this? Because that parallelism no longer serves the purpose it had when Jesus' sayings were being transmitted orally. Repetition in oral communication is good style. The ear needs to hear again what has already been said. Such repetition satisfies the mind and emotions of the hearer. The teaching sinks in and is better retained in the memory for further use when the hearer becomes the teacher of others.

This is the most natural explanation for the poetic structure of Jesus' teaching. And, so long as these teachings were transmitted orally, this poetic structure would retain its functional value. There is nothing to keep an evangelist from retaining the parallelism of oral teaching in the process of written transmission. But once Jesus' teaching in this oral form has been faithfully reduced to writing, something new is introduced into the process of transmission. There is now no longer the same necessity for synonymous parallelism. The eye takes over, and the repetition of the same thought in a second line sometimes appears redundant. The eye can do easily what the ear cannot do easily. The eye can quickly go back and reread as many times as the mind requires what has been written. But not the ear. For the ear to recapture what has been said, the hearer needs to have the line repeated—and repeated in ways that satisfies the inner ear of the mind—so artistry comes in and we call this poetry.

To make the evangelist Matthew, while engaged in the *literary* process of composing his Gospel (including copying Mark), responsible for the basically *oral* form of Jesus' teaching, is to create one more 'epicycle' for the already overburdened theory of Marcan priority.

3. *Luke 17.26-30*

Goulder misconstrues my reasons for conjecturing that Luke probably had access to a special source at 17.26-30. As I clearly stated: 'Luke 17.26-30 exhibits synonymous parallelism, and may be in a more original form than its parallel in Matthew 24.37-39'. 'Adhoc-ery-pokery' in this case would have encouraged me to explain away the evidence from parallelism which required me to posit a 'Q'-like common source between Luke and Matthew. I instead followed the criterion of Semitic parallelism. This has led me to conjecture something Goulder doesn't believe in: a '"Q"-like' document. On the disbelief in 'Q' as an extensive source of Jesus' sayings, Goulder and I are in agreement. We agree that Luke made extensive use of

Matthew and that that offers the best explanation for most of what, on the two-document hypothesis, is explained by Matthew and Luke independently copying 'Q'. And subsequent linguistic analysis of Luke 17.26-30 suggests to me Lucan dependence on Matthew, after all. But Luke's use of Matthew in general does not preclude Luke's knowledge and use of special source material which, on some occasions, parallels material in Matthew. Such cases have to be studied passage by passage. And it should occasion no surprise that sometimes Luke's *Sondergut* has preserved the more original form. In these cases, Burney's method provides us an objective test that will help us to make our critical decisions.

4. *Rejudaizing*

Goulder regards the view that Matthew is rejudaizing Mark as 'normal'. It is 'normal' only if Matthew copied Mark and this establishes what is 'normal'. On all other grounds, the idea of a later author taking an earlier document and 'rejudaizing it' is 'abnormal'. This procedure is not impossible, but it clearly goes against the sociological principle of the 'mother and daughter' law. A Swedish Lutheran theologist in St Paul, Minnesota, can take an ealier book written in Sweden and modify it for the use of the Swedish Lutherans in America. But it violates the 'mother-daughter' law for a Swedish Lutheran theologian at Lund to take a book written in St Paul, Minnesota, and rework it for the use of Lutherans in Sweden. Such reversals of the normal processes of sociological and theological development are not impossible. But the development generally and normally goes the other way. For example, Greek philosophy was generally accepted in Rome. But Roman philosophy was not generally accepted in Greece. Greek drama was well received in southern Italy. But Roman drama exerted little or no influence over dramatic compositions created in Greek cities. For this reason, the critic normally would expect that Mark and Luke, which are better adapted for the use of Gentile churches, though both remain *very* Jewish, are later than Matthew which, by comparison, though adaptable for use in some Gentile churches, remains (on geographical, cultural, and religious terms) closer to the Jewish Christian and Palestinian beginnings of the Christian movement.

5. *The shadowy figure of Mark*

Goulder's point that no clear motive emerges for Mark's action in the composition of his Gospel if he is using Matthew and Luke is well taken. Certainly, more work needs to be done at this point. In the meantime, it is the claim of those critics who work with Mark, assuming his use of Matthew and Luke, that Mark is less of a 'shadowy figure' on this view than on any other. One hundred years of work with Mark, assuming this Gospel to be the earliest, has produced no consensus among the Marcan priorists which can begin to compare to the consensus shared by all critics who regard Mark as third: Mark is a unifying figure, a reconciling churchman, a mediating, but self-consistent, theologian—dynamic in his irenicism.

NOTES

1. Cf. E. Zeller, 'Studien zur neutestamentlichen Theologie 4. Vergleichende Uebersicht über den Wörtervorrath der neutestamentlichen Schrifteller', *Theologische Jahrbücher* 2 (1843), pp. 443-543; and H.J. Holtzmann, *Die synoptischen Evangelien. Ihr Ursprung und geschichtlicher Charakter* (Leipzig, 1863), pp. 271-358. Both Zeller and Holtzmann utilize what we have termed the 'inadvertent' criterion for determining dependence, and then resort to what we term the 'hap-coinage' criterion to explain away the anomalous data that works against their respective hypotheses.

THE ORDER OF A CRANK

Michael Goulder

University of Birmingham
P.O. Box 363, Birmingham 15

B.H. Streeter gave two reasons for dismissing 'the obvious suggestion that Luke knew Matthew's Gospel'. (1) Taken against the Marcan order, Luke's and Matthew's placing of Q material never agree. 'If Luke derived this material from Matthew . . . he must have proceeded with the utmost care to tear every little piece of non-Marcan material he desired to use from the context of Mark in which it appeared in Matthew—in spite of the fact that the contexts in Matthew are always exceedingly appropriate—in order to re-insert it into a different context of Mark having no special appropriateness. A theory that would make an author capable of such a proceeding would only be tenable if, on other grounds, we had reason to believe he was a crank. (2) Sometimes it is Matthew, sometimes it is Luke, who gives a saying in what is clearly the more original form' (*The Four Gospels* [London, 1924], p. 183). Other arguments have been adduced since, but it is these two which still hold the centre of the discussion. I shall not in this paper treat the second argument; criteria for assessing 'what is clearly the more original form' have varied, and often seemed slippery, and the point can only be handled *seriatim*, in a commentary on both Gospels. But the order argument has seemed to many decisive on its own, and it is this which I am considering here.

Clearly Streeter's picture of Luke's supposed activity is grossly implausible; but is it our only option? I do not think so. Let us suppose that Luke was a 'minister of the word' writing in about 90; he has had a copy of Mark since the early 70s, and has used it regularly as the basis of his preaching; he has had a copy of Matthew since the early 80s, and has made much use of this too for instructing his congregation. He wishes now to write a Gospel of his own, and for this purpose will need to combine his two primary sources. (We may leave aside the complication of what other sources, if any, Luke used; but we may suppose that Mark and Matthew were not the only Gospel-authors, and that Luke knew of other such writers.) How then should we expect him to proceed?

Our first response might be, 'Like a 19th century *Leben Jesu* writer; how else?' Luke would clearly be facing the same problem as any harmonist, and we know that the problem of order was felt acutely with respect to the Gospels only a generation after Luke, for Papias is concerned, with such guesses and evasions as he can muster, to justify both Mark's and Matthew's τάξις. Luke appears to feel the same, for the following translation seems to take up the natural stress of his opening period: 'Since many [Mark, Matthew, and the rest] have tried to set an account in order . . . it seemed good to me too, having followed everything accurately from the beginning, to write to you in order, most excellent Theophilus, that you may know the sure truth of the matters in which you have been instructed' (Luke 1.1-4). We cannot escape the combined force of ἀνατάξασθαι and καθεξῆς: Luke is concerned to get his order right.

There may however be some differences between Luke's situation and that of a modern harmonist, and I suggest four. (a) It is not so important for teaching material to be in order as for the incidents. Matthew is pretty faithful to Mark's order of incidents, but he moves Mark 13.9-13, 'They shall hand you over . . . ' to Matt. 10. Luke is similarly careful with Mark's incidents, but he moves Mark 10.42ff., 'The kings of the nations lord it over them . . . ', to the Last Supper. He might take a similar licence with the Matthaean teaching matter. (b) It may be desirable to break up long units of teaching material into more manageable sections. Thus Luke abbreviates Mark's Harvest Parable Discourse from 34 verses in Mark 4 to fifteen verses, Luke 8.4-18, omitting the Seed Growing Secretly and the conclusion, and transferring the Mustard Seed. (c) Matthew has formed his Discourses mainly by expanding Mark (whether with Q/M traditions, or in his own idiom); thus Matt. 10 is built on a foundation of Mark 6 and Mark 13. If Luke's policy were to take Mark in large sections—as it is—without intrusions from Matthew, then of necessity he will have to have the non-Marcan material out of the Marcan context: so two missionary discourses, in Luke 9 from Mark and in Luke 10 from Matthew, would be quite a rational procedure. (d) Streeter thought in terms of 'conflation': his Matthew has a copy of Mark to one side, and of Q to the other, and he 'conflates', a phrase from here, a word from there. I think such a proceeding very unlikely. My Luke has probably a cramped writing table with space for his own scroll and the one he is using as his base-of-the-moment. Mark and Matthew take turns to go on the floor. Where there are overlaps and minor agreements and such things, it is from reminiscence of a familiar parallel text.

I

Well, then, if we were Luke, on such a hypothesis, how would we begin? With Matthew, because he starts with Jesus' legal ancestry, his virginal conception announced by an angel, his birth at Bethlehem, his youth at Nazareth, etc. We may choose between further hypotheses. In my view Luke totally rewrote the Matthaean infancy story, with his own meditation on the OT prophecies and stories that Matthew had used; others will prefer Baptist, Anawim and other traditions. But there is no difficulty to supposing that Luke knew Matt. 1–2; he has just improved on it. He has left out the Magi because he does not believe in astrology and magic. When he comes to John's Preaching, Jesus' Baptism and Temptations, he remains with Matthew, because Matthew is fuller and more interesting; though now there are some echoes of the familiar Marcan wording where it overlaps, especially in the Baptism. But down to Luke 4.13 the story follows Matthew without a waver, to Matt. 4.11.

At this point, if you are Luke with Matthew before you, you face a second decision. Not far ahead, at Matt. 4.25, are the crowds from many lands, followed at 5.1 by the mountain sermon; but it is not till Mark 3.7ff. that Mark has a parallel scene, in which there are crowds from the same places, followed by Jesus going up into a mountain at 3.13. So here, I suggest, Luke does his first reconciliation. Matt. 4.12-16 tells of Jesus' settling in Capernaum, followed by his beginning to preach in 4.17; and surely, Luke might feel, this corresponds very closely to Mark 1.21-34, Jesus' first day at Capernaum, followed by his first preaching tour in Mark 1.35-9. Did Luke really make this equivalence? He seems to have done, for there are two changes in the Marcan order which agree with Matthew. First, Matt. 4.13 notes that before Jesus settled in Capernaum, he left Nazara, as Matthew spells it here; and in just the same place in the sequence Luke inserts the story of Jesus' rejection at Nazareth—only he also spells it Nazara,

and here alone. Many commentators have Luke make the transfer
'for theological reasons', 'for his programmatic sermon', etc.; but my
Luke is trying to get the (chronological) order right, and would not
move a scene from Mark 6 without a text to justify it. Second, if we
make Luke's supposed equivalence, the Call of the First Apostles will
present him with a problem. In Matthew, at 4.18-22, the Call follows
the settling at Capernaum and the mission; in Mark it precedes them,
1.16-20 before 1.21-39. Now Luke agrees with Matthew here, not
Mark; he has the Call at 5.1-11, *after* the scenes at Capernaum, 4.31-
41, and the mission, 4.42-44. So it seems that we have two pieces of
evidence for Luke making the suggested equivalence, Matt. 4.13-17
= Mark 1.21-39.

There is still a long way to go to the crowds and mountain at Mark
3.7ff.; but fortunately Matthew gives the possibility of a second
equivalence, for at 4.23 he writes of Jesus' tour of Galilee preaching
and healing every kind of sickness, and Mark 1.40–3.6 gives a full
account of exactly such activity. Thus Luke is able, on my hypothesis,
to make a second satisfactory reconciliation. He can follow Mark in
his fuller and better-told story of the early healings and controversies,
with a verse from Matthew that covers the same ground; and he can
arrive at the mountain for Mark 3.13 and Matt. 5.1 at the same time.
Is there any indication of such a procedure in the text? Again, there
seems to be; for the Marcan section ends with (a) 3.7-12, the
gathering of great crowds, and (b) 3.13-19, the call of the Twelve; but
in Matthew, the gathering of the great crowds runs directly into the
Sermon, 4.24–5.1. Once again, Luke reverses the order of the Marcan
units, and so brings the crowds directly before the Sermon, as they
are in Matthew.

So Luke is back to Matthew again for the Sermon, without
deserting him once. But now he does reduce the Matthaean volume—I
would suggest for manageability, as with the Parables Discourse in
Mark 4. Matthew's Sermon was a guide to the spiritual life; Luke has
just had the apostles called, and to him the apostolic life is one of
poverty and persecution. So he limits the Beatitudes to these matters,
and expounds them from the end of Matt. 5, on loving our persecutors,
and Matt. 7, not judging them, etc. Other topics can await a more
leisured moment for exposition. Then, having already had the Leper
(Matt. 8.1-4) at 5.12ff. in the Marcan sequence, he moves on to the
Centurion's Boy, Matt. 8.5ff. = Luke 7.1-10.

There is now a break in the Matthaean sequence for the first time:

John's Question, and the material following, are brought forward (on my hypothesis) from Matt. 11.2-19. I have argued elsewhere (*The Evangelists' Calendar* [London, 1978]) that Matt. 11–13 were intended for use over the festal season New Year–Atonement–Tabernacles, as Matt. 26–28 were intended for Passover–Easter. Jesus' healings were a sign that God's reign had begun, the theme of New Year; his preaching as the greater than Jonah, and the Pharisees' rejection of forgiveness in Matt. 12 were a topic for Atonement; the harvest parables of Matt. 13 were a Christian message for Tabernacles. It was a strong support for this that the same topics were to be found in Mark: Mark 1, the coming of God's reign, Mark 2, forgiveness, Mark 4, the harvest parables. We should then have an explanation for the similar sequence in Luke: 7.18-34, the Baptist's Question (as in Matthew); 7.36-50, the Sinner forgiven (with echoes of Mark 2, already used for Atonement); 8.4-18, the harvest parables, for Tabernacles. For the argument, I must refer the reader to my book.

But even without the Lectionary hypothesis, there is little difficulty explaining Luke's bringing forward the Baptist's Question. Julius Wellhausen, *Das Evangelium Lucae* (Berlin, 1904), suggested that Luke has now had the preaching to the πτωχοί following the leper and other healings in chs. 5–6; he only requires a raising story (7.11-17) and some blind people (rather hurried on in 7.21) to enable Jesus to come out with the famous answer. Indeed, my theory is only a liturgical form of Wellhausen's; he offers a topical, I a calendrical urgency for claiming the fulfilment of the Isa. 35 and 61 prophecies.

This insertion, and the (L) Sinner following, bring us to the end of Luke 7, and there are three verses, 8.1-3, before we return to the Marcan sequence. Jesus goes preaching, accompanied by the Twelve, and certain women who had been healed (τεθεραπευμέναι) from evil πνεύματα and ἀσθενείαι; Mary from whom seven δαιμόνια had gone out, and many others who ministered (διηκόνουν) to them. Now it is at such a moment that hypotheses like ours can be put to the test. If Luke has really been following Matthew as carefully as I have been suggesting, then he should be doing so here too. Well, we left Matthew at the Centurion's Boy, 8.13, and the next story is the healing of Peter's mother-in-law: we have had her in the Marcan section, but she ministered to him (διηκόνει). Then, 8.16f., Jesus was brought many δαιμονιζομένους, and he cast out the πνεύματα and healed (ἐθεράπευσεν) the sick, so fulfilling Isaiah, 'He took our ἀσθενείας'. That is a lot of words to find in common, and it suggests a process of which we shall find a number of examples, a process which I shall call 'substitution': that is, *where Luke has already used a topic in the Marcan sequence, he may provide a similar substitute when he reaches that topic in the Matthaean sequence.*

This brings us to Matt. 8.18, 'And Jesus, seeing a crowd about him, commanded to depart to the other side', with the Storm to follow. The fuller account of the Storm, and succeeding incidents, is in Mark 4.35ff., but the crowd might be from the preceding Marcan Parables Discourse, which Luke has not yet given. He therefore turns over to Mark 4.1, and follows Mark, virtually in sequence, though with minor and major omissions, almost to the end of Mark 9. As he had left Mark at Mark 3.19, the Call of the Twelve, all that has been left out is the Beelzebul story and the Mother and Brothers. The latter he appends deftly to the Sower sermon at Luke 8.19-21; the former he prefers to tell in its fuller Matthaean form. This is not the place for an account of Luke's omissions from Mark in Luke 9; but we may see that he must leave Mark before Jesus reaches the borders of Judaea at Mark 10.1; there is a lot of Galilaean matter from Matthew to fill in before he gets that far.

II

What then does Luke seem to do with the rest of Matthew's Galilaean ministry? Mark 9.30ff. speaks of Jesus travelling through Galilee with a view to his passion, so Luke opens the Journey at 9.51 with Jesus' setting his face for Jerusalem. He then moves over to Matthew once more, and as he had left Matthew at 8.18 with the Storm, he begins from the omitted section, Matt. 8.19-22, the aspiring disciples and the sayings about foxes and burying the dead. These are linked with the refusal of the Samaritans to accept him; so (we are to understand) Jesus could not travel south, but turns east along the Galilee–Samaria border, where he still is at Luke 17.11.

Matt. 8–9 had been mostly close to the Marcan text, and the next considerable new section is Matt. 9.35ff., 'The harvest is plenteous', which prepares for the Mission Discourse in Matt. 10. These are the topics next covered in Luke, then (10.1-16): 'The harvest is plenteous' (Matt. 9.37f.), the first part of the Discourse (Matt. 10.7-16), and its last verse (Matt. 10.40). As Luke shortened the Marcan Parables Discourse, so does he here. Matthew expanded Mark 6.7-13 with much material on persecution, and this Luke leaves by as not immediately relevant; but he does allow the mention of Sodom and Gomorrah (Matt. 10.15 = Luke 10.12) to attract in the Tyre and Sidon logia from Matt. 11.21-23 (Luke 10.13-15).

The first nineteen verses of Matt. 11 have been taken already, the Baptist's Question; so this brings Luke to Matt. 11.25-27, the logion on the wise and the babes. He interprets this, as Matthew does, of the acceptance of the gospel by the disciples and its rejection by the leaders of Israel, but emphasizes the mission situation as its occasion (Luke 10.17-22). Again he draws in a subsidiary saying to stress his point. The Son has revealed the gospel to his disciples; 'Blessed are the eyes which see what you see . . .', follows on aptly from Matt. 13.16f.

Matthew proceeds to the Yoke logia (11.28-30), and to an expanded version of the Marcan Cornfield (12.1-8). Luke has told the Cornfield already, but there is a brief note in Matthew's expansion which is close to Luke's heart, 'I desire ἔλεος and not sacrifice'; and this, I suggest, he expands. The same theme is to be found in the story of the Great Commandment, for there the scribe had said that to love one's neighbour was more than all holocausts and sacrifices. Matthew has Jesus say (12.6), 'A greater than the Temple is here'. So Luke brings forward the story of the scribe who asked about the Great Commandment, and he has Jesus reply with the story of the priest and the Levite who left the wounded man by the roadside, while the Samaritan was a true neighbour to him, and did mercy (ἔλεος) with him. I think there may be another reason for so bold a transfer; but I do not think Luke lacked a Matthaean text to justify his order.

But what of the Yoke logia? Here is my boldest suggestion. I think that Luke liked the teaching but was repelled by the image; for 'burdens' hard to bear were imposed by the lawyers in Luke 11.46, and the Law was a 'yoke' with which the Lucan church had dispensed (Acts 15.10). So in Luke 10.38-42 he draws the picture of Mary sister of Martha coming to Jesus and receiving rest for her soul, while Martha is cumbered about with the yoke of service. In 11.1-13 Jesus lays on his disciples the light yoke of his discipline—to say the Lord's Prayer, and to keep praying. There is no verbal support for these suggestions, and there might be other reasons for the order here—I have suggested elsewhere that Luke took the Lord's Prayer as a Christian substitute for the *Shema*'; or there is the influence of the Elisha cycle.

With 11.14ff., the Beelzebul story, we are back to Matt. 12 without any hesitations. In 12.22-30 Matthew describes the controversy itself, and Luke follows him closely in Luke 11.14-23, though he draws in some words from the similar incident in Matt. 9.32-34, and the request for a sign from Matt. 12.38. Matthew rounds the story off with three appendages, 12.31-37 on blasphemy, 12.38-42 on the sign of Jonah, and 12.43-45 on the seven demons. As usual Luke prefers a more compact story, and the piece that rounds off an exorcism tale most effectively is unquestionably the seven demons, which he transcribes in 11.24-26. We have not long to wait for the other two appendages; and Luke 11.16, on the sign, suggests that the sign appendage was in Luke's *Vorlage*.

After Beelzebul, Matthew returns to Mark, with the Mother-and-Brothers at 12.46-50: whoever does the will of Jesus' Father is his true family. Now we come upon a second striking substitute. Luke has already told this story at 8.19ff. in the Marcan section, and he tells of a brief incident in which a woman in the crowd spoke of Jesus' mother being blessed, but he replied, 'Blessed rather are those who hear the word of God and keep it'. It looks as if Luke is following the Matthaean order, and has composed a substitute for Matt. 12.46-50 to save the duplication, much as he did at 8.1-3.

At Luke 11.29-36 we have the omitted Sign of Jonah from Matt. 12.38-42. Luke takes the Sign to be not so much the Resurrection as the preaching, so there is some restyling; and the theme is then expanded with some other material. Luke thought the gospel was a light to lighten the Gentiles, so he adapts Matt. 5.15 with the lamp on the stand giving light to all who enter the house; and he adds the light sayings from Matt. 6.22-23.

III

Luke has now covered Matt. 1-12, and faces a new decision of policy: for in Matt. 1–12 there is an enormously expanded form of Mark 1–3, while Matt. 13–28 is only a mildly expanded form of Mark 4–16. In Matt. 1–12 there are considerable divergences from the Marcan order; Matt. 13–28 virtually follows the Marcan order. But Luke has already given the events of Mark 4–9, and he means to return to Mark for the order of Mark 10–16. So all he has to do now is to cover the little pieces which Matthew has added to Mark in the second half of his Gospel; and these are to a large extent concentrated in Matt. 23 and 24.37–25.46. Luke could have ploughed straight on through

Matt. 13, but he feels no compulsion to do this. All that remains is sayings material, and Luke no doubt knew that the sayings were not in chronological order in either of his predecessors. What he in fact does is to combine the washing controversy of Matt. 15.1ff. with the controversy in Matt. 23 on washing cups, and other matters. Once he is in Matt. 23, he stays there; we will consider in a moment what he does with the enormous chasm he has overleapt. For the moment he abbreviates Matt. 23, as he has every other discourse. Matthew had seven Woes addressed to the scribes and Pharisees. Luke cuts these in half, just as he turned Matthew's eight Beatitudes into four Beatitudes and four Woes in ch. 6; he selects the three most cogent instances of hypocritical piety with which to reproach the Pharisees (tithing, seating, and being hidden tombs), and the three best charges of oppression for the lawyers (loads hard to bear, prophets' tombs, and the key of knowledge). The prophets' tombs do not fit the lawyers very well.

Luke shows us, as he opens ch. 12, that he has not done with the theme of Pharisaic hypocrisy from Matt. 23, and he expounds it by rewriting 'There is nothing hidden which shall not be revealed . . .' from Matt. 10.26ff. But the particular form of hypocrisy Luke is concerned about is described in Matthew's rewriting of Mark in Matt. 24.9-14, 'Then they will hand you over to tribulation and will kill you . . . Then many will be scandalized . . . and the love of many will wax cold.' This passage naturally then leads him further into Matt. 10, since it was there that Matthew gave a fuller and more memorable account of Christians under persecution for their faith— and indeed Luke postponed this section of Matt. 10 till the topic should come up. So once more we have a kind of substitute; only this time it is with a linked passage of Matthew. Luke draws in the 'fear not . . . ' passage, 'your hairs are numbered', confessing and denying the Son of Man and the inspiration of the Holy Spirit from Matt. 10; and adds the blasphemy against the Spirit from Matt. 12.

Luke 12.13-40 is a long section on the coming judgment; it opens with the (L) Rich Fool, and closes with the Thief in the Night from Matt. 24.43f. The latter is preceded by a shortened form of the Bridesmaids from Matt. 25.1-13; the Christians' lights are to be burning, and they like men (this time) waiting for their Lord on his coming from his wedding—blessed are those servants whom the Lord on his coming will find awake. So the climax of the section is drawn from the end of Matt. 24 and beginning of Matt. 25; and the

Rich Fool carries the same moral, except that Matthew still expected judgment to come with the Lord's Parousia, while Luke has come to think of it at our death. Between the Fool and the Marriage Luke has inserted the long passage on wealth from Matt. 6, which takes up the themes of caring for one's soul, gathering corn into one's barns, and laying up treasure on earth; but the judgment sections before and after show that the stress is on 'a treasure that fails not in heaven'.

Luke 12.41–13.9 continues the theme of judgment, which is expanded into repentance. It opens with the parable of the faithful and wise Servant, and the wicked Servant, from Matt. 24.45-51. Luke expands this with other texts from elsewhere in Matthew which he bends to his purpose: the 'five in a house' which Jesus' coming divides, from Matt. 10.34-36 (but perhaps Luke's 'five' have come from the five bridesmaids—note the νύμφη); the cloud rising in the west, perhaps suggested by Christ's coming on the clouds for judgment in Matt. 24.30; and the settlement on the road before judgment from Matt. 5.25f. The L material on repentance in 13.1-9 reaches its climax in the parable of the Fig-Tree, which is often taken to be a parable form of Mark 11.12-14 // Matt. 21.18f.; but there is reference to the parable of the Fig-Tree in Matt. 24.32 also. Thus the leading theme of the section is drawn from Matt. 24.45ff., and Luke may either have elaborated this from elsewhere as he pleased, or he may have substituted again for topics in the surrounding discourse.

We have not left Matt. 24–25 in the section following, on the condemnation of Israel. The (L) Bent Woman is concerned with the rejection of Jesus by the synagogue rulers (13.10-17); 'so he said', says Luke making a connection, that the Church will grow into a great tree full of (Gentile) birds (Matt. 13.31-33). But the paragraph then moves on to our need to enter the narrow door, lest the Lord shut it, and we are left standing outside knocking; we may knock, but he will say, 'I know you not'. Luke has had the first part of Matt. 25.1-13, readiness for the return of the Lord from his wedding, at Luke 12.35ff.; now he has the close of the parable, 'The door was shut . . . Lord open to us . . . I know you not' (Matt. 25.10-12). He introduces this with an adaptation of the gate in Matt. 7.13f., and there is a further adaptation of the 'Many will come from east and west . . .' logion in Matt. 8.11. But the scene is not based upon these texts, but upon the Judgment scene in Matt. 25. Luke's 'Then (τότε) you will begin to say, We ate and drank before you . . . And he will say (ἐρεῖ), Depart from me, all workers of injustice', goes back to Matthew's

'Then he will say (τότε ἐρεῖ) also to those on the left, Go from me, you cursed . . . For I was hungry and you gave me not to eat, I was thirsty and you gave me not to drink.' Matt.. 7.22f. is printed alongside Luke 13.26 by Aland and Greeven, but the details are different, and also the meaning. For Luke is concerned with eating and drinking, not prophesying and miracles, and Matt. 25 is primary; even 'There shall be weeping and gnashing of teeth' is probably drawn in via Matt. 25.30.

IV

So, according to our hypothesis, Luke has now run through the non-Marcan sections of Matthew. Sometimes he has copied the matter word for word (especially in the early sections, the Baptist's Sermon and Temptations); sometimes he has emended freely, so much so that we need our Ariadne's thread to find our way through the labyrinth after him. But he has gone through Matt. 1–12 and 23–25, we may feel, carefully and in order, even if he has made a number of surprising omissions. And now, dear reader, you are St Luke, and there is the scroll of Matthew on the table before you, and the rolled up portion is Matt. 1–25, and the next words in Matt. 26 open the Passion narrative. You are aware that you have not even been through Matt. 13–22 for non-Marcan gems: what would be your policy? Well, I hope you will not think me a crank for suggesting it; but the obvious move seems to me *to go back through the rolled up scroll, and to take the missing pieces as they come, backwards.* It is true that this will involve sacrificing the principle of order; but then Luke has only teaching, no incidents, to concern himself with in the gleaning process—and in fact his leap from Matt. 12 to Matt. 23 necessarily involved gleaning in some form, and therefore the sacrifice of the Matthaean order *in toto.*

Policies often spring from small decisions, and we may first notice a small point. After the Great Assize, Jesus says (Matt. 26.2), 'You know that after two days is the Passover, and the Son of Man is handed over to be crucified'. After the Lucan Assize, 13.24–30, Jesus says, 'I cast out demons today and tomorrow, and the third day I am perfected'; he explains that he means his death in Jerusalem. Now this is not a Q-logion, but it looks very like another of the substitutes, an L-logion in place of a Matthaean redaction of Mark, which we found with the ministering women and 'Blessed rather are those who hear the word of God and keep it'. But the death of Jesus at Jerusalem draws in the thought of Matt. 23.37-39, 'O Jerusalem, Jerusalem . . . ' The rolled up section is reopened a short length, and an instinct is on the way to becoming a policy.

In his Woes in ch. 11 Luke covered the second half of Matt. 23 extensively, but the first part barely. There remain from the chapter (a) the opening verse on the scribes and Pharisees laying down the law in an oppressive manner, (b) their pride in taking the chief seats at dinners, etc., (c) 23.12, 'Whoever shall exalt himself shall be humbled, and whoever shall humble himself shall be exalted', (d) material on oaths, etc., which is a little precious for Luke. However in 14.1-14, immediately following 'Jerusalem, Jerusalem . . . ', he gives us a scene in which all the first three points crop up: (a) 14.1-6, the man with dropsy, who is healed in the teeth of legalist objections by 'the lawyers and Pharisees', (b) 14.7-14, in which the dinner-guests choose the chief seats, and are warned against such pride, and (c) 14.11, 'Everyone who exalts himself shall be humbled, and he who humbles himself shall be exalted'. So Luke has now done and re-done Matt. 23.

Turning back, then, to Matt. 22, we find the latter two-thirds of the chapter to be solid Marcan material, which Luke will expound in Luke 20. There is, however, an important Matthaean innovation in the parable of the Royal Wedding Feast, 22.1-14, and here, next in the Lucan order, at 14.16-24, comes Luke's version of the same, the Great Dinner. Luke cuts out the impossible allegorical element with the army, and reduces the royal scale to his familiar middle class, but he leaves behind traces of other Matthaean details in the surrounding matter. Thus Matthew had a Wedding Feast, Luke a dinner; but in the setting of the parable Jesus says, not very pointfully, 'When you are invited by anyone to a *wedding*'. Matthew closed the parable with the unworthy guest who was cast into outer darkness; cf. the Lucan disciple of 14.34, who will not detach himself from his possessions— ἔξω βάλλουσιν αὐτό. Not one diamond shall be lost from the Matthaean tiara: all must be included.

The Cost of Discipleship, Luke 14.25-35, is a subject close to our evangelist's heart, and not to be dismissed so briefly. He opens it with a version of Matt. 10.37f., 'He who loves father or mother . . . ', and closes it with a form of Matt. 5.13, 'If the salt has lost its taste . . . ' But the substance of the section is the two short parables, the man who wished to build a tower (πύργον οἰκοδομῆσαι), and the king who sent (ἀποστείλας) an embassy of peace. Now if our scroll-rolling hypothesis is correct, we ought to find something that could serve as a suggestion for these two parables in Matt. 21, before the Wedding Feast. Matt. 21 ends with the **Marcan** Husbandmen: 'A householder man planted a vineyard, and built **a wall** round it and dug a press in it and built a tower (ᾠκοδόμησεν πύργον) . . . and at harvest-time he sent (ἀπέστειλεν) his servants'. Although the words are not too uncommon, these are the only two occasions in the NT when someone builds a tower, and the connection of a subsequent embassy in both cases is not negligible; we have here yet another possibility of a Lucan substitute, an L passage taking the place of the next piece in the Matthaean order, where Matthew is over-writing Mark.

Immediately before Matthew's Husbandmen comes a further Matthaean intrusion, 21.28-32, the rather colourless little parable that begins 'A man had two children'. One of the sons refused to work in his father's vineyard, but later repented and did; and he is said to be like the publicans and harlots who will enter the kingdom. The other son said Yes, but didn't work, and he is said to be like the Jewish leaders, who did not repent. Now in the next scene in Luke after the Cost of Discipleship, Jesus is found preaching to publicans and sinners with a crowd of murmuring Pharisees to criticize him. He develops the theme of the Lost Sheep from Matt. 18.12ff. which is concerned with God's joy at the repentance of sinners, before telling his own incomparable version of the Two Sons parable. He opens, like Matthew, 'A certain man had two sons'. The first of these does not want to work in the family estate, and goes off and spends his patrimony; but afterwards he comes to himself, goes back to confess his fault and is willing to work with his father's hirelings—he is the repentant sinner. The other does the work, but resents his father's good-heartedness to the prodigal—he is the Pharisee. It would be difficult to think of a more striking candidate for Lucan substitute, though this time it is for what has traditionally been regarded as an M passage rather than one where Matthew is rewriting Mark.

There is only one considerable Matthaean intrusion into the previous two and a half chapters of Marcan incident: the Labourers in the Vineyard. Luke has left this out; perhaps he thought it rather similar to the Two Sons in the vineyard which he has just used; or perhaps he felt that he had taken its theme, 'The last shall be first . . .', not long since at Luke 13.30. The rest he will take up in the Marcan sequence in Luke 18–19. So that brings him back to Matt.

18, where there is indeed considerable new Matthaean material; and where in fact he has already begun to press his thinking, with the Lost Sheep. Matt. 18 ends with a parable on the importance of remitting debt, that is sin. There are three characters in the story: the king (i.e. God) who is owed a fabulous sum by his 'servant' (who is 'us'), and who in turn is owed a small sum by a 'fellow-servant' (who is the man who has offended against 'us'). The king makes an account (λόγος) with the servant, and lets him off; the servant demands of his fellow-servant, 'pay what you owe! (ἀπόδος εἴ τι ὀφείλεις)', and refuses to let him off; and the king then sends the unremitting servant to hell. The parable following the Two Sons in Luke is the Unjust Steward, which has the same structure, and the same moral. There is an owner who says to his steward, 'Give an account (λόγος) of your stewardship!' The account is temporarily stayed, and the steward summons his sub-debtors, saying to each, 'How much do you owe (πόσον ὀφείλεις)?' He then remits a suitable part of the debt, and so secures his future from their goodwill. The evangelists concur. How foolish, says Matthew, to insist upon the trivial wrongs done to us, when our eternal future depends upon the forgiveness of God! How wise, says Luke, to remit debts due to us, and so secure our eternal future with the angels in heaven! Luke cannot abide Matthew's fairy-tale style, though, with its oriental despot, its multi-millionaire satrap, its torture-chamber and the rest. He goes for down-to-earth situations as always, with believable debts payable in familiar produce, and a colourful ambiguous hero given to Lucan-style soliloquy. The parable would have been a great success if only Luke could have resisted the temptation to complicate it with the stewardship theme from Matthew's Talents; but that is another story.

The train of thought of the next Lucan paragraph, 16.14-31, is a standing problem. It contains the following elements: (a) the Pharisees were money-lovers, and Dives goes to hell for his love of money and contempt of the poor; (b) the Pharisees justify themselves before men, and are odious to God; (c) the law and the prophets were till John, but now the kingdom is preached, and everyone forces his way in; (d) nevertheless (δέ) it is easier (εὐκοπώτερον) for the universe to pass away than for one tittle to fall—i.e. presumably to become invalid (cf. later 'they have Moses and the prophets'); (e) remarriage is no better than adultery. Luke does not write inconsequential nonsense elsewhere, and we should consider, at least from motives of charity, whether there may be some rational explanation for such an apparent muddle. Now our labyrinthine thread has given us an opportunity not open to those before us. On our hypothesis Luke is sitting looking at a scroll of Matthew open at the end of Matt. 18. He has just rolled back a good length, two and a half chapters. It would not be implausible for his eye to fall on Matt. 19; and it may be an encouragement to think so when we notice the rare word εὐκοπώτερον at Matt. 19.24, 'It is easier for a camel to pass through the eye of a needle than for a rich man (πλούσιον) to enter the kingdom of God'. But the Lucan parable is about riches as a bar to heaven! Here is point (a), the Pharisees' cupidity, illustrated by 16.19, 'There was a certain rich man (πλούσιος)', and his subsequent tormented afterlife. Furthermore, the Rich Ruler in Matt. 19 is the clearest text we have for the teaching that the gospel requires more than the Law (viz. 'selling all'); and this will provide a pointful meaning for the contrast in point (c), 'The law and the prophets were till John; from then the kingdom is evangelized'. Indeed, in Matthew the rich man asked how he should gain eternal life, and he was told, 'keep the commandments'; so there is point (d), no tittle shall fall from the law, they have Moses and the prophets. Jesus specifies in the Matthaean text, 'Thou shalt not murder, thou shalt not commit adultery, μοιχεύσεις'; and here we have point (e), remarriage is adultery. In the Marcan, and both the Matthaean versions of the remarriage text, 'he commits adultery' is μοιχᾶται—only Luke has μοιχεύει. So the verb could come from Matt. 19.18; and the closest form of the remarriage text to Luke is the Vaticanus version of Matt. 19.9, which is read by Greeven. The two have in common, against both Mark and Matt. 5.32, (i) 'he commits adultery', absolutely, at the end of both sentences, (ii) ὁ ἀπολελυμένην γαμῶν/–ήσας, participial, in the second clause.

So it looks as if we have the key to Luke's thinking. The only missing point is (b), the Pharisee's justification of himself before men; and this seems to come from Matt. 6.1-18, where the Pharisees do their righteousness to be seen of men, but God sees in secret. Luke has just concluded the Steward with the Mammon saying from Matt. 6.24. For the rest, as he looks at Matt. 19 he thinks of the rich man as a proud Pharisee, just as he turned the innocent Simon of Mark 14 into Simon the Pharisee of Luke 7. These people derided Jesus in their self-conceit, thinking they could force their way into the kingdom; but now we have not only to keep the law, but to give away our possessions as well. The rich man in Matthew refused to see this.

But the whole law is still valid—for instance the marriage law which the Pharisees also disputed in Matt. 19.3-9. In fact so far from giving all to the poor, they live like Dives, and to hell they will go. It is Matt. 19 which shows us the thrust of this over-compact section. It would have been neater if Luke had put Dives, etc., before the Steward, as Matt. 19 is before Matt. 18 in our supposed scroll-rolling; but I am not arguing for neatness, but for plausibility.

With Luke 17.1-10, on πίστις, we are on easier ground. Luke has covered the Remission of Debt parable; now he moves back to the first half of Matt. 18. First he treats Matt. 18.6f., the scandalizing of the little ones, and the millstone; then Matt. 18.15, 'If your brother sins, rebuke him . . .'; then Matt. 18.21f., forgiveness seven times and more. The discussion of who was greatest, Matt. 18.1-5, Luke has given in the Marcan sequence; the Lost Sheep, Matt. 18.12-14, he has expounded already. Visiting sinners with witnesses, etc., is a bit legalistic for Luke. But with only four verses out of the first half of Matt. 18, he needs more material to make a lesson, and moves back into Matt. 17. The Coin in the Fish's Mouth he also omits, but before that, at Matt. 17.20, is πίστις as a grain of mustard seed, the only other Matthaean introduction into a Marcan chapter; illustrated by the Servant of All Work, a parable of faithfulness.

Luke 17.11-19 is the Ten Lepers. The story is opened with the astonishing comment that Jesus is passing through Samaria and Galilee en route for Jerusalem. It contrasts the grateful Samaritan with the nine thankless Jews, as he kneels before the Lord who has 'had mercy on him' (ἐλέησον). We cannot come so far without noting that N-A[26] puts 'Mt 17.15!' alongside, for there Matthew tells of the father who knelt before Jesus and asked him to have mercy (ἐλέησον) on his son; and Christ had lamented the faithless generation he must be with. The Lucan context suggests (17.19 [cf. 17.5]; 18.8) that he thinks of gratitude as πίστις, so the central point, and the contrast with 'this faithless generation', and the image of the kneeling man are the same. Luke has taken Mark's possessed boy in Luke 9, so here is another of his 'substitutes', the leper material coming from Mark 1 and 4 Kgdms 5. The journey through Galilee to Jerusalem is taken from Matt. 17.22, 'While they were gathering in Galilee, Jesus said to them, The Son of Man is to be delivered . . .'

And so we come to the last Q pericope in the Journey, 17.20-37, the Day of the Son of Man. Synopses print Matt. 24 sections alongside it, but not in sequence, and commentators note some uncomfortable veering of thought. Why the Pharisees' opening question (ἐπερωτηθείς), when the discourse is to the disciples? Why 'the kingdom of God comes not with watching', when the discourse gives the signs of the Day of the Son of Man? Why, when we are being told that the Son of Man will come like lightning, is it said, 'But first he must suffer many things and be reviled from this generation'? How can it be sensible to say of that Day, 'He that would gain his life shall lose it, and he who loses his life will preserve it'? Well, before Matt. 17 comes Matt. 16, and Matt. 16 opens with the Pharisees questioning (ἐπηρώτησαν) Jesus and asking for a sign; but, he replies, they shall have no sign but the sign of Jonah. Then (after two Marcan incidents) Matthew gives his version of the teaching on Jesus' coming sufferings, and his return in judgment. 16.21, 'He must suffer many things from the elders . . .'; 16.25, 'He that would save his life shall lose it, and he who loses his life for my sake shall find it'; 16.27, 'For the Son of Man is to come in the glory of his father with his angels, and then will he render to every man after his work'; 16.28, 'They will see the Son of Man coming in his kingdom'.

As with Luke 16.14ff., there is a hidden thread on which the Matthaean pearls are strung. Luke takes the Matt. 16 verses in order, 16.1, 4, 21, 25, while the Son of Man's coming (vv. 27f.) is the leitmotif of the whole. The Matt. 24 verses are not in order, and are used to expound the Matt. 16 text as is convenient. The Pharisees' question comes first, and Jesus' answer, 'No sign', is interpreted as 'not with watching . . . here or there', as in Matt. 24.23; and the 'here or there' of Matt. 24.26, and the ἀστραπή logion following, are resumed in 17.23-24. Luke then returns, somewhat inconsequentially, to Matt. 16.21, 'First he must suffer' (17.25), before resuming the theme of the day of the Son of Man. The beckoning text for this is the Noah logion (Matt. 24.37-39), to which Luke adds a Lot parallel of his own. 'Remember Lot's wife' leads him back to Matt. 16.25, 'He who would save his life . . .', for she was saving hers, and lost it. And so to the couples in bed and at the mill, and to the eagles. The actual imminent coming of the Son of Man to judgment (Matt. 16.27f.) is developed in the parable of the Widow and the Judge: 'I say to you, he will vindicate them soon. But when the Son of Man comes, will he find faithfulness on the earth?' (Luke 18.8). Thus the Matt. 16 texts provide the string, and the Matt. 24 texts the pearls.

* * *

Well now, men and brethren, what shall we say to these things?
We have seen reason to think that, if Luke were familiar with
Matthew as well as Mark, he would have been likely to attempt a
reconciliation of them. For 1.5–9.50 there seemed to be evidence that
this is what he has done: following Matt. 1–4.11 (with replacements)
down to Luke 4.13, and Matt. 5.1–8.10 from Luke 6.20–7.10; and
skilfully using the Matthaean summaries to bring in blocks of Mark.
Thus Matt. 4.12f. was used to bring in the Rejection at Nazara, Luke
4.14-30; Matt. 4.13b-17 was taken as equivalent to Mark 1.21-39,
Capernaum and the first mission, Luke 4.31-44; the Call of the first
disciples then fell in the Matthaean sequence, Matt. 4.18-22 // Luke
5.1-11; Matt. 4.23 then gave opportunity for Jesus' healing ministry
of Mark 1.40–3.6 = Luke 5.12–6.11; and Matt. 4.24f., the great
crowds, accounted for the reversing of the crowds (Mark 3.7-12) and
the Call of the Twelve (Mark 3.13-19) in Luke 6.12-19. There was a
similar use of Matt. 8.14-17 in Luke 8.1-3. The overall neatness of
this account was disturbed by the bringing forward of the Baptist's
Question and following matter, Matt. 11.2-19, for which I offered my
own calendrical explanation, or, as an alternative, Wellhausen's
topical theory.

For the first part of the Journey, we found an extension of this
process. Luke could be seen as resuming Matthew where he had left
off, with the Aspiring Disciples, Matt. 8.19-22 // Luke 9.56-60; and
following him with 'The harvest is plenteous . . .', Matt. 9.37f. //
Luke 10.2, the Mission Discourse, Matt. 10.7-16, 40 // Luke 10.3-16,
the Woes on the Cities, Matt. 11.21-24 // Luke 10.13-15, 'I thank
you, Father . . .', Matt. 11.25-27 // Luke 10.21f., the Beelzebul
pericope, Matt. 12.22-45 // Luke 11.14-26, 29-32, and Jesus' True
Family, Matt. 12.46-50, cf. Luke 11.27f. The last raised an interesting
question, because it appeared that Luke was writing a substitute for
the next unit of Matthew, which happened to be a Matthaean
redaction of verses in Mark which Luke had had earlier, at 8.19-21. If
so, then it seemed that Luke knew Matt.R, or in other words
Matthew; and it was possible to suggest that the 'missing' pieces of
Matthew in Matt. 11.28–12.7 had also been substituted for, 'I desire
mercy and not sacrifice' with the Good Samaritan, the Easy Yoke
with Mary and the Lord's Prayer.

Luke not only seems to substitute on occasion; he also may be seen
as adding in texts from elsewhere which are to his point, as he added
'Blessed are the eyes . . .' to the Babes logion. This realization

delivers us from the wooden interpretations that draw lines between tables of pericopae, and purport to show little relation of order between Luke and Matthew after Matt. 12. In fact a reason can be offered for Luke to have pretermitted the mainly Marcan matter in Matt. 13–22; and Luke 11.37–13.33 seem to rest on a chain of Matthaean texts in Matt. 23–26.2. The Woes on Pharisees and Lawyers, Luke 11.37-53, follow Matt. 23; Fearless Confession, Luke 12.1-12, follows sections of Matt. 10, whose original context was Mark 13 = Matt. 24.9-14; Readiness for the Hereafter, Luke 12.13-40, follows Matthew's Thief, 24.43f., and his Return from the Marriage, 25.1ff., amplified by the Cares logia from Matt. 6; Repentance, Luke 12.41–13.9, expands Matt. 24.45-51, the Two Servants; Judgment, Luke 13.10-30, takes up the end of the Marriage parable in Matt. 25.10-13, and the rejection of the reprobate in Matt. 24.30-46; and the Two-Days-then-Martyrdom saying, Luke 13.31-33, looks like a version of Matt. 26.2. Here again it seems possible to account for the Lucan order on the basis of Luke's knowledge of Matthew. Most of the links in the chain are obvious. Of the two 'substitutes', the Fearless Confession is plausible without being evident, but the coincidence of order and content with Matt. 26.1f. is rather impressive, and again with Matt.R.

It is the second half of the Journey which seems to me to settle the question. The process suggested, that Luke set out to cover Matthew's additions to Mark in Matt. 13-23 by going back up the scroll, is psychologically believable. The remaining Lucan material till he rejoins Mark runs from 13.34 to 18.14, and it has been possible to suggest correspondences (often multiple correspondences) for the whole of this section down to 18.8. This covers ten pericopae, and they follow the (reversed) order of Matthew continuously, with the sole exception of the Matt. 19 parallels following the Matt. 18.23-35 parallels. The Matthaean matter used starts from 'Jerusalem, Jerusalem ...' just before where Luke has got to, and goes back to the beginning of Matt. 16; and Luke has either used from Mark, or deliberately omitted, most of Matt. 13–15.

The correspondences may be seen most clearly in a table:

13.34f.	Jerusalem, Jerusalem	Matt. 23.37-39
14.1-14	Pharisaic legalism, best seats, humility	Matt. 23.6-12
14.15-24	The Great Dinner, based on	Matt. 22.1-14
14.25-35	The Tower-Builder and Embassy, based on	Matt. 21.33f. R

15.1-31	Pharisees and Sinners: The Two Sons, based on	Matt. 21.28-32
16.1-13	The Steward who remitted debts, based on	Matt. 18.23-35
16.14-31	Harder for the rich to enter heaven . . .	Matt. 19.9, 16-26R
17.1-10	Offences, Forgiveness, Faith	Matt. 18.6-21; 17.20
17.11-19	Ten Lepers, based on	Matt. 17.14-23
17.20–18.8	The Coming of the Son of Man, based on	Matt. 16R, with 24.

(R indicates a passage where Matthew is rewriting Mark.)

It is impossible that such a sequence should occur by accident; and several of the passages are Matt.R.

Our task has in some ways resembled that of an archaeologist uncovering a building that has been twice rebuilt. The pillars and stones of the first building (Mark) were in part incorporated as they stood by the second builder (Matthew), and in part moved and refashioned. It has been clear for many years that the third builder (Luke) was working on a modification of the original structure (Mark); the question has been whether he was aware of the second builder. We have seen that the third builder in fact modifies the second design as well as the first over Luke 1.5–13.33; and in places that he uses the refashioned stones, or supplies similar ones (substitutes). But over 13.34–18.8 he has done something much easier to see, once we are looking for it. He has taken out the second builder's additions to, and some adaptations of, the first, and built them into an extension of his own; and he has taken them in sequence. So Luke's knowledge of Matthew seems to be multiply confirmed, and his ordering of Matthew shown to be, on the whole, careful, rational and indeed sophisticated. I should like to propose that Canon Streeter owes St Luke an apology.

THE CREDIBILITY OF LUKE'S
TRANSFORMATION OF MATTHEW

H. Benedict Green CR

College of the Resurrection
Mirfield, West Yorkshire

If Luke had known the gospel of Matthew, could he have used it with the freedom that the hypothesis requires that he did? In the practice of the critical mainstream this has been virtually reduced to a rhetorical question, the repetition of which is held sufficient to dispense the scholar from serious consideration of evidence that might bear the other way;[1] the case is never really heard. To treat it as, on the contrary, a real question, as I propose to do, implies the possibility of an affirmative answer, which, while it will not itself establish the hypothesis, ought (in the best of possible worlds) to allow a fair hearing to what evidence there is in its favour.

Austin Farrer[2] was here before me. It would involve too much of a digression to analyse in detail the reasons why his argument failed as a whole to carry conviction with those to whom it was directed;[2a] briefly, though he correctly identified the objections and answered some of them effectively, he allowed himself to be sidetracked into a typological account of what Luke was about, where most of his readership could not follow him. I shall endeavour to stay closer to those I am arguing with.

I follow Farrer, however, in not seeking to dispense with Mark as a source as well as Q. That was being done in his time by Abbot (now Bishop) Butler in the interests of the Augustinian solution;[3] the inheritors of the Benedictine tradition of Matthaean priorism in this country have now gone over to the Griesbachian.[4] I do not find the newer fashion an improvement so far as understanding Luke is concerned, for the Augustinian hypothesis at least allowed Luke access to Mark as well as Matthew, and without this no plausible solution is likely to emerge. To derive Luke, with Griesbach, from Matthew alone seems to involve the same difficulties, especially in the order of the earlier chapters and the apparently less 'developed' form of the non-Matthaean versions of the narratives, as to derive Mark from Matthew with Augustine. (I also find it impossible to reconcile what I am not alone in seeing as the literary power and originality, to say nothing of the theological depth, of Mark[5] with the account of its genesis that the Griesbach hypothesis offers—but that is another story.)

What is there about Luke's presumed treatment of Matthew that is found difficult to credit? The central difficulties raised have to do with the differing ways in which Luke has used his two putative sources, following the Marcan narrative for long stretches while breaking up Matthew's great discourses into small pieces and redistributing the bulk of these to fresh contexts. The meticulous care which, on this view, he has taken not to reproduce the latter in the same Marcan contexts in which he found them in Matthew Streeter thought only possible in a crank.[6]

A new version of these basic objections has recently been propounded by F.G. Downing, in the course of a comparison of Luke's literary methods with those of Josephus,[7] which shifts the weight from the contexts in which only one source is discernible to those in which they overlap. While he still finds the rehandling of Matthew's discourses by Luke which our hypothesis would require more drastic than his model would lead him to expect,[8] for Downing the really 'complex and laborious task' that the process would have demanded from Luke lies in his apparently systematic avoidance of the literary methods used by Josephus on his (predominantly biblical) sources.[9] Where Josephus has two sources before him and they agree, he follows them without a demur; where they conflict in a straightforward way he follows the '*older and* fuller';[10] only where they conflict in detail does he give up and rewrite the passage himself. Luke on the other hand seems to go out of his way to avoid doing this with Mark and Matthew; where they agree he mostly refuses what Downing calls this 'ready-made conflation',[11] and where Matthew has largely rewritten Mark, Luke follows neither but rewrites in a way that takes him still further from Mark.[12]

This is a fair challenge, in view of the literary *genre* to which, at one level, the Lucan writings undoubtedly belong;[13] other things being equal, we should expect Luke to follow the same general conventions as Josephus. But in fact other things are not all equal, and among the unequal things in this case are the character of the sources used, and the author's own relation to them. First, Josephus worked from a number of parallel biblical sources; whether or not he was aware of the literary dependence of some of them upon others,[14] they were all sufficiently removed from him in time, and hallowed by their acceptance as scripture, to be handled by him in essentially the same way. Luke on the other hand stood very close in time to his sources; if his second source was Matthew its author may well have been still living when Luke wrote, and he had already incorporated the substance of Luke's first source (Mark) into his own work. Such a situation would inevitably have complicated the literary conventions as to what constituted plagiarism.[15] Where Matthew had lifted a passage of Mark unaltered and Luke was aware of the fact, this would have brought more and not less pressure on him to modify it in his own version.[16]

Secondly, the fact that Josephus's major sources were already part of scripture implies that no one of them had an established priority over the others for him. With Luke it was different. If the literary and chronological relationship between Mark and Matthew is what the majority take it to be (and I have indicated that I am with the majority here), then Luke will have known Mark for a great deal longer than he has known Matthew[17]—will have used it week by week in the worship of the Church, preached from it, taught from it, and lived with it as the only written gospel; and if his project of a new and enlarged gospel was forming in his mind for any length of time, it will have been in terms of Mark that it was originally conceived. When the work of Matthew, another enlarged version of Mark but made with rather different preoccupations, came into his hands, the following possibilities were open to him: (i) to continue as he had begun, and to find ways of incorporating material from Matthew where this seemed desirable; (ii) to start again, using his two sources together and switching from one to the other at his own discretion in the same way as Josephus does;[18] (iii) to discard Mark and make Matthew his primary source throughout. Possibility (ii) would certainly have posed considerable problems in the earlier chapters where the order of the two gospels diverges widely; and there were a number of good reasons for avoiding (iii). The emphasis of his own work was to be on narrative, as can be seen from his second volume; a gospel that was essentially a re-run of Matthew (in which there is really no continuous plot, at any rate after the opening chapters, before ch. 12) would not have made a suitable companion piece for this. Nor could he have produced (as the literary conventions of his time required) a *different* book, yet of comparable length (a significant factor, as that of Acts confirms), which did not both omit a proportion of Matthew's content and break up its systematic arrangement. The indications are therefore that he would have opted for (i). Is this conclusion compatible with the redactional methods exhibited by Josephus, as well as with the internal evidence of his gospel?

It is clear enough that Luke prefers to follow one primary source at a time, using the second, where they overlap, chiefly as a source of minor verbal variations. This was standard practice with ancient authors,[19] and is a commonplace when stated in terms of Mark and Q, where the overlap, even on Streeter's earlier view,[20] is comparatively small. It is the very large overlap between Mark and Matthew that makes the difficulty. Why does Luke follow Mark for such long stretches with only such insignificant influence from Matthew?[21] Our provisional answer must be that for much of the narrative material Mark does in fact offer the fuller, as well as the older, version. But it will still need to be shown that where Matthew's account is the fuller Luke works from that, as well as to make sense of his redistribution of the Matthaean sayings material, to which I now turn.

It is at best a half-truth to say with Farrer[22] and John Drury[23] that Luke prefers Mark for narrative and Matthew for teaching. There are several stretches of teaching unrelieved by narrative in Mark, and four of Matthew's Five Discourses have simply been expanded from them. For two of these, the parables discourse and the Little Apocalypse, Luke has elected to stay with Mark, in content as well as in context; though he has handled the material, especially in the latter case, with considerable freedom, the modifications represent an adaptation of Mark to his own standpoint, not an assimilation of it to what we find in Matthew. The loosely knit series of paradigms and other sayings that occupies the space between the second and third passion predictions in Mark (9.33–10.31) is worked up by Matthew into two separate discourses: that of ch. 18, the fourth of the Five, and a further one at 19.1–20.16 which opens his new section after the change of scene corresponding to Mark 10.1. For Luke this section in Mark provides both the general literary model and, in Mark 10.32 (anticipated at Luke 9.51), the starting-point for his own journey section; structurally speaking he is still following Mark here,[24] though it is significant that he includes in his own section such non-

Marcan material from Matt. 18 as he uses, and that he concludes it more or less where Matt. 18 ends, before his own parallels to Mark 10.

Of the remaining two of the Five Discourses, the Sermon on the Mount has no counterpart in Mark, neither in content nor, strictly speaking, in context. It has been, so to say, 'exploded' out of the 'teaching with authority' of the suppressed synagogue episode of Mark 1.21ff., as the assembly of miracles which follows it in Matt. 8–9 has been 'exploded' out of the authoritative exorcism of Mark 1.27, with a disintegrative effect on the narrative sequence of Mark, which is not taken up again until after the fresh start of Matt. 11. This is turn means that the mission discourse which comes next in Matthew (ch. 10), though initially parallel to Mark's in content, has no corresponding Marcan context in Matthew. Here Luke has chosen both to stay with Mark in the Marcan narrative sequence and to provide a parallel to Matthew in what, as I hope to show, is for him a Matthaean context.

So much then for the objection that Luke goes to great pains to remove Matthaean material from its Marcan context in Matthew and insert it in a different Marcan context; not only, as Farrer had already observed,[25] does he not insert it in a Marcan context at all, but in the case of the two discourses on which he has drawn most he has not strictly taken it from a Marcan context either. How much of it he has in fact removed, and how far he has removed it, are matters that will occupy us further on. One aspect of this question, connected with the small scale and essentially narrative character of his two-volume work, is the limitation of the length of his spoken set-pieces. The speech of Stephen in Acts 7 (52 verses) is exceptional; those of Peter in Acts 2.11ff. (20 verses) and of Paul in Acts 13.16ff. (26 verses), 20.18ff. (19 verses), 22.1ff. (20 verses), and 26.2ff. (25 verses) are the longest of the remainder. The discourses in Matt. 5–7 (107 verses), 10 (38 verses), 13 (46 verses), 18 (32 verses), and 23–25 (132 verses)[26] are wholly out of scale with this as they stand. Where he has stayed with Mark, Luke has reduced the parables discourse from 31 verses in Mark to 18 verses, and the Little Apocalypse (his own additions notwithstanding) from 31 verses to 28 verses. That he would reduce the much longer discourses in Matthew to a comparable scale was altogether to be expected.

But significant as the Five Discourses are for the structure and interpretation of Matthew, they are not the only substantial bodies of sayings material that the evangelist has expanded from or added to

Mark.[27] The second discourse is followed by a further section which
occupies the whole of ch. 11, and the fourth, as we have already seen,
stands similarly back to back with 19.1–20.16. The parables discourse
of ch. 13 is preceded by the sayings material arising from the
Beelzebul controversy which runs continuously from 12.25-50.
(Chapter 23 might possibly be related in the same way to 24–25,
though I remain convinced by the arguments for seeing it as an
integral part of the discourse.[28])

The immediate relevance of this to our argument is that there is a
particular concentration of material in this category in Matt. 9.35–
12.50, and the bulk of it is reproduced in Luke 9.51–12.59. Of 126
verses of Matthew, Luke has parallels to 78, 17 in his scaled-down
version of the mission charge, and another 33 (making a total of 50)
subsequently in these chapters, and only 28 elsewhere in the gospel,
of which 16 are from the section Matt. 11.2-19 which could not be
used at this point because John the Baptist has already been reported
dead at 9.7-9, and had therefore to be brought forward.[29] Of the 48
verses in Matthew which Luke has not reproduced here, 29 have
Marcan parallels which Luke has already followed in their Marcan
context, and of the remainder only two passages are more than two
verses in length, the Matthaean conclusion to Jesus' thanksgiving to
the Father (Matt. 11.28-30) and the long formula quotation at Matt.
12.17-21. The first of these would have been inappropriate to the new
context which Luke has constructed for the verses which precede it
in Matthew, the response of Jesus to the returning missioners, and its
conception of Jesus as embodying in his own person the true counterpart of Torah is one to which Luke is not elsewhere receptive.[30] The
second passage is rooted in its Marcan context in Matthew to which
Luke has no parallel either here or elsewhere.

There is so far no justification for the claim that Luke has
systematically redistributed the material from these three chapters of
Matthew to other contexts; though he has rearranged it, as was
necessary to his purpose of keeping the mission discourse short,[31]
the greater part of it has been retained within the same overall
context, and there is sufficient explanation for the one significant
exception. But the 167 verses of these Lucan chapters also contain no
less than 70 verses of material which Matthew has used in other
contexts, both earlier and later in his gospel but particularly in the
Sermon on the Mount. Our next task is therefore to identify further
concentrations of non-Marcan material in Matthew which would

have caught Luke's eye in the same way, and discover how far it would have been possible there also for him to leave the material in the context in which he found it.

Two of these concentrations are to be found near the beginning of the gospel. The first of them comprises the preaching of John the Baptist, the temptations of Jesus and the return to Galilee; this material is inseparable from its context at the beginning of the ministry, and Luke has not attempted to displace it; it will be considered in that context later on. The second consists of the Sermon on the Mount, followed by the healing of the centurion's boy and the hard sayings to would-be disciples at Matt. 8.18-22. We have already shown reason why Luke could have been expected to avoid reproducing the Sermon *in extenso*; we can now show further reason why he does not use it even in part to inaugurate his account of the ministry of Jesus.

1. While the Matthaean sermon presupposes the kerygma recorded in outline in the previous section,[32] it is not itself to be classed as kerygma. Luke, whose second volume, especially in its early chapters, is dominated by speeches embodying an appropriate form of the kerygma, could be expected to open his account of the ministry of Jesus with such a sermon on the lips of the original proclaimer of the good news—as indeed, with anticipation of Mark 6.1-6 and references to Isa. 61 which echo the opening Matthaean (but not Lucan)[33] Beatitudes, he has. There was no room at the beginning of his narrative both for this and for the non-kerygmatic sermon of Matthew.

2. Though Luke depicts Jesus as personally obedient to the Mosaic law, he shows little or no interest in him as its definitive interpreter, which is what the Sermon on the Mount, especially in its first part, is basically concerned with[34]—a further reason why he would not have wished it to stand at the head of his account of Jesus' mission.

3. Writing as he did more explicitly within the Hellenistic milieu, Luke (whether or not he numbered Jews among his readership) was not under the same pressure to proclaim the Christian message *against* Jews. Comparisons between what was said to men of old and the message of Jesus (especially if the real object of the attack was what afterwards came to be called the oral law),[35] or aspersions on the sincerity of conventional Jewish piety, were at best marginal to his purpose in writing. Therefore, while a number of single items in the Sermon commended themselves to him, the framework of the antitheses and of the tripartite section on true and false piety did not.

4. We have seen that the nearest thing to a Marcan context for the Sermon in Matthew is the gap left by the suppressed synagogue exorcism at Capernaum (Mark 1.21). But the mountain of Matt. 5.1 is derived not from this context but (with some typological assistance) from Mark 3.13,[36] the scene of the appointment of the twelve. Luke has noticed this, and made the latter the occasion for his own reduced version of the Sermon, an allocution to the twelve on the nature of discipleship.[37] Not all the Matthaean material was equally suitable for this, let alone the outline in which Matthew presents it.

As the Sermon on the Mount has displaced the synagogue exorcism in Matthew, so the Sermon on the Plain and the material that follows it have displaced the Beelzebul controversy and the sayings associated with it in Luke. He makes room for these later on, but using Matthew's version[38] and in the general context of his borrowings from Matthew 9.35–12.50. He had also to find a place for those sayings which for reasons of space or content he could not use in his version of the Sermon but still wished to include in his gospel. Having excluded them from the Sermon itself he was hardly likely to insert them as a sort of appendix in its immediate vicinity. The alternative was to reserve them for his next major stretch of insertions into the Marcan outline, which is what he has in fact done.

Matthew's sermon concludes with the comparison of the two houses, followed by the regular repeated formula used by him after each of the Five Discourses, and then by the healings of the leper and the centurion's boy. Except for the leper, which he has used already in its Marcan context, Luke's ending reproduces this sequence; his echo of the characteristic Matthaean formula is particularly striking,[39] as is the fact that while his introduction to the episode of the centurion differs widely from Matthew's, the dialogue at the heart of the story is reproduced almost word for word. Matthew's treatment of the Marcan miracle stories shows a marked tendency, as H.J. Held's analysis has demonstrated,[40] to reduce narrative to dialogue. It would be surprising if just in this case (his only non-Marcan miracle story) the reduction was the work of his source; and if it was not, from where else could Luke have derived it?

Finally (having passed over another brief episode, that of Peter's mother-in-law, which he has used in the Marcan sequence) Luke picks up the two short apothegms to would-be disciples at Matt. 8.18-22. Sayings in this form were unsuitable for inclusion in a continuous set-piece like the Sermon; their content, on the other hand, made them very apt for the theme of a journey in the company of Jesus, and Luke therefore defers them to the beginning of his journey section, and there adds a third to round off the composition and make a link with the Elijah-typology[41] with which the journey begins.

We have not quite finished with Luke's first interpolation. It has already been observed that the material in Matt. 11 concerned with John the Baptist could not have been used at the corresponding point in Luke because by then John is already dead. There is no Marcan context for this material, and Luke had no real alternative to including it in his one major interruption of the Marcan sequence so far, the section we have been considering. But he has felt necessary to prepare the context, perhaps a little hastily, for a saying pointing to the miracles of Jesus as signs of his Messiahship. Luke has already recorded the healing of a leper (5.12ff.) and of a paralytic (5.17ff.); and the good news has been proclaimed to the poor both in Nazareth (4.18ff.) and on the plain (6.19). But Jairus's daughter, Bartimaeus and the deaf/dumb demoniac of 11.14 are still to come. He has therefore not only constructed a verse (7.21) describing miscellaneous healings, including the restoration of sight to the blind; he has also followed up the healing of the centurion's boy who is at the point of death with the raising of the widow of Nain's son who is actually dead and on his way to burial. Since the latter is both a mirror-image of the raising of Jairus's daughter with the sexes reversed (as Drury has shown)[42] and an instance of the Elijah-typology which as applied to Jesus is a special Lucan characteristic, it is, *pace* Downing,[43] hard to resist the conclusion that he composed it himself for this position. It is unlikely that Luke would have gone to such lengths to provide an apposite context for the reply to John the Baptist if he had not found it in one in his source, which implies that the latter was more like a narrative gospel than a collection of sayings. In Matthew (11.4-6) the reply arises naturally out of what has been related in chs. 8–9. It is Matthaean in style and Septuagintal in formulation,[44] and only the pressure of the Q hypothesis has obliged scholars to postulate an independent origin for it.

The remaining concentration of non-Marcan material in Matthew is that of chs. 23–25 (with which we should probably include 22.1-14). Here, as we have seen, Luke has opted to stay with Mark, or rather to adapt Mark's version on different lines from those preferred by Matthew. Luke's dramatic perspective is that from which the historical Jesus speaks; the setting up of the desolating sacrilege is replaced by (or interpreted as) the investment of Jerusalem by the Roman armies in the war of AD 66-70, an event already past for Luke,[45] and the horrors that attended it are carefully distinguished from the cosmic disturbances which will usher in the parousia. For Matthew on the other hand the desolating sacrilege, whatever it may be (he says only that it will be located in the temple area)[46] is still in the future, and will be the sign that the end is imminent; the church is living in the phase preceding this,[47] in which the end is held up while the gospel has to be proclaimed to all nations, and the delay is long enough for some Christians to lose their first fervour—but the destruction of Jerusalem and the temple is already past, and the previous chapter with its denunciation of the Pharisees and its lament over Jerusalem implicitly interprets this as God's judgment on the old Israel that had rejected Christ.[48] Matthew and Luke are not in fundamental disagreement about the point on the grid where the contemporary church is to be located. But the points from which they respectively project the future are different, and for this reason (over and above the question of length) it would have been very difficult for Luke to find room for additional material from Matthew within the context of his own (previously worked out) adaptation of Mark. He had therefore to find an earlier position in his gospel for any that he wanted to use than that in which they are found in Matthew's. And this kind of anticipation is hard to combine effectively with a planned composition; its effects on Luke's are not difficult to discern.

Of the passages displaced, the hardest to reaccommodate was without question the denunciation of the Pharisees. In Matt. 23 this rises to a great crescendo in the coda to the Seven Woes with its message of retribution for the murderers of the prophets, followed by the finality of the lament over Jerusalem at its conclusion. No earlier position in the story of the ministry of Jesus would have been appropriate for this as it stood, apart from any considerations of length. Luke's only alternative to omitting it was to de-dramatize it sufficiently for it to be accommodated earlier on without an explosive effect on the development of his plot. The journey section was the obvious general area for this, but the lack of general connection with what precedes and follows it there is painfully obvious and suggestive of late insertion,[49] and the inclusion of Luke 11.49-51 (Luke's parallel to the Matthaean coda), which breaks into the pattern of three woes against Pharisees and three against lawyers, has the appearance of a last minute addition of material which Luke had found it difficult to incorporate into his reduced version of the Woes, yet still wanted to bring in.[50] The lament over Jerusalem would not have made a fitting conclusion to Luke's non-climactic woes, nor have had much appropriateness to its original position if left by itself. It may then be asked why Luke did not transfer it to mark Jesus' approach to Jerusalem in ch. 19, instead of composing what is clearly a fresh lament of his own. It was actually disqualified for this position by the acclamation of its final verse (Matt. 23.39b = Luke 13.35b), which would then only repeat what has just been proclaimed during the triumphal entry. Luke may already have prepared his own lament for this point, since its content anticipates the alterations he has made independently to the Marcan apocalypse;[51] but it is also possible that it was the Matthaean lament, which for reasons of content he was compelled to use earlier and in a very contrived context, that suggested its Lucan counterpart.[52]

The problems posed by the Matthaean parables of warning (Matt. 24.37–25.46) were a little less intractable, though the Great Assize (Matt. 25.31-46) evidently proved to be inseparable from its context in the account of the Last Things and is simply omitted,[53] and the Ten Virgins (Matt.25.1-13) for similar reasons is only drawn on for isolated excerpts used in association with other material of eschatological flavour taken from the earlier parts of Matthew or provided by Luke himself.[54] The dialogue at the heart of the parable of the Talents (Matt. 25.14-30) is provided with a new narrative frame,[55] a rather crude allegory of the ascension of Christ and his return,[56] which is offered, a little maladroitly, as background to the entry into Jerusalem (Luke 19.11-27). The Matthaean parable of the Great Supper (Matt. 22.1-14), which in Matthew stands in the same relation to that of the Wicked Tenants which precedes it as does the apocalypse of ch. 24 to the judgment on the historical Israel in ch. 23, has been (if indeed it *is* the direct source of the Lucan parallel)[57] de-eschatologized and de-nuptialized and placed with a series of other parables and sayings concerned with the paradoxes of Christian hospitality (Luke 14.16-24). The Thief in the Night and the Faithful (and Unfaithful) Steward (Matt. 24.42-51) are used more or less as they stand in a context prepared for by one of Luke's generalizing parallels to the Ten Virgins (Luke 12.38-46). Finally the little parable of Noah's Flood (Matt. 24.37-39) is given a second strophe by Luke[58] and together with a number of other minor Matthaean additions to the Marcan apocalypse, all concerned either with the suddenness of the end or its unmistakableness, is worked up into an additional apocalyptic discourse under the rubric of 17.20f., and placed, without great regard to context, at the conclusion of the journey section.

The point to make about all these transpositions, both forward from the Sermon on the Mount and backward from the apocalypse, is that they are not just a laborious series of alterations for alteration's sake; what Luke has done with them was the alternative, on his scheme, to omitting them altogether. We may not, perhaps, consider that it was well done, but we need feel no particular wonder that it was done at all. In fact, as the accompanying table shows, he redistributes only where necessary, and then no further than necessary. Thus virtually none (only three and a half verses) of what he uses in the Sermon on the Plain is drawn from the later parts of Matthew, and of the materials from the Sermon on the Mount held over by him, three-quarters is used in his next Matthaean section. Similarly two-thirds of what he takes from Matt. 9.35–12.50, and over two-thirds of what he takes from Matt. 13–18, he uses in the corresponding section of his own gospel. Only in what he has lifted from Matt. 19–25 is this pattern not followed, for reasons which we have already explored; the material is divided more or less equally between this and the two preceding sections, but it may be observed that in Luke 9.51–12.59 it amounts only to a quarter of the total Matthaean material, in 13.1–18.14 to nearly a half, and in 18.15–22.30 to the whole.

Lucan parallels to Matthew in terms of their Matthaean contexts

Mt Lk	5.3-8.22	9.35-12.50	13-18	19-25	Total Matthaean	Total verses
6.20-49	*22*	3	1	-	26	30
7	6	15	-	-	21	50
9.51-12.59	30	*50*	6	34	120	167
13.1-18.14	10	5	*14*	22	51	184
18.15-22.30	-	-	-	*21*	21	37*

*Exclusive in this case of verses with Marcan parallels in context (not applicable in other sections).
The figures in italics are of verses which are found in the corresponding sections of the two gospels.

There remain the parallels in the opening chapters. Both Matthew and Luke offer extended counterparts to the Marcan prologue (Mark 1.1-13), and there is a close structural correspondence between their respective versions. Both have an infancy narrative divided into two clearly defined sections, pre-natal and post-natal. Both amplify the content of the Baptist's preaching (the additions peculiar to Luke, though their tone is very different, seem to presuppose those which he shares with Matthew),[59] supply content for the temptations of Jesus, and elaborate the notice of his return to Galilee. The case for their total independence of one another has rested mainly on the wide divergence of the content of their infancy narratives; it is generally maintained[60] that Luke could not have known Matthew's without reproducing more of it in his own than the basic data of Davidic descent, virginal conception, naming of the child by divine command, birth at Bethlehem, and later residence at Nazareth[61] which are undeniably present in both. This argument is ripe for re-examination, on a number of counts.

(a) The dominant interest of Matthew's narrative is to establish the claim of Jesus to be, despite his supposed Galilean origins, the Messiah.[62] Its first chapter introduces him into the Davidic line by means of a legal fiction, and its second claims in effect that he was not really a Galilean at all, but a Bethlehemite refugee. The argument seems to be directed at a particular form and phase of Christian-Jewish controversy which was not necessarily relevant to Luke's own apologetic concerns. He would hardly in any case have wanted to begin a work intended for a cultivated Greek readership with a Chronicler's genealogy. It is all the more striking, therefore, that he should introduce a genealogy of his own, though as an argument for Jesus' representative humanity rather than his Abrahamic-Davidic descent, later on (3.23-38). What prompted him to do this?

(b) The story of the recognition of the child as king by mysterious visitors from beyond the eastern frontiers of the empire would have had a distinctly subversive ring to loyal subjects of Rome, especially if repeated in the reign of Trajan.[64] Luke in any case avoids direct involvement of Gentiles in the life story of Jesus. What has been called 'Mark's Gentile mission' (Mark 6.45–8.21) is entirely omitted by him;[65] the centurion of Capernaum communicates with Jesus only through intermediaries, and the centurion at the foot of the cross (23.47) is reduced to a witness to his innocence, the first Graeco-Roman confession of faith being reserved for the centurion of Caesarea in Acts 10 and a point in the story where it would be historically more plausible. Here in the infancy narrative Luke's shepherds are indigenous and politically neutral, but nevertheless, with the help of the Nunc Dimittis,[66] enable him to make the universalist point in his own way.

(c) The massacre of the innocents and the flight into and return from Egypt are part of the logic of events set in motion by the story of the magi, and could hardly have stood in isolation from it. The anticipations of future rejection and passion with which they are loaded[67] are, once again, conveyed by Luke in his own terms: the lack of room at Bethlehem, the sword that was to pierce Mary's soul, and the three-day disappearance in Jerusalem.

(d) That leaves only Matt. 1.18-25 as a foundation for Luke to build on, a story with two serious omissions: it said nothing of how Mary came to be with child by the Holy Spirit, and virtually nothing of the circumstances of the child's birth at Bethlehem (it seems to be tacitly assumed that the parents were already living there, but this is nowhere expressly stated). The license of the *darshan* to supply gaps in a narrative[68] could be assumed to operate in such a case.

(e) By introducing the parallel account of the birth of the Baptist, and by giving him priestly as well as prophetic antecedents, Luke deals in his own way with the Old Testament roots of the Messiah as well as the problem of his precedence over the forerunner (who salutes him from the womb in the Visitation story),[69] and is able to inaugurate the pattern of beginning from Jerusalem which dominates both his volumes.

So if Luke sets aside most of the detail of Matthew's narrative, he retains and expresses in other terms enough of its inner meaning to suggest that, so far from being unfamiliar with it, he had in fact read it with penetration and discernment. If he was inhibited from transmitting it as it stood, the very fact that it was now current in the Church would have made it impossible for him to remain silent at this point in his story; that would only have left Matthew in possession of the field. He had therefore no alternative to a fresh composition.

If then it is allowed that Matthew's infancy narrative could have served both as starting-point and as indirect source for Luke's, is it reasonable to see his account of the baptism of Jesus as the starting-point and major direct source for Luke's? If it is true, as Downing says,[70] that Luke here 'follows his fuller source, with one or two supplements from the shorter one', is there any insuperable objection to the identification of the 'fuller source' as Matthew? I shall argue that there is not, if the significance of certain of Luke's divergences from his sources is correctly understood.

(i) Matthew, in distinction from Mark, asserts (a) the continuity of John the Baptist's kerygma with Jesus', by assimilating his summary of the one to his summary of the other,[71] (b) the discontinuity of the baptism received by Christian converts with John's baptism, which he will not allow to convey forgiveness of sins, that being rooted in the death of Christ.[72] Luke stands with Mark on both points. For him Jesus' proclamation of the kingdom is inaugurated with the sermon at Nazareth (4.16ff.), and what differentiates the baptism of John from Christian baptism is not that the latter alone forgives sins, but that it alone confers the Holy Spirit.[73]

(ii) Whereas both Mark and Matthew represent John's baptism as an ongoing activity, for which people resort to him over an extended period,[74] Luke (perhaps by assimilation to Christian practice as he knew it) thinks rather of a single mass baptism of the people (λαός) after suitable preparation.

(iii) In Matthew the religious leaders of the Jews are among those who present themselves for baptism, sincerely or otherwise. In Luke this is clearly not the case (cf. 7.29f.).

(iv) Luke elsewhere alters or suppresses passages in his sources which identify the Baptist with Elijah in his role of immediate precursor of the Messiah.[75]

If the parallel versions are now examined with these points in mind, it will be observed, first of all, that Matthew and Luke agree in providing a temporal link with the foregoing chapters, introduced by Ἐν . . . δέ. In Matthew this is indefinite in content; in Luke it has been expanded into his effort at synchronized multiple dating (3.1f.) which in turn has affected the terms in which John is introduced. The principal biblical model is Jer. 1.1-3, and the prophetic call of Jeremiah provides an alternative OT type for John to Elijah (as found in Matt. 3.4 [= Mark 1.6], which Luke therefore omits; see (iv) above). In his next verse (3.3) Luke introduces the Marcan account of John's preaching κηρύσσων βάπτισμα μετανοίας εἰς ἄφεσιν ἁμαρτιῶν.

In Mark this is apparently meant for a summary of the content of the preaching, for which Matthew has substituted his own summary in direct speech (see (i) above); in Luke, on the other hand, its function seems to be rather to provide the heading for an actual piece of kerygma which is to follow. This is borne out by his expansion of the Isaiah text which in both gospels comes next. In Matthew this is simply a fulfilment quotation; in Luke it serves also, and more prominently, as the opening text of a sermon, to which the omission of Matt. 3.4-6 (see (ii) above) allows the evangelist to proceed forthwith.[76] His source and model here is Matt. 3.7-10; but whereas for Matthew this is a warning (in characteristic Matthaean language) to Pharisees and Sadducees which clearly anticipates (and gets) no positive response, Luke by addressing it to the whole company (see (iii) above) makes it the content of John's baptismal kerygma, to which his hearers respond, as at Acts 2.37, by asking to be told what to do. The ethical instruction which follows is manifestly Lucan in its concerns as it is in the width of its vocabulary.

In Matthew the words of warning run on from vv. 7-12 without a break, incorporating at v. 11 the Marcan prediction of the coming of the mightier one in a form close enough to Mark to have been derived from Mark alone without any conflation with a second source, yet so integrated with its context in Matthew that it is impossible to detach it and still make continuous sense of what remains. Luke's additions interrupt the sequence and require the construction of a bridge passage (3.15-16a) in order to rejoin Matthew. Luke 3.16b-d is clearly structured on Matt. 3.11, with its μέν . . . δέ antithesis; but in 3.16c he has followed Mark's wording, doubtless preferring Mark's image of a slave to Matthew's image of a disciple as an account of the Baptist's relation to the mightier one.[77] This is only one of a number of passages in which he re-conflates Matthew with Mark.[78] In 3.16d-17 he is back with Matthew. 3.18-20 anticipates what is said at Matt. 4.12 (which Luke does not use in that context), and fills it out with material from Mark 6.17f., which he likewise omits in its context.

Luke presents the baptism, as we have seen (in (ii) above), as a general baptism of Israel, and Jesus participates in it as an obedient son of his people; there is no direct confrontation recorded between him and John (whose role is not emphasized), and therefore no need for the dialogue of Matt. 3.14f. His description of the scene is generally closer in its wording to Matthew than to Mark,[79] except that the voice from heaven is addressed to Jesus, as in Mark, and not to the bystanders. Though the accompanying phenomena are described in quasi-physical terms, Luke sees the revelation as given to Jesus himself rather than to Israel at large, as is implied by Matthew.

There is, I submit, nothing in this section of Luke that makes it implausible to regard Matthew as his major documentary source, and not a little to suggest that if a hypothetical source is posited it will be found to resemble closely what we have in Matthew.

There remains the Temptation narrative. There is now a great preponderance of exegetes who take the view that Matthew's is the earlier as well as, from a literary point of view, the superior version of this;[80] and Conzelmann's account of the principles of Luke's redaction offers at least three reasons why he should have altered the story in the way he has: the inappropriateness of a mountain, normally the place for revelation and communion with God, as the scene for a temptation; the central part played by Jerusalem in the beginnings of the gospel story; and the fact that it is after the return of Jesus to the city that the devil's attack is resumed.[81]

To summarize the argument so far: Matt. 1–2 is the source that Luke departs from, Matt. 3 is the primary source that he follows, and Matt. 4.1-11 the only source (after his first two verses) that he has. Taken as a whole, the contents of Matthew's opening section (1.1–4.16) are sufficient to explain Luke's. That Luke's runs to 183 verses against Matthew's 81 is the consequence of his characteristically more extended narrative in the infancy stories.

While a few reminiscences of Matt. 4.12-16,[82] as well as of other passages in Matthew,[83] are to be found in the transition to the story of the rejection at Nazareth, the latter is clearly an anticipated development of Mark. 6.1-6[84] (which Luke omits in its Marcan context), and the section which it opens has Mark for its primary source both of content and order. Luke 4.14–9.50 runs parallel to Mark 1.14–9.40, except for the omission of Mark's 'Gentile mission' (Mark 6.45–8.21). If the 70 verses of the latter are excluded from the count, Luke's Marcan model for this section contains 280 verses; his own version comprises 275, though his omissions and abridgments have made it possible to include the 83 non-Marcan verses at 6.20–8.3 in the reckoning. The close correspondence in length is unlikely to be sheer coincidence, especially in the light of what follows.

We have seen that Luke's central section (9.51–18.14) is an insertion by him into the Marcan framework, and that the first half of it (9.51–12.59) draws extensively on Matt. 9.35–12.50 for its content. The parallels do not stop at that point. The chapter that immediately follows this section in Matthew is that devoted to the parables. Luke has already given his version of this in the Marcan context at 8.4ff.; it is therefore striking that the only parables from the Matthaean chapter to which he offers a parallel, the Mustard Seed and the Leaven (Matt. 13.31-33), are placed by him half way through his own ch. 13 (13.18-21). Again, Luke's parallels to the themes and, so far as he uses it, to the material found in Matt. 18 are reserved by him for the closing chapters of this section:[85] repentance in ch. 15 (using the Lost Sheep of Matt. 18.12-14);[86] debt in ch. 16 (though with a different emphasis from Matt. 18.23-35); offence to little ones at 17.1f. (cf. Matt. 18.6f.); forgiveness at 17.3f. (cf. Matt. 18.15f., 21f.); (the confident faith of 17.5f. is also parallel to Matt. 17.19f.). Finally, Matt. 9.35–18.35 amounts to a total of 349 verses, and Luke 9.51–18.14 to 351. Since the figure for Matthew includes the Marcan material in Matt. 13–17 which Luke has used already in its Marcan context, there is no way (barring, once more, sheer coincidence) by which he could have arrived at this agreement if he had only worked from Matthew's supposed non-Marcan source. The correspondences in length, in outline, and for part of the way in content all point to Luke's familiarity with Matthew.

In the last main section, where all three gospels march together, Luke, as we have seen, once again follows Mark in preference to Matthew, down to and including the Empty Tomb narrative. Mark 10.1–16.8 contains an aggregate of 293 verses, Luke 18.15–24.12 of 301 verses (the 440 verses of Matt. 19.1–28.8 include his enlargement of the Marcan apocalypse and his additional parables). But after the point at which Mark fades out, Luke agrees with Matthew in offering an extended resurrection section incorporating appearances of the Risen One; his, as befits his narrative emphasis, is once more the longer (41 verses, as against Matthew's 12) and more circumstantial, but the themes of the Matthaean commission—the authority of the glorified Christ, the command to evangelize all nations, the promise of supernatural assistance[87]—are his also, expressed in his own characteristic style. His version, like his infancy stories, is not derived from so much as inspired by Matthew's. And, despite its comparative brevity, it is to be reckoned as a fresh section in which Luke has switched once more from following Mark to following Matthew.

There are then five of these sections, which can be arranged in terms of their primary source thus: Matthew–Mark–Matthew–Mark–

Matthew. Of the three that go back, in some sense, to Matthew, the third does not replace something already present in Mark, but only supplies something missing from his account. The second is substituted for a much shorter section in Mark; its content is mostly independent of Mark, though it does contain at 11.14-32 an important parallel to a Matthaean passage which has been expanded from Mark.[88] But the first (1.1-4.13) has replaced the short prologue of Mark 1.1-14 with a much fuller one part inspired by, part actually derived from Matthew's. Here, if anywhere, we should recognize that preference for the fuller account which has been observed in Josephus and postulated for Luke.[89]

I have attempted no more than an overall view of what is involved in claiming that Luke could have used and altered Matthew. It will not as it stands satisfy those (and they are not a few) whose sticking point is a particular passage in Luke which they cannot accept as having been altered by him from Matthew: e.g. the Beatitudes,[90] the Lord's Prayer,[91] the mission charge, the Beelzebul controversy.[92] These will need to be tackled in detail; it was one of the flaws in Farrer's essay that he attempted to deal with them summarily on the spot,[93] instead of reserving them for the only form of treatment that would be likely to convince. But it still has to be said that the case that I have been arguing here is not of the sort that can be falsified simply by the production of a single contrary instance. We are not dealing with inductive generalizations,[94] but with the work of human authors. To allow that Luke knew and used Matthew does not in principle rule out the possibility that the two had at the same time independent access to common traditions.[95] The second of these propositions must be argued on its merits in each case. But as one who formerly saw a solution to the synoptic problem in combining the two,[96] I can testify that once the first has been admitted, the pressures of Occam's razor[97] will ensure a fresh angle on the second.

NOTES

1. For examples see V. Taylor, 'The Order of Q', *JTS* 4 (1953), p. 31; 'The Original Order of Q' in A.J.B. Higgins (ed.), *New Testament Essays: Studies in Memory of T.W. Manson* (Manchester, 1959), p. 267; T. Schramm, *Der Markus-Stoff bei Lukas* (Cambridge, 1971), pp. 57-59.

2. A.M. Farrer, 'On Dispensing with Q' in D.E. Nineham (ed.), *Studies in the Gospels: Essays in Memory of R.H. Lightfoot* (Oxford, 1955), pp. 55-86.

2a. For these see M.D. Goulder, 'Farrer on Q', *Theology* 88 (1980), pp. 190-95.

3. B.C. Butler, *The Originality of St. Matthew* (Cambridge, 1951).

4. As represented by B. Orchard, *Matthew, Luke and Mark* (Manchester, 1976); and see now his *Synopsis of the Four Gospels* (Edinburgh, 1983).

5. For the impression made by Mark on one secular literary critic, see F. Kermode, *The Genesis of Secrecy* (London, 1979); and cf. some wise remarks of A.D. Jacobson, 'The Literary Unity of Q', *JBL* 101 (1982), p. 368, esp. n. 11: 'It [the Griesbach hypothesis] would appear . . . to deny theological intentionality to the structure of Mark'.

6. B.H. Streeter, *The Four Gospels* (London, 1924), p. 183. The substance of the argument continues to be repeated; cf. W.G. Kümmel, *Introduction to the New Testament* (Eng. Tr.; London, 1966), p. 50; J.A. Fitzmyer, 'The Priority of Mark and the Q Source in Luke', in *Jesus and Man's Hope* (Perspective I; Pittsburgh, 1970), pp. 147-55.

7. F.G. Downing, 'Redaction Criticism; Josephus' Antiquities and the Synoptic Gospels', *JSNT* 8 (1980) (=I), pp. 46-65; 9 (1981) (=II), pp. 29-48. Cf. his earlier article 'Towards the Rehabilitation of Q', *NTS* 11 (1964-65), pp. 169-81.

8. II, p. 42.

9. II, p. 43f.; cf. I, pp. 61-63.

10. I, p. 62 (italics mine). Can it be assumed that the fuller version is necessarily the older—or that Josephus would have known that it was?

11. II, p. 43. I am unhappy with Downing's use of this expression. If the purpose of conflating two different accounts is factual, to provide an amalgam of the information contained in them, then to talk of 'conflating' two identical accounts is paradoxical; if it is verbal, to avoid word-for-word reproduction of either, then it is not served in this case by leaving the common version unaltered.

12. Downing claims (II, p. 43) that in such cases Luke does not as a rule 'reconflate' Matthew with Mark. I find, on the contrary, that he has done so in a number of significant places: Luke 3.3, 16, 21f. (see above, pp. 145f.); 4.1f.; 11.24 (ἐφ' ἑαυτήν); 11.29; 12.10 (see my other essay here, pp. 162f.); 17.2 (περίκειται . . . εἰς τὴν θάλασσαν); 17.31 (εἰς τὰ ὀπίσω).

13. Cf. H.J. Cadbury, *The Making of Luke–Acts* (London, 1958²), especially pp. 169ff.

14. Downing (I, p. 61) allows the possibility of this.

15. See Cadbury, *Luke–Acts*, pp. 160f.

16. It is interesting that the more striking instances of Luke's avoidance of 'ready-made conflation' cited by Downing (cf. II, pp. 43f.), and at least one which he has passed over, are to be found in passages where Luke is, on the thesis of this essay, following Matthew as his primary source. Though a separate explanation can be found for each (Downing accepts this for Matt. 3.4-6 par.; for 12.29 par., 46-50 par.; see my other essay, pp. 162, 164f.), an

objection to reproducing Mark at second hand may still have operated.

17. J.B. Tyson, 'Sequential Parallelism in the Synoptic Gospels', *NTS* 22 (1976), p. 293, suggests that certain problems for the Augustinian solution might be eased by assuming that Luke had begun by working from Mark alone and only had access to Matthew at a later stage. He was anticipated in this conclusion by the Benedictine scholar J. Chapman, *Matthew Mark and Luke* (London, 1937), pp. 110, 178f. Tyson's article nowhere considers the Farrer solution; but the difficulties which it raises are not very different from those of the Augustinian so long as attention is confined to Luke.

18. Downing, I, pp. 61f.

19. See Cadbury, *Luke–Acts*, pp. 159f.

20. In his contribution to W. Sanday (ed.), *Oxford Studies in the Synoptic Problem* (Oxford, 1911), pp. 165ff., Streeter argued for a documentary overlap between Mark and Q. In *The Four Gospels*, pp. 186ff., this was reduced to Marcan reminiscence of Q tradition encountered at the oral stage. Had he been influenced by early work of the *formgeschichtliche Schule*?

21. Cf. Downing, II, pp. 42f., who skilfully inverts the older argument against Q from the minor agreements of Matthew and Luke against Mark. But see my other essay, pp. 159ff.

22. Farrer, 'Q', p. 67.

23. J. Drury, *Tradition and Design in Luke's Gospel* (London, 1976), p. 121.

24. And very occasionally in content too; cf. Luke 14.34f. par. Mark 9.50.

25. 'Q', pp. 66, 82; possibly in dependence on H.G. Jameson, *The Origin of the Synoptic Gospels* (Oxford, 1922), pp. 15f. (cited by W.R. Farmer, *The Synoptic Problem* [New York and London, 1964], pp. 292f.).

26. 94 if ch. 23 is excluded.

27. It is a major defect of Taylor's two articles (see n. 1) that they ignored this fact.

28. See R. Hummel, *Die Auseinandersetzung zwischen Kirche und Judentum im Matthäusevangelium* (Munich, 1963), pp. 85ff.; J. Schmid, *Das Evangelium nach Matthäus* (Regensburg, 1965⁵), p. 333; F.W. Beare, *Matthew* (Oxford, 1981), p. 446.

29. Already noted by Farrer, 'Q', p. 74.

30. The conclusion substituted by Luke (10.23f. par. Matt. 13.16f.) is in its Matthaean context part of Matthew's redaction of Mark, and its presence there can be sufficiently explained without assuming any further source.

31. He would in any case hardly have given a more elaborate commission to the Seventy than to the Twelve.

32. See J. Jeremias, *The Sermon on the Mount* (London, 1961), pp. 24f.

33. So, rightly, H. Frankemölle, 'Die Makarismen (Mt 5.1-12, Lk 6.20-23): Motive und Umfang der redaktionelle Komposition', *BZ* 15 (1971), p. 60.

34. See W.D. Davies, *The Setting of the Sermon on the Mount* (Cambridge,

1963), especially pp. 93ff.

35. See Davies, *Setting*, pp. 265ff.

36. So Farrer, 'Q', p. 80.

37. For this see H. Schürmann, *Traditionsgeschichtliche Untersuchungen* (Düsseldorf, 1968), pp. 290-309.

38. See my other essay in this volume, pp. 157ff.

39. See Butler, *Originality*, pp. 45f.

40. H.J. Held, 'Matthew as Interpreter of the Miracle Stories', in G. Bornkamm, G. Barth, H.J. Held, *Tradition and Interpretation in Matthew* (Eng. Tr.; London, 1963), pp. 165ff.

41. Cf. Luke 9.54-56, and see n. 75 below.

42. Drury, *Tradition*, p. 71.

43. Cf. Downing, II, p. 37; also B. Lindars, *Jesus Son of Man* (London, 1983), p. 132.

44. For LXX influence on the wording of Matt. 11.5f. see K. Stendahl, *The School of St. Matthew* (Philadelphia, 1968²), p. 91. S. Schulz, *Q: Die Spruchquelle der Evangelisten* (Zürich, 1972), p. 196, recognizes (with acknowledgment to Dibelius) the poetic style of the logion; compare the comments of Frankemölle, 'Makarismen', pp. 56, 74, on the Matthaean Beatitudes. The incidence of internal rhyme is in fact very marked in both. Schulz, p. 190, resists any attempt to detach the logion from its narrative matrix and places it firmly in a Hellenstic Jewish milieu. Jacobson, 'Unity', pp. 372f., similarly regards it as a very late accession to Q. The parallels between the situation they posit for it and that usually assigned to the first gospel hardly need underlining.

45. The arguments to the contrary of C.H. Dodd, *More New Testament Studies* (Manchester, 1968), pp. 69-83 (=*JRS* 37 [1937], pp. 43-54) have not been found generally convincing, despite their revival by J.A.T. Robinson, *Redating the New Testament* (London, 1976), pp. 27ff.

46. Matt. 24.15 (diff. Mark).

47. This is convincingly argued by W. Marxsen, *Mark the Evangelist* (Eng. Tr.; Nashville, 1969), pp. 198ff., and D.R.A. Hare, *The Theme of Jewish Persecution of Christians in the Gospel according to St Matthew* (Cambridge, 1967), pp. 177-79, against A. Feuillet, 'Le Sens du mot Parousie dans l'Évangile de Matthieu: Comparaison entre Matt. 24 et Jas. 5.1-11', in W.D. Davies and D. Daube (eds.), *The Background of the New Testament and its Eschatology* (Cambridge, 1956), pp. 261-80, who was subsequently supported by Hummel, *Auseinandersetzung*, pp. 90-94.

48. See Hare, *Persecution*, pp. 152-56.

49. The context on either side of Luke 11.37-52 shows signs of disturbance. At 11.36 there is a clumsy attempt to construct a combined moral for the two separate logia at 11.33, 34f., and 12.1 introduces, rather abruptly, a saying parallel to Matt. 16.6 par. (The interpretation of the 'leaven' as hypocrisy suggests Matthew as the ultimate source of Luke's redaction.) It is a not

unreasonable conjecture that 11.33 was originally intended to introduce 12.2ff., especially in view of the parallel to both at 8.15f.

50. This and the non-eschatological context account for the change of address at 11.49a, on which, since R. Bultmann (*The History of the Synoptic Tradition* [Eng. Tr.; Oxford, 1963], pp. 114, 152) so much fragile hypothesis has been built. The near-unanimous preference for Luke's version as the original (see Schulz, *Q*, p. 336 n. 96) rests on prior assumption of Q; i.e., the possibility of Luke's having known Matthew's version *in context* has not been considered.

51. Compare 19.43 with 21.20.

52. J.H. Neyrey, 'Jesus' Address to the Women of Jerusalem (Luke 23.27-31)—A Prophetic Judgement Oracle', *NTS* 29 (1983), p. 80, points out the identical structure of Luke 19.41-44 with 13.34f., and concludes that the latter provided Luke's model for the former.

53. It may however have influenced the Acts account of Paul's conversion (. . . why do you persecute *me*?): Acts 9.4 etc.

54. Cf. Luke 13.25-27 par. Matt. 7.22f.; 12.35-38.

55. Compare Luke's procedure at 7.1-10 par. Matt. 8.5-13.

56. See C.H. Dodd, *Parables of the Kingdom* (London, 1936), pp. 146-53; J.T. Sanders, 'The Parable of the Pounds and Lucan Anti-Semitism', *TS* 42 (1981), pp. 660ff. (especially p. 666).

57. J.D.M. Derrett, *Law in the New Testament* (London, 1970), pp. 126ff., though he does not claim dependence of Luke on Matthew, argues for a prehistory of the parable in which the Matthaean features were present from an early stage. M.D. Goulder, *Midrash and Lection in Matthew* (London, 1974), pp. 59, 62, and Drury, *Tradition*, p. 146, maintain direct dependence.

58. Butler, *Originality*, pp. 58f., found Luke's additional strophe the one item that he could not readily account for on his theory of the sources. The admission did more credit to his candour than to his resourcefulness; Schulz, *Q*, pp. 279f., has no difficulty about attributing it to post-Q redaction, though he stops short of making Luke the author.

59. See above, pp. 145ff.

60. Most recently by Downing, II, p. 42.

61. Most of these items are listed by G.D. Kilpatrick, *The Origins of the Gospel according to Saint Matthew* (Oxford, 1946), p. 54.

62. On this see especially K. Stendahl, 'Quis et Unde?' in W. Eltester (ed.), *Judentum, Urchristentum, Kirche* (Festschrift für J. Jeremias; Berlin, 1960), pp. 94ff.

63. On the Lucan genealogy see M.D. Johnson, *The Purpose of the Biblical Genealogies* (Cambridge, 1969), pp. 229-52; Farrer, 'Q', pp. 87f.

64. For reasons which favour dating Luke as late as this see Drury, *Tradition*, p. 22; more radically (Hadrian rather than Trajan, which is probably too late), J.C. O'Neill, *The Theology of Acts in its Historical Setting* (London, 1970), pp. 21f.

65. For the only satisfactory explanation of this see Drury, *Tradition*, pp. 96-102.

66. Luke 2.32.

67. See B. Lindars, *New Testament Apologetic* (London, 1961), pp. 216-18.

68. Cf. G. Vermes in P.R. Ackroyd and C.F. Evans (eds.), *Cambridge History of the Bible*, I (Cambridge, 1970), pp. 207-209.

69. Luke 1.41, which serves the same purpose as Matt. 3.13-15.

70. II, p. 34.

71. Cf. Matt. 3.2 with 4.17.

72. Cf. Matt. 26.28. Note that Matthew omits the thought of sharing Jesus' baptism from his version of Mark 10.38f.; cf. 20.22f.

73. Cf. Acts 2.38; 11.16; 19.1-7; and see G.W.H. Lampe, 'The Holy Spirit in the Writings of St Luke', in *Studies in the Gospels* (see n. 2 above), pp. 197f.

74. N.b. the imperfect ἐβαπτίζοντο in Matt. 3.6 par.

75. See H. Conzelmann, *The Theology of St Luke* (Eng. Tr.; London, 1960), pp. 166f.

76. Compare the pattern at 4.16ff.

77. The antecedent of the relative pronoun οὗ in Matt. 3.12 (par. Luke 3.17, and therefore Q to those who assume that hypothesis) must be the subject of 3.11 which is Marcan in substance. The formidable difficulties which this poses for the Q hypothesis have been pointed out by Butler, *Originality*, p. 111, and R.T. Simpson, 'The Major Agreements of Matthew and Luke against Mark', *NTS* 12 (1965), p. 27. Neither has ever, to my knowledge, been answered.

78. See n. 12 above.

79. Matthaean are βαπτισθῆναι, the participial form βαπτισθείς, the verb ἀνοίγειν, and ἐπ' αὐτόν; Marcan only ἐγένετο and ὡς (Matt. ὡσεί) περισσεράν.

80. H. Schürmann, *Das Lukasevangelium* (Freiburg, 1969), p. 218, is the only significant recent exception; see Schulz, *Q*, p. 177 n. 2; I.H. Marshall, *The Gospel of Luke* (Exeter, 1978), p. 167.

81. See Conzelmann, *Theology*, pp. 27-29.

82. ὑπέστρεψεν may reflect Matthew's ἀνεχώρησεν. For the form Ναζαρά see n. 84 below.

83. For φήμη cf. Matt. 9.26; for ἐδίδασκεν ἐν ταῖς συναγωγαῖς αὐτῶν cf. Matt. 4.23 = 9.35.

84. See however C.M. Tuckett, 'Luke 4,16-30; Isaiah and Q', in J. Delobel (ed.), *LOGIA* (BETL, 59; Leuven, 1982), pp. 343ff., for the view of H. Schürmann and others that Luke is also drawing on Q at this point. Much is made of the form Ναζαρά, found only at Matt. 4.12 and Luke 4.16. But (i) Ναζαρά is apparently the reading of the 3rd century p[70] (our earliest witness) at 2.23 (see Nestle–Aland[26] *ad loc.*); (ii) the form Ναζαρά is consonantally closer to Ναζωραῖος; (iii) Matthew is too consistent a writer

for it to be at all likely that he used different forms of a name (even under the influence of a source) in two contexts which not only lie close to one another but are parallel in their formulation (note the occurrence of ἀκούσας, ἀνεχώρησεν εἰς, ἐλθὼν κατῴκησεν, and the formula quotation in both); cf. B.M. Nolan, *The Royal Son of God* (Fribourg & Göttingen, 1979), pp. 103, 139. Matt. 21.11, the only other occurrence of the name in the first gospel, is much further on, and reflects the influence of Mark 1.9 in its wording. Thus while Ναζαρά in Luke is indicative of a source, the same form in Matthew can equally well indicate what that source was.

85. They may have originally been meant to stand even closer to the end of the section, if the 'Lucan apocalypse' of 17.20ff. was in fact a later insertion. Note that while the parable of the Unjust Judge (Luke 18.1-8) belongs thematically with the apocalypse, that of the Pharisee and the Tax-collector (18.9-14) belongs more naturally with sayings concerned with sin, forgiveness, and unprofitable servants (cf. 17.10).

86. On the priority of the Matthaean form of this parable see E. Linnemann, *Parables of Jesus* (Eng. Tr.; London, 1966), pp. 65ff.

87. Matt. 28.18-20; cf. Luke 24.46-49.

88. See my other essays in this collection, pp. 157ff.

89. See p. 132, above.

90. I have a detailed study of these in hand.

91. Farrer himself made an exception for this, treating the two versions as deriving from separate liturgical traditions. But cf. M.D. Goulder, 'The Composition of the Lord's Prayer', *JTS* 14 (1963), pp. 32ff.

92. On this, which is singled out by Downing, II, pp. 43f., as a passage of special difficulty for the position I am defending, see my other essay here.

93. Cf. 'Q', pp. 63-65.

94. Cf. Jacobson, 'Unity', p. 366 n. 4: 'A source hypothesis seeks to explain a unique event, the genesis of the gospels; it does not seek to explain what is typical. Therefore, a source hypothesis has no predictive power. Since it cannot predict anything, it cannot be tested and falsified in the way ordinary scientific hypotheses can be tested and falsified.'

95. As Farrer tacitly admitted; see n. 91 above, and cf. Goulder, 'Farrer on Q', p. 194.

96. See H.B. Green, *The Gospel according to Matthew* (Oxford, 1975), pp. 5ff. and *passim*. This position is to be distinguished from that of R. Morgenthaler, *Statistische Synopse* (Zürich / Stuttgart, 1971), p. 303, and W. Wilkens, 'Zur Frage der literarische Beziehung zwischen Matthäus und Lukas', *NovT* 8 (1966), pp. 48ff. (see also his 'Die Versuchung Jesu nach Matthäus', *NTS* 28 [1982], pp. 479ff.), which argues for Luke's use of Matthew without relinquishing the Two-Document hypothesis!

97. *Entia rerum non praeter necessitatem multiplicanda.*

MATTHEW 12.22-50 AND PARALLELS:
AN ALTERNATIVE TO MATTHAEAN CONFLATION

H. Benedict Green CR

College of the Resurrection
Mirfield, West Yorkshire

Matthew 12.22-50 par. Luke 11.14-32 is the most extended section of
separate items in virtually the same internal sequence in the so-called
Q material. That in itself makes it a test case for any form of the
hypothesis that one of the two evangelists derived it from the other.
At the same time the greater part of it is paralleled in Mark 3.20-35,
and the problem of overlap that this poses for the Two-Document
theory is a standing invitation to the advocates of alternative
solutions to argue their case in detail; an invitation which is here
taken up on behalf of the Ropes–Farrer–Goulder position.[1]

Though in both gospels the passage is found approximately half-
way through the book, its relation to the narrative development in
Luke is quite different from what it is in Matthew. Matthew in the
first half of his gospel uses Mark, as he does his other sources,
selectively for his presentation of Jesus as Messiah. It is only in ch. 12
that he begins to follow the Marcan order of events consistently,
which he then continues to do, with added material of his own, but
with few omissions and even fewer displacements, to the end of his
gospel. The section which we are examining is fully integrated into
the Marcan context, and no component of Mark 3.20-35 is unrepre-
sented in it. Matthew retains, and by his additions intensifies, Mark's
understanding of the Beelzebul slander as a climactic point in the
rejection of the mission of Jesus by the Jewish authorities, which is
then taken up and given theological interpretation in the parables
chapter that follows.

There is nothing of this in Luke. The Beelzebul slander would
have come much earlier in his gospel if he had recorded it in its
Marcan context, since Luke presses on with the Marcan outline in

the first half of the book and has handled the major part of this before he reaches his central section. But in fact it has been displaced by the Sermon on the Plain and the other inserted material that follows, and the Marcan order is rejoined at the parables discourse. Whether his reasons for doing this were literary (an inappropriate sequel to the Sermon on to the reply to John the Baptist, or a preference for the fuller version of Matthew) or theological (e.g. his understanding of the Galilean ministry as a privileged period in which no harm can come to Jesus or his followers),[2] Luke passes over the episode in his narrative of the Galilean ministry and then reproduces material elsewhere associated with it in his central section, where there is no narrative context for it to be integrated into, and no developing action for which it could be significant.

It is all the more striking that Luke's version of these verses contains an equivalent to every section in which Matthew corresponds to Mark (with the single exception of the sin against the Holy Spirit, which is deferred rather than omitted; see below), and in the same order; and at the same time a parallel to every item that Matthew has added to Mark (apart from the saying about the tree and its fruit, which he has already drawn on at 6.45), and in the same sequence (with the minor exception of the displacement of the sign of Jonah). If Luke was not familiar with Matthew's treatment of Mark, then the independent version which lies behind him and Matthew ran so closely parallel to Mark in content and order as to be more like a narrative gospel than a sayings source.[3]

On the latter view Matthew has conflated the independent version with Mark; Luke either represents the unconflated version or, if he did conflate (since *ex hypothesi* he knew Mark), did so independently of what Matthew had done. Does this account convincingly for the evidence before us? The question has to be answered section by section, bearing two considerations in mind: (i) if Matthew's text can, given his known methods of redaction, be plausibly derived from Mark alone, this weakens the argument that any conflation has taken place, and thus that there was any independent version for Luke to work from; (ii) where Matthew has unquestionably added material to what he found in Mark, we should on the conflation theory expect Luke's version, where parallel, to represent (with due allowance made for the possibility of his own redaction) more or less what has been added. Is this what we in fact find?

To this examination we now proceed.

1. *The Beelzebul slander*
Matt. 12.22-24 // Mark 3.20-21 // Luke 11.14-15

Mark introduces this with the imputation of madness to Jesus by his own relatives, Matthew and Luke with a miracle. The substitution is a likely enough one for a redactor to have made for himself, though where two have done so it cannot be simply assumed that they worked independently. Matthew's miracle is a comprehensive healing/ exorcism of a blind and dumb demoniac; Luke's simpler exorcism is parallel not to Matt. 12.22-24 but to Matt. 9.32-34.

A word needs to be said first about the relation of the two texts in Matthew. Matt. 9.32-34 is preceded by the healing of two blind men at 9.27-31 which is similarly paralleled by that of the two blind men of Jericho at 20.29-34. These and their connection with the two healings of single blind men in Mark have been fully examined by Held;[4] Matt. 20.29-34 conflates the two Marcan healings in the Bartimaeus context, and Matt. 9.27-31 is a throwback from this into his collective miracles section. It does not require us to postulate another literary source for the latter version. The same holds by analogy for 9.32-34 in relation to 12.22-24. Moreover when the Beelzebul slander itself is reached, 9.34 (assuming that the text is sound[5]) is in fact closer in its wording to Mark 3.22 than is 12.24. There is nothing to support the inference that Luke is here following Q in preference to Mark. On the face of it he is, on a point of detail, agreeing (not for the first or last time) with Matthew out of context against Matthew in context. And this, I shall argue, is part of a larger phenomenon, the most familiar form of which is the minor agreements of Luke with Matthew against Mark in Marcan contexts,[6] though it also includes the less commonly recognized agreements of Luke with Mark against Matthew in non-Marcan contexts—some of which will also be indicated in the course of this study.

2. *Jesus' answer: (i) Can Satan cast out Satan?*
Matt. 12.25-28 // Mark 3.24-26 // Luke 11.17-20

It would appear that the Two-Document theory is as far as ever from providing a convincing answer to the baffling question of the relation between Mark's version of this logion and Matthew's.[7] All the more reason, therefore, for examining a wider range of possibilities than can be accommodated within that hypothesis.

To begin with what is undisputed: Matthew's version adds vv. 27-28. These are recognizably a quatrain (though slightly obscured by the addition of the glossing comment διὰ τοῦτο αὐτοὶ κριταὶ ἔσονται ὑμῶν in v. 27b). The quatrain (with gloss) is reproduced in Luke with only a single variation in the wording, δακτύλῳ instead of πνεύματι (to which we shall return). But next, vv. 25-26, both in Matthew and Luke, are also a quatrain, of the same general form. Either (a) the four verses already belonged together in the tradition, and Matthew substituted them for Mark's balder three-membered form, or (b) Matthew (but not, of course, Luke) conflated the first two with Mark's version, or (c) Matthew assimilated the content of Mark's version to the form of vv. 27-28, or (d) Mark's version is derived from Matthew's and/or Luke's. It will be observed that whereas (a) (and, less relevantly, (d)) leaves open the relation of Luke's version to Matthew's, (b) requires a Q-type answer to this, while (c) definitely excludes it.

If in the light of these alternatives we now compare Luke's version of these two verses with Matthew's, Luke's will be found to differ at three points:

(i) His second line καὶ οἶκος ἐπὶ οἶκον πίπτει is at first sight quite different. Luke has a tendency to vary parallelism, but not as a rule to eliminate it altogether, and οἶκος ἐπὶ οἶκον is therefore rightly taken, with most translators,[8] as an elliptical construction pointing to the presence of a participle in his *Vorlage*, which has been suppressed as a gesture towards crisper Greek style. As the two significant words[9] introduced here are ones for which Luke shows a distinct preference, the most natural conclusion is that the alteration is his own, and the *Vorlage* not necessarily different from Matthew.

(ii) The third line omits (after εἰ δὲ καὶ ὁ σατανᾶς) τὸν σατανᾶν ἐκβάλλει. An equivalent to this stands as the heading to Mark's version of the saying, and Matthew's insertion of it into the body of the argument is the one component of his text that could plausibly be attributed to conflation of Mark with another version. But:

(iii) The gloss that Luke adds to the fourth line, 'because you say that I cast out demons by Beelzebul', seems to indicate that he was aware of a missing stage in the argument in his version, and this is entirely compatible with his having suppressed the missing words himself.[10] A desire to simplify Matthew's overloaded line would be sufficient motive, and the absence of the words from his version would be a further, negative, instance, as his substitution of ἐφ' ἑαυτὴν for καθ' ἑαυτῆς in the first line is a positive one, of his agreement with Mark against Matthew in a non-Marcan context.

The effect of the two latter alterations is thus to cancel one another out; and the variants in Luke's text offer minimal encouragement to the proponents of conflation in Matthew's. Is it then possible that Matthew's version of vv. 25-26 is derived from Mark's alone? If Matthew is recognized as a creative reshaper of his sources (and the case for this hardly calls for further argument now), there is no insuperable difficulty about this. Though the form of the lines has been tautened, and their rhythm assimilated to that of vv. 27-28, the stages of the argument (kingdom–house–Satan) remain unaffected, and every word but two in Matthew's version will be found to be represented in Mark's also. (The intruders are ἐρημοῦται, an understandable substitution to relieve the monotony of the thrice-repeated 'cannot stand' in Mark[11] (itself an argument against the literary dependence being in the other direction), and the bracketing of πόλις with οἰκία, a combination found also at Matt. 10.14,[12] again in a redactional context).

There remains the question of the original word in Matt. 12.28 // Luke 11.20. The past twenty years have seen the beginnings of a movement back towards the position of Harnack and Schlatter, that Matthew's πνεύματι is the original word; Dupont,[13] writing in 1969, could cite five authorities in favour of this in addition to himself,[14] and Schulz's list of a year later, though it included only two of these, was able to add the important name of Käsemann.[15] The arguments of T.W. Manson in the contrary direction,[16] which have been influential in this country,[17] have been effectively disposed of by Hamerton-Kelly and Goulder.[18] It is not claimed that this shift has so far affected more than a minority. What is significant is that all the scholars mentioned except the last-named start from the assumption of Q. If even a minority of those without any methodological bias in favour of Matthew can nevertheless conclude for his originality here, a hypothesis which stands or falls by the latter conclusion cannot on that account be ruled out as impossible. The question, 'Given on other grounds the general priority of Matthew, can Luke's text here be satisfactorily explained as his own alteration of Matthew?', can now claim an affirmative answer.

3. *Jesus' answer: (ii) The strong man disarmed*
Matt. 12.29-30 // Mark 3.27 // Luke 11.21-23

Matthew here follows Mark almost word for word, adding only the brief epigram at 12.30. Luke, though his essential meaning is the same, departs almost completely from both in his wording, ἰσχυρός being the only significant word they have in common. It used to be claimed that his is the Q version of the logion, but in view of the absence of any trace of it in Matthew, as well as of the greater sophistication of its vocabulary, this has been generally, and wisely, abandoned[19]. His version contains two NT hapax legomena (καθωπλισμένος, σκῦλα),[20] four more words not used by the other synoptists (νικήσῃ,[21] πανοπλίαν,[22] διαδίδωσιν,[23] ἐπελθών),[24] one which is strongly characteristic of his personal style (ὑπάρχοντα[25]) and the conjunction ἐπάν which he elsewhere introduces redactionally.[26] It is evidently a rhetorical paraphrase in his own wording, and there is no reason to conclude that what he was paraphrasing was any different from what we have in Mark and Matthew. It is all the more striking that he places it in the same position relative to 11.14-20 (par. Matt. 12.22-28) as Matthew does, and that like Matthew he adds the concluding epigram at 11.23.

There remains the question why, if he used both Matthew and Mark as sources, he thought it necessary to depart so radically from wording in which they substantially agree, thus refusing what has been called a 'ready made conflation'.[27] The answer in this case is to be found in a neglected observation of Austin Farrer,[28] that Luke has assimilated the logion to that of the house swept and garnished which he has placed immediately after it (11.24-26). Possible reasons for this rearrangement and its relation to the whole section are discussed below.

4. *Jesus' answer: (iii) The sin against the Holy Spirit*
Matt. 12.31-32 // Mark 3.28-30 // Luke 12.10

The Lucan counterpart to Matthew 12.31f. par. Mark 3.28ff. is not found in the same context. But it has not been moved very far away,[29] only to Luke 12.10; nor is it difficult to suggest a reason for its transposition, and with it an argument for the possibility of Luke's having found it in the context in which it appears in the other gospels. Both Mark and Matthew connect the saying closely with the

Beelzebul controversy in its narrative context, the sin against the Holy Spirit being the ascription of Jesus' exorcisms to diabolical power. Luke, as we have seen, does not include the controversy in his narrative of the Galilean ministry, and his transposition of the saying to a context which speaks of fearless confession (Luke 12.2ff.) is probably to be understood in terms of the tendency in later NT times to reinterpret the saying with reference to apostasy after baptism.[30]

The logion is commonly cited as a characteristic instance of Matthaean conflation of sources, and it is not difficult to see why. What Mark has said once, with a simple contrast between the other sins and blasphemies of the sons of men and blasphemy against the Holy Spirit, Matthew has found necessary to say twice over, contrasting first the other sins and blasphemies of men with blasphemy against the Holy Spirit, and secondly speaking against the Son of man with speaking against the Holy Spirit. But there is no need to invoke the hypothesis of a second source, with or without the support of suggested translation variants,[31] in order to understand what he has done; one need only recognize that Mark's expression 'sons of men' represents (despite its Hebraic roots) an unacceptable level of ambiguity for Matthaean theology. In Matthew's gospel, as Kingsbury has convincingly shown,[32] 'Son of man' is a public title used for Jesus personally which awaits full elucidation of its meaning; it is not a designation that he shares with others. It has therefore in the nature of things no plural, and the contrast between its referent and the generality of men is one which the evangelist is at pains to emphasize in a number of passages generally agreed to be redactional. Thus at 16.13 the first question of Jesus to the disciples asks 'Who do men say that the Son of man is?', and at 9.6-8 'the Son of man' (= Jesus personally) in v. 6 is distinguished from the collective 'men' in v. 8, which includes him but will not always remain restricted to him.[33] In the present passage Matthew is at pains to distinguish *men*, who are sinners and blasphemers and in need of forgiveness, from the *Son of man*, who is both (like the Holy Spirit, but less culpably, since his true identity is not yet disclosed) the object of their attack and the one who (in all but the reserved instance) bestows forgiveness. What Mark actually meant would have been sufficiently conveyed by the substitution of 'men' for 'sons of men', which is more or less what Matthew has done in the first half of his version. But because he is practising midrash on what for him was a sacred text,[34] he has been constrained to attend not only to the meaning but to the wording of

it, and to construct a variant form of the saying which retains 'Son of
man', but in the singular and referred unambiguously to Jesus
himself.

If the argument is sound so far, there should be no difficulty about
deriving Luke's text from the second half of Matthew's. Apart from
the substitution of ὃς ἐάν εἴπῃ λόγον by πᾶς ὃς ἐρεῖ λόγον (the
exchange of synonymous words being a form of verbal tinkering very
characteristic of Luke),[35] the only real divergences from Matthew—
the replacement of κατά by εἰς, and the use of βλασφημεῖν in the
second half (Luke's habit of variation again)—both draw on Mark's
version: a minor agreement of Luke with Mark against Matthew in a
non-Marcan context, and an instance of conflation not by Matthew
but by Luke!

5. *Jesus' true kin*
Matt. 12.46-50 // Mark 3.31-35 // Luke 11.27-28 (cf. 8.19-21)

This is the remaining passage in the section in which Matthew runs
parallel to Mark, and I therefore take it next. He follows Mark in it as
closely as he normally does, and there is nothing that requires us to
postulate an additional source. The content of Luke's version is
different at this point, and at first sight apparently independent. He
has however already made use of Mark's version in a context much
closer to that in which he found it; it is the one item from Mark's
Beelzebul sequence that he has salvaged and included, with some
degree of assimilation to its new context, in his version of the parable
discourse which follows immediately in Mark (8.19-21). He has there
altered the punch-line of the paradigm to run: my mother and my
brothers are οἱ τὸν λόγον τοῦ θεοῦ ἀκούοντες καὶ ποιοῦντες (8.21).
Since most of this reappears as the climax of 11.27-28, μενοῦν
μακάριοι οἱ ἀκούοντες τὸν λόγον τοῦ θεοῦ και φυλάσσοντες it can
be inferred that he saw or intended a connection between the two.
The wording of the introductory part of the latter pericope is
reminiscent of 23.29 (part of the reply of Jesus to the women of
Jerusalem, which has all the marks of Luke's own composition),[36]
and also of the infancy narratives.[37] ἐπαίρειν,[38] βαστάζειν,[39]
φυλάσσειν[40] are all relatively more characteristic of Luke than of
other NT writers, and their occurrence together within the space of
these two verses help further to stamp the latter as his. Luke has
constructed them himself, and he has done so with the express object

of providing a parallel to Matt. 12.46-50 without repeating his earlier parallel to Mark 3.31-35.

The implications of this are that Matthew knew no other version of the pericope to conflate with Mark, and that Luke knew none that was independent of Mark. His construction of a version of his own to insert in this context can only mean that he had Matthew before him to indicate the context.

6. *Three Matthaean Logia*
Matt. 12.33-45

There remain the three logia (two composite, one unitary) which Matthew has inserted between 12.32 and 12.46. They have no counterpart in the context in Mark, and the question of conflation by Matthew thus does not arise directly. But all have parallels in Luke, two of the three in the same context if not the same order, and they are therefore relevant to the thesis that Luke knew and used Matthew.

Goulder[41] has pointed out that they correspond in the inverse order (i.e. chiastically) to the three conditions (possession, blindness, dumbness) of which the sufferer is cured in the comprehensive miracle of Matt. 12.22. This is *prima facie* evidence that it is Matthew himself who has assembled them in their present context and sequence. What reasons, if any, might Luke have had for modifying this?

(a) Luke does not use the parable of the tree and its fruit (Matt. 12.33-37) at this point, because he has already drawn heavily on this version of it in his parallel to Matt. 7.16-20 at 6.43-45 (another case of his agreement with Matthew out of context against Matthew in context).

(b) The transposition of the Sign of Jonah sayings to the end of the section allows Luke to place the parable of the house swept and garnished (Matt. 12.43-45 // Luke 11.24-26) directly after the other sayings about exorcism and, as we have seen,[42] to assimilate the form of one of the latter to it; he may well be treating the whole section as commentary on Jesus' practice for the guidance of the later Church. His divergences from Matthew at this point are very minor ones, and no obstacle to regarding Matthew as his source here.

(c) Luke not only makes the Sign of Jonah sayings (Matt. 12.38-42 // Luke 11.16, 29-32) the climax of the whole section, but by his anticipation of them at v. 16 suggests that for him the theme runs concurrently with the whole exorcism sequence. He may be using them to convey a warning that exorcism must not be practised to impress the onlooker with its spectacular aspects; the proper response to it is not admiration but *metanoia*. The division of his material to express something of this kind is surely an author's literary device rather than a feature of the tradition, as is confirmed by examination of the parallels.

Matthew's version is a further instance of what I have called Matthaean throwback. The Marcan source is Mark 8.11-12, to which Matthew's parallel in context is Matt. 16.1-2a, 4. Matt. 12.38-39 paraphrases 16.1-2a, and reproduces 16.4 unaltered apart from the addition of τοῦ προφήτου. So far there is no need at all to postulate a second source; all is well within Matthew's redactional capacity, and his most significant alteration, the substitution of the mysterious 'sign of Jonah' for the blanket refusal of a sign in Mark 8.12, introduces a theme in which he alone in the NT, apart from this single parallel in Luke, evinces any interest.[43]

Luke 11.16, 29-30 is found in a context parallel to Matt. 12.38-39, but once again Luke is found agreeing on details with Matthew out of context against Matthew in context, and this time simultaneously, as we shall see, with Mark against Matthew in a non-Marcan context. Thus Luke 11.16 agrees with Matt. 16.1 in the position of πειράζοντες and its lack of an expressed object, and in using the preposition ἐκ/ἐξ as opposed to ἀπό, but with Mark 8.11 in the use of the verb ζητοῦν followed by παρ' αὐτοῦ. Luke 11.29 agrees with Matt. 12.39 and 16.4 in the general form of the saying, and with 16.4 against 12.39 in omitting τοῦ προφήτου. It retains from Mark 8.12 the expression ἡ γενέα αὕτη (though qualifying it as πονηρά as do the two Matthew versions) and the uncompounded form ζητεῖ (though it inverts the order of verb and object as does Matthew in both places). It would appear that there is conflation in these verses, but that once more it is Luke, not Matthew, who is the conflator.

For what remains, Luke 11.30-32, there is only the one Matthaean parallel at Matt. 12.40-42. Luke differs from this at two points: (i) in omitting the comparison between Jonah in the whale's belly and the Son of man in the heart of the earth; (ii) in inverting the order of the witness of the Ninevites and that of the queen of the south. Item (ii) can be explained as Luke's alteration on a number of levels: variation for its own sake,[44] or to avoid the offence of plagiarism;[45] a pedantic concern for the correct historical sequence of the persons named;[46] or, as suggested above, a desire to emphasize repentance rather than the spectacular by making Jonah the climax.

Some of these considerations may apply also to (i), but here the case is more complicated. The formal structure of the two versions is identical, but the content so totally divergent, that the usual criteria for distinguishing the more from the less developed simply do not apply. Either one of the evangelists (or his source, or a later interpolator), knowing the other version, has substituted his own for it, or both have been substituted for a similarly structured original now irretrievably lost. The latter alternative seems not to be followed very rigorously even by its principal advocate R.A. Edwards,[47] since he tacitly reverts to treating Luke's version as a probable clue to the content of the original.[48] In this he approximates to the great majority of commentators[49] who, starting from the first alternative, assume that the fuller version (i.e. Matt. 12.40) must be the later, though there are no invariable laws of development that require this.[50]

In the face of this consensus it is tempting to the dispenser with Q to follow Stendahl[51] in attributing Matt. 12.40 to a post-Matthaean interpolator,[52] especially since even a veiled reference to the resurrection seems at first sight out of place at that point in the gospel. This short cut to the resolution of the difficulty must however be resisted, both because Stendahl's arguments for Justin Martyr's ignorance of the present text of Matthew, on which his whole case rests, are not finally convincing,[53] and because the claims of Luke 11.30 to represent a less developed version do not stand up to closer examination. The main objections are these:

a. The starting point of the whole complex is the modification of 'no sign at all' to 'no sign except the sign of Jonah', and the argument for Lucan priority here has to begin by assuming that this took place at an early stage of the oral tradition.[54] Since the text in its present form has been built up by additions to what we find in 11.29, we have further to suppose that the cryptic exception originally circulated without explanatory comment. How likely is this?

b. Luke 11.30 does not by itself tell us in what sense or by what means Jonah was a sign to the Ninevites; clarification of that has to wait for the double logion of 11.31-32. As only half of this is concerned with Jonah or repentance the present context can hardly have been its original setting in the tradition. 11.30 can really be understood only in terms of its function in this context, as a bridge[55] between 11.29 and 11.31-32, and this is redaction, not tradition.[55a]

c. The explanation when it comes is more than a little forced. The OT says nothing of any unusual visual impact made by Jonah on Nineveh. Ezekiel dumb or Isaiah naked[56] is a sign to Israel; Jonah is not a sign to the Ninevites in that sense, but simply a prophet at whose message they repented.[57] Only the parallel with Solomon, the impression his wisdom made on the queen of Sheba, does anything to prepare for the thought of Jonah as a sign: Solomon supplying the sign and Jonah the repentance (is that the real reason why Luke places them in this order?).

The redaction that has produced the Lucan version of this passage is thus both subtle and artificial, and more readily attributable to the author of a self-consciously literary work than to an anonymous hand in the formation of the oral tradition behind him. Did Matthew then know Luke's version, or is the dependence the other way after all? Let us begin by comparing them at the points at which we have found problems for Lucan priority.

a. There is no need to call in form-critical considerations in order to make sense of the textual data found in Matthew; all can be accounted for in terms of Matthaean redaction. 16.4 is his own modification of Mark 8.11, and 12.39 is simply throwback from this.

b. 12.40 is offered as an explanation of what is meant by the sign of Jonah, and as such can stand independently of the two following verses, though these serve to carry the general theme further.

c. In order to argue convincingly that both redaction and explanation are the work of Matthew himself, it is still necessary to show what he understood by the sign of Jonah and why he thought it significant, on lines which will respect his known methods of interpreting scripture, be consistent with his general message, and appropriate to the point in the gospel narrative at which each passage is found. The following is an outline of how this may be done:

(1) 12.39ff. is not the first instance of Jonah-typology in this gospel; it has already appeared in the narrative of the stilling of the Storm (8.23-26), where reminiscences of the LXX of Jonah 1, which are not absent from Mark's version,[58] are considerably enchanced by Matthew's redaction.[59] Here, as often in Matthew,[60] the antitype is contrasted with the type: whereas the ship that carried Jonah could only survive by throwing him overboard, the boat that carries Jesus is saved by having him on board. In his well-known essay on this

pericope Bornkamm[61] sees here a prefiguration of the Church as 'ark of salvation'. While the evangelist may well be leading the minds of his readers towards an eventual understanding of this kind, the use of the word ἄνθρωποι, which is both reminiscent of ἄνδρες used of the ship's crew in Jonah 1.16 LXX and suggestive of the presence of others in the boat besides disciples,[62] seems to imply that so explicit an ecclesiological reference would be premature at this point in the gospel. The typology of the passage is nevertheless a valuable indicator of the aspect of the Jonah story that Matthew found specially significant.[63]

(2) The 'generation' whose representatives approach Jesus at 12.38 is contemporary Israel[64] whose rejection of its Messiah is summed up in its attribution of his exorcisms to the agency of Beelzebul. Having denounced the brazenness of their demand for a sign, he is hardly to be understood as proceeding to comply with it. The only sign that will be offered is a negative one, that will convey nothing to the unbeliever. 'This generation' is typified in the Jonah story by the ship's crew, who throw Jonah overboard, and that is the last they see of him. That he disappears not simply beneath the waves but into the belly of the whale, which is at once a symbol of death and a means of deliverance from it, remains hidden from them. So will it be with those who in order to preserve the old Israel as it is conspire to do away with Jesus; they will be unable to see beyond his death.

Thus while Matthew's readership may be expected to pick up an implicit reference to the passion of Christ, and beyond it to his *descensus ad inferos*[65] and even, more obliquely, to his resurrection,[66] as the mystery behind the sign, these are strictly not part of the sign itself, which remains visual and negative and directed at unbelievers. The same applies, so far as this context is concerned, to the hint of post-resurrection mission to Gentiles conveyed by the reference to Jonah's reappearance in Nineveh. The Ninevites are a reproach to 'this generation', not a type of it, and Jonah, as we have seen, is not a sign to them but a prophet.

(3) Yet this is not the last that we hear of the sign of Jonah in this gospel. We have had the Christological interpretation; there remains, as so often in Matthew, the ecclesiological, and it is reserved for that section of the gospel (13.53–18.35) which contains, in a Galilean setting,[67] its principal adumbrations of the future Church[68] and of the Gentile world in which that future lies.[69]

There are a number of recurrent motifs in these chapters: the sequence: feeding of the thousands—crossing of the lake—Christo-logical confession is found both in ch. 14 and chs. 15–16, and in both instances the figure of Peter plays a significant part. The lake crossing in the first sequence, the Walking on the Water (14.22-33), contains several echoes of the Stilling of the Storm in 8.23-26,[70] but there has been some development of the symbolism; where the stilling in the earlier episode is effected by keeping Jesus aboard a craft with a mixed crew, the reassurance in the later one is brought about by taking him (now accompanied by Peter) aboard a boat manned, it would appear, by disciples only. The corresponding crossing in the second sequence is the immediate prelude to the confrontation with Pharisees and others[71] (16.1-4) in which the latter again demand a sign and are once more offered only the sign of Jonah—this time without explanation, and in a symbolic context which the interpretation given at 12.40 does not fit, since the thought of the mission to Gentiles is never far from the surface[72]. It would be uncharacteristic of Matthew to leave the reader without any clue to his meaning here, and the key is supplied a little further on in the same section at 16.17, where the σημεῖον Ἰωνᾶ of 16.4 is picked up by the address Σίμων Βαριωνᾶ.[73] This is surely paranomasia and not coincidence; and its meaning is that there remains a visible sign of the presence and activity of the Son of man whom the old Israel has rejected, a counterpart to what he was in the days of his flesh. This is the Church founded on and represented by the figure of Peter;[74] but it is to be found (like Jonah after his deliverance) in the countries of the Gentiles. For those who continue embattled in the old Israel it can only be, once again, a sign of contradiction.

It is thus possible, I would claim, to offer a coherent account of the meaning of the sign of Jonah within the general framework of the Matthaean *Heilsgeschichte*.[75] Why then should Luke have been dissatisfied with it? It is of course possible that he did not understand it, and if so he was, evidently, not the last. But it is usually unsafe to assume that early Christian writers were unable to pick up each other's allusions, particularly in the field of exegesis, and it is more likely that he understood Matthew's meaning well enough, but found it not to his purpose at this point, since he reserves the theme of conspiracy against Jesus' life for the time after his arrival in Jerusalem,[76] and that of the future Church and its Gentile setting (apart from oblique allusions, as at 4.24-7) for his second volume.[77] Either way he had sufficient motive for reworking the saying;[78] and the relative lameness of what he has substituted is evidence not of closer proximity to primitive tradition, but of a certain maladroitness in the handling of sayings material in particular which can sometimes be observed in his writings. There is another example only four verses further on.[79]

Conclusion

It has been argued, first, that Matthew's version of these verses is an elaborated version of Mark's, retaining its order unchanged and needing no continuous second source to account for it; secondly, that Luke's version corresponds, in content entirely and in order very largely, to Matthew's as we have it and not to what remains of it when its Marcan core has been extracted; and, thirdly, that there are no individual passages which when analysed in depth resist this conclusion. The parallels are set out in the accompanying table. Their implications for current majority assumptions about source-analysis hardly require emphasis.

Mark		Matthew	Luke
2.23-28	Gleaning on the sabbath	12.1-8	
3.1-6	Healing in the synagogue	12.9-14	
3.7-12	Summary of healings	12.15-17 (leading to formula quotation at 12.18-21)	
3.13-19	Appointment of the twelve	(already used at 10.1-4)	
3.20-22	Beelzebul slander	12.22-24	11.14-15
3.23-26	Jesus' answer (i) Can Satan cast out Satan?	12.25-26 (27-28)	11.17-18 (19-20)
3.27	Jesus' answer (ii) The strong man disarmed	12.29 (adds 12.30)	11.21-22(23)
			11.23
3.28-30	Jesus' answer (iii) The sin against the Holy Spirit	12.31-32	(12.10)
		12.33-37 tree and fruit: heart and mouth	(used at 6.45)
		12.38-42 The sign of Jonah	11.16, 29-32
		12.43-45 The house swept	11.24-26
3.31-35	Jesus' true kin	12.46-50	11.27-28 (cf. 8.19-21)

NOTES

1. See J.H. Ropes, *The Synoptic Gospels* (Cambridge, Mass., 1934; Oxford, 1960²), p. 37; A.M. Farrer, 'On Dispensing with Q', in D.E. Nineham (ed.), *Studies in the Gospels: Essays in Memory of R.H. Lightfoot* (Oxford, 1955), pp. 55-88; M.D. Goulder, *Midrash and Lection in Matthew* (London, 1974).

2. See H. Conzelmann, *The Theology of St Luke* (Eng. Tr.; London, 1960), pp. 27ff.

3. A conclusion reached on other grounds by T. Schramm, *Der Markus-Stoff bei Lukas* (Cambridge, 1971), especially pp. 185ff.

4. H.J. Held, 'Matthew as Interpreter of the Miracle Stories', in G. Bornkamm, G. Barth, H.J. Held, *Tradition and Interpretation in Matthew* (Eng. Tr.; London, 1963), pp. 165ff.

5. The verse is omitted by D a k sy^s Hil, followed by R. Bultmann, *History of the Synoptic Tradition* (Eng. Tr.; Oxford, 1963), p. 212, who sees it as a later insertion from 12.24. But it is needed to prepare the reader for 10.25. Bultmann is nevertheless right in rejecting the view that 9.32-34 preserves the source of the episode at 12.22-24.

6. For these see especially F. Neirynck, *The Minor Agreements of Matthew and Luke against Mark* (BETL, 37; Leuven, 1974).

7. The basic solutions proposed have been: (i) a primitive Q version underlying Mark and Matthew, which has been severely scaled down by the tradition behind Mark (so Bultmann, *Tradition*, pp. 210f., followed by S. Schulz, *Q: Die Spruchquelle der Evangelisten* [Zürich, 1972], pp. 203ff.; D. Lührmann, *Die Redaktion der Logienquelle* [Neukirchen, 1969], pp. 32ff., etc.); (ii) two separate traditions have been combined in the Q version, one of which lies behind Mark's (so E. Schweizer, *The Good News according to Mark* [Eng. Tr.; London, 1971], pp. 82ff.; *The Good News according to Matthew* [Eng. Tr.; London, 1976], p. 284). It is not clear in the first case why an evangelist with something like what we have in Matthew and Luke before him should want to reduce it to what we find in Mark, nor in the second how Mark's tradition could be familiar with the terms of the Beelzebul slander, yet unfamiliar with that part of the composite logion which on Schweizer's view directly answers it.

8. All the major modern versions except RSV; for details see I.H. Marshall, *The Gospel of Luke* (Exeter, 1978), p. 474 (though Marshall himself favours the RSV rendering). Schulz, *Q*, p. 205, also construes Luke in the same way as RSV, but regards his version as secondary and resting on a misunderstanding of his source.

9. οἶκος, πίπτω (which Luke however never uses in the sense required by RSV).

10. So Bultmann, *Tradition*, pp. 90, 327.

11. See Goulder, *Midrash*, p. 332. Is there an echo of the disputed ἔρημος

at Matt. 23.38?

12. Cf. also 5.14f.; see Goulder, *Midrash*, p. 332.

13. J. Dupont, *Les Béatitudes*, II (Paris, 1969), p. 109n.

14. F. Gils, A. Richardson, C.S. Rodd, J.A. Yates, R.G. Hamerton-Kelly, A. George.

15. Schulz, *Q*, p. 205 n. 218; E. Käsemann, 'Lukas 11.14-28', in *Exegetische Versuche und Besinnungen*, I (Göttingen, 1960), p. 244. The list should now include also P.D. Meyer, *The Community of Q* (Dissert. Ph.D. Iowa, 1967), pp. 71f.: Goulder, *Midrash*, p. 333; J.M. Van Cangh, '"Par l'esprit de Dieu— par le doigt de Dieu" Mt 12,28 par Lc 11,20', in J. Delobel (ed.), *LOGIA* (BETL, 59; Leuven, 1982), pp. 337-42.

16. *The Teaching of Jesus* (Cambridge, 1935), pp. 82f.

17. See especially C.K. Barrett, *The Holy Spirit and the Gospel Tradition* (London, 1947), pp. 62f.; W.D. Davies, *The Setting of the Sermon on the Mount* (Cambridge, 1963), p. 91n.

18. R.G. Hamerton-Kelly, 'A Note on Matt. 12.28 par. Luke 11.20', *NTS* 11 (1964-65), pp. 167-69; Goulder, *Midrash*, p. 333n. E. Schweizer, art. πνεῦμα, *TDNT*, VI, p. 405, points out that Luke never speaks of the Spirit as the agency by which Jesus' miracles are performed, and Meyer, *Community*, pp. 71f., connects this with his avoidance of any suggestion that Jesus was subordinate to the Spirit (see Barrett, *Spirit*, p. 101; Conzelmann, *Theology*, p. 180); he concludes: 'Luke possibly altered the saying because it conflicted with his carefully thought out pneumatology'. Cf. also C.M. Tuckett, 'Luke 4,16-30, Isaiah and Q', in *LOGIA* (see n. 15), pp. 349-51.

19. See Schulz, *Q*, p. 203 n. 200; Marshall, *Luke*, pp. 476f., resists this conclusion, but can claim real support only from H. Schürmann, *Der Paschamahlbericht* (Münster, 1953), p. 2.

20. Both common in LXX.

21. Luke 1, Paul 3, Johannine corpus 7, Rev. 17; common in LXX.

22. Luke 1, Eph. 2; LXX 11.

23. Luke 2, Acts 1, John 1; LXX 12.

24. Luke 3, Acts 4, others 2; common in LXX.

25. Matt. 3, Luke 15, Acts 25, Paul 12, others 5; common in LXX.

26. See 11.34; elsewhere in NT only at Matt. 2.8.

27. See F.G. Downing, 'Redaction Criticism: Josephus' *Antiquities* and the Synoptic Gospels' (II), *JSNT* 9 (1981), p. 43. Cf. my other essay in this volume, p. 132.

28. Farrer, 'Q', pp. 70f.

29. Especially if the suggestion in my other paper, n. 49, is accepted.

30. See Barrett, *Spirit*, pp. 106f.

31. For the well-known suggestion of Wellhausen see Barrett, *Spirit*, p. 103.

32. J.D. Kingsbury, *Matthew: Structure, Christology, Kingdom* (Philadelphia and London, 1975), pp. 103-22.

33. See G. Strecker, *Der Weg der Gerechtigkeit* (Göttingen, 1962), pp. 221f. The argument of M. Pamment, 'The Son of Man in the First Gospel', *NTS* 29 (1983), pp. 116ff., that 'Son of man' in Matthew has a collective reference throughout, is not convincing. If there is tension here between what is unique to Jesus and what is extended to his followers, that is not, as she claims, peculiar to the title 'Son of man'; it is true also of 'Son of God' (cf. 5.9, 45 with 16.16; note the reminiscence of Hos. 1.10 LXX behind both 5.9 and 16.16, and see E. Lohmeyer–W. Schmauch, *Das Evangelium des Matthäus* [Göttingen, 1956] on 5.9). In either case the primary thought is of what is unique to Jesus.

34. Cf. M. Black, *An Aramaic Approach to the Gospels and Acts* (Oxford, 1967³), p. 109: 'Matthew is faithfully targumising Mark as well as conflating with Q'. The truth of his first statement does not stand or fall by that of his second!

35. See H.J. Cadbury, *The Making of Luke–Acts* (London, 1958²), especially pp. 173ff.

36. See J.H. Neyrey, 'Jesus' Address to the Women of Jerusalem (Luke 23.27-31)—A Prophetic Judgement Oracle', *NTS* 29 (1983), pp. 74ff., especially p. 84.

37. Cf. 1.42, 48.

38. Matt. 1, Mark 0, Luke 6, Acts 5, John 4, Paul 2, rest of NT 1.

39. Matt. 3, Mark 1, Luke 5, Acts 4, John 5, Paul 6, Rev. 3.

40. Matt. 1, Mark 1, Luke 6, Acts 8, John 3, Paul 3, Pastorals 5, others 4.

41. *Midrash*, pp. 331f.

42. See above, p. 162.

43. To treat it in isolation, as does R.A. Edwards, *The Sign of Jonah* (London, 1971), is to get it seriously out of proportion.

44. See Cadbury, *Luke–Acts* (n. 35 above); *id.*, 'Four Features of Lucan Style', in L.E. Keck and J.L. Martyn (eds.), *Studies in Luke–Acts* (Nashville, 1966 / London, 1968), pp. 87-102, esp. pp. 91f.

45. See Cadbury, *Luke–Acts*, p. 195.

46. See T.W. Manson, *The Sayings of Jesus* (London, 1949), p. 91.

47. Edwards, *Sign*, p. 82.

48. *Ibid.*, p. 85.

49. See Schulz, *Q*, p. 252 n. 520. Among those who have supported the minority view have been A. Schlatter, *Der Evangelist Matthäus* (Stuttgart, 1929), p. 416; J. Schniewind, *Das Evangelium nach Matthäus* (Göttingen, 1956⁷), p. 162; Barrett, *Spirit*, p. 90; Meyer, *Community*, p. 9; R.T. France, *Jesus and the Old Testament* (London, 1971), pp. 80-82.

50. See E.P. Sanders, *The Tendencies of the Synoptic Tradition* (Cambridge, 1969), pp. 46ff.

51. K. Stendahl, *The School of St Matthew* (Lund, 1954 / Philadelphia, 1968), pp. 132f.

52. This is said by way of retraction; see H.B. Green, *The Gospel according*

to Matthew (Oxford, 1975), p. 129.

53. The arguments of Strecker, *Weg*, p. 103, are not all equally convincing or even consistent with one another, but he seems to have established (i) that Justin (*Dialogue* 107) is not quoting verbatim, since his introduction to the citation is a mixture of Matt. 12.38 and 16.1; (ii) that his quotation of 12.41 is also free, and it cannot therefore be argued that he would have cited 12.40 verbatim if he had known it.

54. So Edwards, *Sign*, pp. 70ff.

55. This remains true whether the verse is seen as a later construction made to link 11.29 and 11.31f. (so Lührmann, *Redaktion*, p. 41) or the three verses 11.30-32 are regarded as having been added simultaneously (so Meyer, *Community*, p. 9). Either position is preferable to that of Schulz, *Q*, p. 252 n. 527, and authorities cited by him (see now also A.D. Jacobson, 'The Literary Unity of Q', *JBL* 101 [1982], p. 382), that the verses were added to 11.29 successively in the order in which they now stand.

55a. The same is true of B. Lindars's proposal (*Jesus Son of Man* [London, 1983], pp. 42f.) to treat 'except the sign of Jonah' in Luke 11.29 as itself the bridge between the tradition represented by Mark 8.12 and Luke 11.30 (here claimed as an authentic Son of man saying). To attempt to harmonize two such contradictory sayings would have been a fairly sophisticated redactional exercise.

56. Ezek. 24.15-24, esp. v. 24; Isa. 20.2ff.

57. Jacobson, 'Unity', p. 382, argues that a sign is here not a prodigy but a warning about the future; but this is certainly not the sense in which a sign has been demanded. Cf. J. Jeremias, 'Ἰωνᾶς', *TDNT*, III, p. 409.

58. With Mark 4.41 cf. Jonah 1.10, καὶ ἐφοβήθησαν οἱ ἄνδρες φόβον μέγαν; also 1.16. Matthew tones this down, but his οἱ ἄνθρωποι (not in Mark) seems to be due to Jonah's οἱ ἄνδρες. Other parallels in Mark are noted by Jeremias, 'Ἰωνᾶς', p. 408.

59. With Matt. 8.24-25 cf. Jonah 1.4-6. Matthew's reflection of Jonah here is pointed out (apparently from a Matthaean priorist standpoint) by the classical scholar A. Pallis, *Notes on St Mark and St Matthew* (Oxford, 1932²), p. 75.

60. See H.B. Green, 'Solomon the Son of David in Matthaean Typology', *SE*, VII (Berlin, 1982), p. 227.

61. 'The Stilling of the Storm in Matthew', *Tradition* (see n. 4 above), pp. 52-57.

62. Cf. the contrast in 16.13f. between οἱ ἄνθρωποι and ὑμεῖς (i.e. the disciples).

63. For rabbinic allusions to the part played by the crew of Jonah's ship, see Jeremias, 'Ἰωνᾶς', p. 409 n. 26.

64. The source of this usage seems to be Mark 8.12, 38. Matthew systematically develops it; cf. 11.16; 12.45; 23.36, and see R. Walker, *Die Heilsgeschichte im ersten Evangelium* (Göttingen, 1967), pp. 35-38. The

Lucan passages in which it is found are always parallel to Matthew, with the exception of 17.25 which is clearly secondary reminiscence of Mark.

65. For parallels to this in contemporary Jewish literature, see A.T. Hanson, *New Testament Interpretation of Scripture* (London, 1980), pp. 148-50.

66. The associations of the 'three days' motif made this inevitable, especially for readers of LXX which repeats it at Jonah 3.4: see Hanson, *loc. cit.*

67. On Galilee in Matthew see Green, 'Solomon', p. 230; *id.*, 'The Structure of St Matthew's Gospel', *SE*, IV (Berlin, 1968), pp. 51-53; B.M. Nolan, *The Royal Son of God* (Fribourg & Göttingen, 1979), pp. 139-42.

68. See especially 14.28-33; 16.17-19; 17.24-27; 18 *passim*.

69. Matthew not only retains Mark's 'Gentile mission' (Mark 6.45–8.21) largely intact, but adds 15.29-31, which reads like a version of 11.2-6 for Gentiles; cf. Green, *Matthew*, p. 148.

70. See Held, *Tradition* (see n. 4 above), p. 206.

71. On Matthew's reference here to 'Pharisees and Sadducees', see Walker, *Heilsgeschichte*, pp. 11-16.

72. See n. 66 above.

73. Contemporary changes in pronunciation make this all the more plausible. 'Itacism' was already affecting Attic Greek usage by the mid-second century AD; see L.R. Palmer, *The Greek Language* (London, 1980), p. 206. That it should have affected the Koine half a century earlier in an area much nearer to the linguistic frontier is not difficult to credit.

74. For the exegesis of Matt. 16.18f. as a midrash on Isa. 28.10ff. contrasting church and synagogue see J. Kahmann, 'Die Verheissung an Petrus: Mt. XVI,18-19 in Zusammenhang des Matthäusevangeliums', in M. Didier (ed.), *L'Évangile selon Matthieu* (BETL, 29; Gembloux, 1972), pp. 261-80; Green, *Matthew*, pp. 246-48.

75. For the appropriateness of this expression cf. Walker, *Heilsgeschichte*; but in fact virtually all the redaction-critical studies of the past twenty years have been concerned with one aspect of it or another.

76. See Conzelmann, *Theology*, pp. 28, 80, 198.

77. See my other essay here, p. 144.

78. Meyer, *Community*, pp. 10-12, argues that Luke reinterpreted the sign of Jonah in terms of the salvation of the Gentiles. On the view outlined above this would amount not to an outright rejection of Matthew, but rather to a preference for Matt. 16.4 as against 12.40.

79. See my other essay here, n. 49.

MATTHEW ON MATTHEW

G.D. Kilpatrick

27 Lathbury Road, Oxford

In my book *The Origins of the Gospel according to St. Matthew* (Oxford, 1946), p. 138, I wrote as follows:

> Mark ii.14 mentions Λευεὶν τὸν τοῦ Ἀλφαίου, but the corresponding passage Matt. ix.9 has just Μαθθαῖον and, while Mark iii.18 has only the name Μαθθαῖον, Matt. x.3 has Μαθθαῖος ὁ τελώνης. It is tempting to assume that these changes have some connexion with the title κατὰ Μαθθαῖον. This gives two possibilities: either the title came out of this change and was subsequent to it, or else the change and the title were both the work of the evangelist and he deliberately gave the book its pseudonymous heading.

I ought to remind you that Mark has after Αλφαίου the words καθήμενον ἐπὶ τὸ τελώνιον, but Matthew has in full ἄνθρωπον καθήμενον ἐπὶ τὸ τελώνιον Μαθθαῖον λεγόμενον (Matt. 9.9). In other words the customs officer is called in Mark, Levi or Levin, the son of Alphaeus, but in Matthew he is called Matthew.

In the discussion in my book I had assumed that Matthew and Luke used our Mark and proceeded to make certain inferences about the ascription of the Gospel to Matthew. I had also assumed that the text at Mark 2.14; 3.18 was in order, i.e. that at 2.14 we read Λευιν and not Ἰάκωβον and at 3.18 Θαδδαῖον and not Λεββαῖον.

Assumptions are now challenged and in the light of such challenges we must look again at our question: why has Mark Λευιν τὸν τοῦ Ἀλφαίου where Matthew has Μαθθαῖον? We may be reminded that Luke has τελώνην ὀνόματι Λευιν καθήμενον ἐπὶ τὸ τελώνιον (5.27), but this still leaves us with our question: why has Matthew Μαθθαῖον where Mark and Luke have Λευιν?

We may suppose, instead of my assumption, that Mark used Matthew or that Luke used Matthew and Mark used Luke, but those who make such assumptions have to explain how Matthew's Ματθαῖον has become Λευιν in Mark and Luke. We can imagine explanations; for example, that the other evangelists took Matthew's text as indicating the authorship of Matthew and regarded such an indication as highly improper. I am sure that the opponents of the priority of Mark can do better than that, but the important question now is: how can the change be explained? In any attempt to answer this question we must try to find out what each Gospel tells us about itself and its author. I hope to point you to one body of material which bears on this question.

Professor Farmer has reminded us in his paper of some problems faced by earlier Oxford scholars in dealing with the problem of Gospel origins, and of what we might learn from them. My solution, you will see, is a little different from Professor Farmer's. I must plead in explanation of some of the differences that, when I wrote my paper, I did not know precisely what Professor Farmer was to say.

Those who were present at the Griesbach Colloquium at Münster in 1976 may recall that one of the speakers said that linguistic criteria had nothing to contribute to textual criticism. Considerable dissent from this opinion was expressed at the Colloquium itself and I repeat this dissent here, for I shall argue that linguistic considerations are important and relevant.

Let me return to Oxford. The man most responsible for Oxford interest in the Synoptic problem was William Sanday, who gathered round him a group of scholars who worked on this problem in his seminar. From this there came an interim report, *Oxford Studies in the Synoptic Problem* (Oxford, 1911), J.C. Hawkins, *Horae Synopticae* (Oxford, 1909[2]), W.C. Allen, *St. Matthew* (Edinburgh, 1912[3]), B.H. Streeter, *The Four Gospels* (5th impr., London, 1936) and C.H. Turner's papers on Marcan usage and the like (*JTS* 25-29 [1924-28]).

It is W.C. Allen's *St. Matthew* that I particularly had in mind. We may infer from Plummer's courteous remarks in his preface to his book, *An Exegetical Commentary on St. Matthew's Gospel* (London, 1909, etc.), that some of Allen's contemporaries found his commentary hard going. Nonetheless to Allen let us go.

Allen's introduction has from our point of view two important items: (a) pp. xiv-xxxi linguistic changes; (b) pp. lxxxv-lxxxvii style and language. In mentioning these I am deliberately avoiding issues of order and of change in order, but, despite the speaker in Münster, I assume that in these matters language does count.

In *Studies in John Presented to Professor Dr. J.N. Sevenster* (Leiden, 1970) I had a paper, 'What John tells us about John' (pp. 75-87), in which I suggested that, if we followed various linguistic criteria, the New Testament writers fall into three classes: (1) the lowest, Mark, John, Revelation, the Pastorals, (2) the middle group, writers such as Matthew, James, 1 Peter, Ephesians, (3) the top group, Luke, Acts, Paul, Hebrews. Later I found that this classification was confirmed in Moulton and Howard, *A Grammer of New Testament Greek*, vol. II, *Accidence and Word-formation*, Part 1 (1919), pp. 1-34.

This opinion may be taken as part of the answer to the question: What does Matthew tell us about Matthew? Relevant to this is a second question: What does Mark tell us about Mark? Next we have to compare the two answers and try to elicit what the comparison may tell us about the relation of Mark and Matthew.

I say, 'part of the answer', because I suggest in my book, treating of financial matters: 'These details together point to a community of greater wealth, accustomed to a much wider financial range than in Mark' (p. 125). More generally Matthew seems to have a greater affinity to city life.

If we may put together the linguistic implications, the suggestions of a wider financial range and the affinity to city life, we have a picture of a much higher level for Matthew and a clearly lower one for Mark. It was on the old hypothesis easier to explain this difference. Mark to a large degree represented a more primitive form of the tradition, but in Matthew we have a rewriting of this in an upward direction. I cannot say that the reverse development, the depraving of features of a tradition in such a way that Mark could derive from Matthew is impossible, but defenders of such a derivation should show that it is not only possible but probable.

It appears that recent discussions of the Synoptic Problem have not looked much at evidence of this kind. We have at this Conference heard two papers which are concerned with the implications of order in the study of the Gospels. Fair enough, but not quite enough. We must try to see what each Gospel tells us about itself and its author, and in this attempt, to study the order of events has its place, but we must look at a wider range of evidence.

It is here that the Oxford school of which I spoke earlier has its importance. It was prepared to look more widely, and particularly to look at the evidence of language. C.H. Turner, in his *Studies*, examined characteristics of Mark's style and the way in which they were treated in Matthew and Luke. Quite clearly these *Studies* argued from the assumption of Mark's priority. In the light of that assumption, he proceeded to state an opinion that the handling of such characteristics in Matthew and Luke had the following purposes: (1) to reduce the excessive use of certain linguistic traits and (2) to improve the style.

We may illustrate this from the use of εὐθέως—εὐθύς, a detail barely mentioned by Turner (*JTS* 28 [1927], p. 153). This word, however we spell it, appears in Mark 42 times, in Matthew 19, Luke 7 and John 6. If we examine the passages in a full textual apparatus, we shall find that sometimes some witnesses avoid the word. For example, Mark 9.8 in the printed texts reads ἐξάπινα, a word which recurs in early Christian literature only once again in the Shepherd of Hermas, but εὐθέως is read in Mark instead by D Θ 0131 28 69 565 *al.* We may suppose that εὐθέως is right here and that ἐξάπινα has no place in Mark's vocabulary (L. Rydbeck, *Fachprosa, Vermeintliche Volkssprache und Neues Testament* [Uppsala, 1967], pp. 167-76).

Allowing for such variation we have to ask: If Mark is secondary, why is there this variation? Why has Mark increased his use of the word? Turner assumed that Matthew altered Mark and, in this instance, may have supposed that Matthew cut down Mark's excessive use of the word.

Another example is instructive. Turner (*JTS* 28 [1927], pp. 20f.) argued that Mark used οὖν rarely if at all. Mark appears to have οὖν 4 times, Matthew some 57 and Luke 31 times. Why is this so? Turner of course argued that Matthew and Luke intruded οὖν into passages taken over from Mark, but if we are not allowed to do this how do we explain the rareness of the particle in Mark?

Turner's treatment of οὖν is part of his discussion of asyndeton and particles in Mark. We may define it more precisely and develop it in certain directions.

First we may look at the history of the language. In Homer and the Attic writers there is a wealth of particles which cannot come first in their clause or sentence (see J.D. Denniston, *Greek Particles* [Oxford, 1959²]). Already in the New Testament these words are on the way out. We may instance τε, δή, γε. Except for one usage which may be of Semitic origin, δή occurs only at Heb. 2.16. Except for Acts and Hebrews τε is very rare. In the end even δέ dropped out of use and we can see early signs of this in Mark. On the other hand the connectives that come first in their clauses or sentences are retained. καί, which is heavily overworked, ἀλλά, ὅτι (= γάρ) can come first in their clauses and survive. Consequently it is not surprising that when we take the relative shortness of Mark into account, it surpasses Luke and Matthew in its use of ἀλλά (Mark 45; Matt. 37; Luke 36).

We may note that quite apart from Mark, the particles at risk survive more frequently in the top group of New Testament writers in contrast to the bottom group. This is characteristic of language in general. Literary Latin of Cicero's day was more conservative than spoken, or non-literary Latin. The same is true for English today as for Hellenistic Greek. Literate Greek reflected tendencies in the language earlier than literary Greek as we can see from the papyri.

In this way Turner's case was stronger than he recognized.

In another direction Turner can be supplemented. In *JTS* 28 (1927), pp. 15-19 he discussed asyndeton without showing awareness that the Greeks had a doctrine for asyndeton (e.g. Demetrius, *On Style* §§ 191-196). Asyndeton gave weight and punch to a style, but could lead to obscurity and ambiguity. Philo certainly showed himself aware of the doctrine (*Quis Rerum* § 198). If this is relevant, we may question Turner's omission of καί at Mark 1.22, his reading at 1.27; 3.35; 10.28; 13.8, 23; 14.3.

This points to a widespread oversight. The Greeks of the first and second centuries AD had a considerable number of books on style and language, especially on vocabulary. It is customary to ignore this literature, as can be seen from the pronouncements on style and the like in Metzger, *A Textual Commentary on the Greek New Testament* (London–New York, 1971). Only by consulting the ancient handbooks can we arrive at an opinion on many matters of style. On others again the history of the language can, as we have seen, throw light. For some things we are left to our own devices. For example, I suspect that scribes did not like the neuter interrogative τί applied to persons. If this is true, we shall find it easier to understand the variations at John 1.21. This however is said subject to correction. At any moment a passage in an ancient author may put us to rights.

The consequences of using this evidence may be unexpected. For instance Mark 10.25, Matt. 19.24 have ῥαφίδος, 'of a needle', but Luke 18.25 has, according to most printed editions, βελόνης with the same meaning. A common view is that ῥαφίδος has been altered to βελόνης by the evangelist: see H.J. Cadbury, *The Style and Literary Method of Luke* (Cambridge, Mass., 1920), pp. 186f. There is in Luke a variation, βελόνης ℵ B D L Φ 157 579 1241 *al*, ῥαφίδος A W Γ Δ

'Ω. Are we to regard βελόνης as the evangelist's stylistic improvement on Mark or as a scribe's stylistic improvement on Luke's ῥαφίδος? Phrynichias 72 is quite clear: βελόνη belongs to the old language, but no one would know what ῥαφίς is.

In general we can go through the New Testament and find variations where one reading is condemned by the ancient authors and the alternative is approved (see my 'Atticism and the Text of the Greek New Testament', in *Neutestamentliche Aufsätze* [Festschrift für J. Schmid: Regensburg, 1963], pp. 125-37). Using this and other evidence we can infer that Matthew and Mark, for example, were writing on different levels of style, and that any view of the relation between these two Gospels must take this into account.

Not everyone sees the matter in this light. G.D. Fee has clearly presented his view on modern textual criticism (e.g. his essay, 'Modern Text Criticism and the Synoptic Problem', in *Griesbach Studies 1776–1976*, ed. B. Orchard & T.R.W. Longstaff [Cambridge, 1979], pp. 154-69). In discussing the variation between ἔφη and the formula ἀποκριθεὶς εἶπεν and the like, he writes:

> The best explanation of all these data, and of the multiple variation in this passage, is *not* the Atticizing of Mark's text, but rather its harmonization either to Mark's more common idiom or to its Synoptic parallel (less likely). If this is so, then either Luke Semitizes Mark or Mark Atticizes Luke! (p. 167).

This fails to note the fact that there is no certain example of ἔφη in Mark, and until a firm example is produced from Mark we cannot speak with any confidence of Luke Semiticizing Mark or of Mark Atticizing Luke in this instance.

Two questions are involved here: first, How far did Mark atticize? secondly, How far did scribes introduce Semitic features into their texts?

About Mark it still has to be shown that he rewrote his text bringing in Attic features. We may suggest this as an alternative explanation of some phenomena, but as far as I can see it is in no way demonstrable.

Secondly, how far did scribes introduce Semitic features into this text? I had said that 'No Greek at any period left to himself would say or write ἀποκριθεὶς εἶπεν' ('Atticism', p. 126). Fee quotes this and then goes on to urge that 'the Greek Fathers were *not* "left to themselves"' ('Rigorous or Reasoned Eclecticism—Which?', in J.K. Elliott [ed.], *Studies in New Testament Language and Text* [Leiden,

1976], p. 191). This is quite true and not only for the Greek Fathers. Lucifer of Caliaris wrote a Ciceronian Latin, but at one point he wrote to the Emperor Constantius: *uidens, uidebis*, 'thou shalt verily see', and we can guess how he came to this.

Fee at the same point notices that Chrysostom twice gives ἀπεκρίθη ὁ ἀσθενὴς καὶ εἶπε or ἀπεκρίθη αὐτῷ καὶ λέγει for John 5.7 'against all known witnesses'. But *L* b has *respondit illi infirmus et dixit* while *L* l has . . . *et ait*. If we look up the passage in Horner, *Sahidic New Testament*, III, pp. 66f., we will find some oriental evidence to support the longer text. I would not be surprised, if I had access to fuller collections of evidence, to find other witnesses to such a reading; cf. G. Messina, *Diatessaron Persiano* (Rome, 1951), p. 165.

In addition Chrysostom quotes as John 8.13 ἀπεκρίθησαν καὶ εἶπον αὐτῷ (*Griesbach Studies*, p. 218). Here at present I have no supplementary evidence, but that does not mean that it does not exist. It would be valuable to hear Père Boismard on this matter. We have also to ask ourselves: How were the homilies on John transmitted? We know that the homilies on Acts were revised, but by good fortune we have an unrevised text of these homilies as well, apparently taken down *verbatim* by shorthand. If the homilies on John were taken down in this way, we would not be surprised if the preacher confused the beginning of v. 13 with the beginning of v. 14, ἀπεκρίθη ὁ Ἰησοῦς καὶ εἶπεν αὐτοῖς. It is surprising what extempore preachers can do on occasion.

Fee is quite right about witnesses not being always 'left to themselves'. We may suspect that in the Biblical codices the LXX has influenced the NT, for example in the spelling οὐθείς, μηθείς, etc., where we may be persuaded that the NT originally had οὐδείς, etc. We may also suspect that nearly all the NT examples of ὡσεί as distinct from ὡς came from the LXX.

None the less, when all is said and done, Fee has still to produce a firm example of ἔφη in Mark. He may want to conclude that ἔφη is Marcan, but he has not produced a proof.

Secondly, how far did scribes introduce Semitic features into their text? We may suppose that some of the NT authors knew a Semitic language, but how many of their scribes subsequently did? It is at least debatable whether even a scholar like Origen knew Hebrew.

Two substitutes for a knowledge of a Semitic language may be suggested. First, the LXX often presents a Greek which has the impress of Semitic idiom, and we may suspect that Luke–Acts for example owes much to the LXX wherever we detect a Semitic background. As we have seen, such imitation does occur, but how far can we point to it as the dominant influence in the textual variation in the second century? Later, Lucifer of Caliaris, as we have seen, addressed an echo of Biblical idiom to the emperor, but normally he was content to write to him in Ciceronian Latin.

This brings us to our next point. From the Flavian emperors onward, if not before, we can discern a fashion in style. I have already called attention to the ancient literature in this subject, but we may note of Lucifer, for example, that, while he writes a Ciceronian Latin, the ordinary Latin of his day was far from Ciceronian. The same was true of second-century Greek. The Apologists are already writing a Greek much nearer to literary fashion. We may, indeed, believe that here and there in the Acts of the Apostles the return to Attic Greek has left its mark. The more the early church moved into the educated, as distinct from the merely literate world, the more its writings, including the Greek Bible, would be influenced in their text by the prevailing literary fashion.

This enables us to consider another argument. Fee says 'The fact that P^{66} (almost alone) conforms to the more characteristically Johannine idiom at two places indicates that even in the second century the tendency to "conform" is at least as great as any tendency to "Atticize", as far as this idiom is concerned' ('Rigorous or Reasoned Eclecticism—Which?', p. 91). We may question this. That a scribe may assimilate one passage to a similar passage in the same book is not inconceivable, though it may not be the true explanation of a similarity in text among certain witnesses, but we question if there was any tendency to 'conform' comparable to the tendency to 'Atticize'. On the contrary we have to reckon with the possibility that the tendency was the other way. Acts shows frequent repetitions, and some readings can be explained as attempts to eliminate or mitigate these features. To this extent we may speak of a nonconformist tendency of scribes.

Let me give an example: Acts 1.10-11 has four examples of the phrase εἰς τὸν οὐρανόν. One of these, the second occurrence in v. 11, is omitted by a number of witnesses. Some scholars have argued that the shorter text here is right, but with four instances in two verses it would be more in keeping with stylistic tendencies for a copyist to cut down the incidence of this phrase.

Fee is concerned to show that internal evidence is secondary to external in the treatment of the NT text, e.g. considerations of language and style must be subordinated to manuscript attestation. We can be led to think that some ancient witnesses are knaves or fools and that knaves and fools cannot be right.

We may think of two recent Synopses, Huck–Greeven and Orchard, as differing in some points in their conception, but we must recognize that in their Gospel text they both find internal considerations decisive. I suggest that they are right in doing so and represent a long tradition including such figures as F.C. Burkitt, W. Sanday, W.C. Allen, C.H. Turner, H. Lietzmann and J. Wellhausen.

This consideration leads me back to the view that in our problems style counts. We cannot enter on NT textual criticism by asserting that such considerations as style and language do not matter.

This leaves us with our principal contention. The study of the language and style of the Gospels suggests that they are properly put on different levels of style. I am not now contending that this conclusion leads to this or that view of Gospel origins, but I do find a tacit agreement that the different levels that we can detect in the several Gospels have nothing to say to the enquiry into Gospel origins.

THE EVIDENCE OF PAPIAS
FOR THE PRIORITY OF MATTHEW

Anthony Meredith SJ

Campion Hall, Oxford

The central purpose of this essay is to examine the external evidence for the priority of Matthew; and as the main evidence of this type is arguably, though not I suspect demonstrably, to be found in the fragments of Papias largely preserved in Eusebius, something must be said about the reliability as distinct from the exact import of the evidence he provides. It has become the fashion to decry Papias himself and consequently the evidence which comes from him by means of an argument that can be reduced to syllogistic form somewhat as follows.

(i) All the available external evidence for the independence and priority of Matthew is derived from Papias.

(ii) But Papias was a 'pinhead' as well as a 'bottle neck'. (For this minor Eusebius's words at *H.E.* 3.39.13 are taken as conclusive evidence.)

(iii) Therefore we can afford to disregard all the external evidence in favour of Matthaean priority.

If (iii) follows logically from a combination of (i) and (ii) then all we need to do to establish it is to prove both of them. As to (i) it seems to be fairly clear that most of the Fathers from Irenaeus onwards accept the priority of Matthew on the basis of what at times appears to be an oversimplification of Papias. This is especially true of the assertion that Matthew wrote in Hebrew, for where Papias says that Matthew was written in the Hebrew dialect, which could mean in a Hebrew style—Old Testament prophecies and Hebraisms are more common with him than with other evangelists—Irenaeus (*Adv. H.* 3.1.2) says quite simply; 'Ita Matthaeus in Hebraeis ipsorum lingua scripturam edidit Evangelii' (cf. Harvey, *Irenaeus*, II, p. 3 n. 1). It does indeed seem in principle possible that the Matthaean priority arguably implied by both Justin at *Trypho* 106.3 and by Clement of

Alexandria in Eusebius *H.E.* 6.14.5 derives from a source independent of Papias. But for the purpose of the argument I shall assume that it is from Papias above all that the main external evidence derives.

It is worth, however, noting at this point that, for whatever reason, the early Fathers betray a marked preference for Matthew and a distinct lack of interest in Mark. This point is well illustrated by a few statistics, largely dependent on the list of quotations collected at the back of most modern editions. So, for example, the first and second *Apologies* of Justin account in Blunt's index for 47 direct quotations from Matthew, 8 from Mark, 23 from Luke and 1 from John. Ignatius has 6 from Matthew, 1 from Luke, 4 from John and none at all from Mark. An overall count from Justin, Irenaeus (*Adv. Haereses*), Theophilus, Athenagoras (*Legatio*) and Clement of Alexandria (*Protrepticus*) yields the following interesting results: Matthew 335, Mark c. 50, Luke 232, John 120. In the second century Matthew was the most and Mark the least used of the gospels. This general preference for the first gospel is borne out by the state of Patristic commentaries on the New Testament. Whereas from Origen onwards and in unorthodox circles perhaps earlier, commentaries on Matthew and John abound, only ten homilies on Mark survive from Jerome and we have to wait for Bede in the eighth century for a full length Latin commentary on the second gospel and for Theophylact in the eleventh for a full length Greek commentary. These facts by themselves indicate a remarkable shift of emphasis and interest from the early church to our own day. I would not, however, wish to argue from this fact that Matthew is primary. Rather the opposite. As was pointed out to me by Fr Barnabas Lindars, if Matthew had in fact preexisted Mark and became subsequently so popular it would hardly have been necessary for Mark to appear at all.

I now turn to (ii), 'that Papias was a pinhead', a view for which evidence is supposed to be provided both by the actual evidence of what he wrote, in this case very little, and by the hostile notice in Eusebius which I have already referred to and to which I now turn. At first sight the words seem clear and damning enough and indeed are not infrequently quoted in order to discredit Papias. But how much weight should be placed upon them? I should put on record at this point my indebtedness to two articles by Johannes Munck, 'Presbyters and Disciples of the Lord' in *HTR* 52 (1959), pp. 223-43, and 'Die Tradition über das Matthäusevangelium bei Papias', in *Neotestamentica et Patristica* (Freundesgabe O. Cullmann; Leiden,

1962), pp. 249ff. He begins by calling into question the impartiality of Eusebius as a historian. There is one particular case of absence of impartiality which I hope now to illustrate.

Eusebius says a certain amount, not much (for reasons which will soon become clear), about Tertullian. The main references occur in *H.E.* 2.2.4 and 3.33.3. In the former passage he writes: 'These facts [sc. about Pilate and Tiberius] were noted by Tertullian, an expert in Roman law and famous on other grounds—in fact one of the most brilliant men in Rome [*sic*]'. This is followed by a quotation from *Apol.* 5. The second passage is again largely concerned with a quotation from *Apol.* 2.6 and deals with Trajan's attitude to the Bithynian Christians, recorded in Pliny *Ep.* 10.96. On one other occasion in *H.E.* Eusebius quotes from Tertullian's *Apol.* 5 again, in *H.E.* 5.5, the famous case of the Thundering Legion, which according to Eusebius and Tertullian secured a shower of rain as a result of their prayers. Eusebius capitalizes on this phenomenon because of its witness to the power of prayer and also because it shows the Christians as willing both to fight and to pray for the empire. And for this purpose he finds the witness of Tertullian of all people of use. Clearly Eusebius is very selective in his treatment of Tertullian. (i) There are few other places in his writings where Tertullian shows himself favourable to the Roman authorities. On the contrary he shows himself determined on a course of radical secularization of the secular. This attitude is explicit in *De Spectaculis* and even more in *De Corona Militis*, strangely at variance with the tone of *Apol.* 30; 32; 39. It is doubtless arguable that Eusebius knew nothing of Tertullian's later life and writings, though I find it hard to believe that he, one of the most learned men of his time, knew nothing about Tertullian's later vitriolic outbursts. (ii) Connected with the above it might be noted that although Eusebius treats of the growth and refutation of Phrygian Montanism (cf. esp. *H.E.* 5.14-16), he *nowhere* connects the name of Tertullian with the movement. Again it may be the case that Eusebius knew nothing of this behaviour on Tertullian's part; or, as some scholars have suggested, Tertullian was merely an advocate of Montanism and not actually a member. I prefer to believe that Eusebius had his own reasons for failing to make the connection; but these will become apparent when some more evidence has been reviewed.[1]

I now pass to the case of Hippolytus. Of him Eusebius writes in *H.E.* 6.22: 'At the same period [sc. the beginning of the third century] Hippolytus, author of many other short works, composed the essay *The Easter Festival*, in which he works out a system of dates for the sixteen-year cycle of Easter ...' Eusebius then mentions other of Hippolytus's writings including the *Answer to all the Heresies*. He omits to mention, however, the fact that Hippolytus had been a rival and bitter critic of the bishops of Rome and that he composed what is now called *The Apostolic Tradition*. What, however, for my purposes is even more revealing of Eusebius's methods is the final sentence of the paragraph: 'Many others are probably to be found in various private collections'. Are we to assume that Eusebius knew nothing at all of the two works *De Antichristo* and *Comm. in Dan.*? Perhaps so. But it is not without interest that in *Comm. in Dan.* 4.9,[2] Hippolytus argues that the kingdom of Christ is counterfeited by the Roman Empire, and implies a sharp contrast between the earthly and heavenly kingdom. In the next section of the same work Hippolytus is discussing the interpretation of Daniel 7.17: 'These four great beasts are the four kings who shall rise out of the earth. But the saints of the most high shall receive the kingdom, and possess the kingdom for ever, for ever and ever.' Hippolytus's interpretation of this text is as follows. The fourth king is the Roman Empire and its arrival is the sign of the end, not as fulfilling the word of God as his last message, but rather as heralding the advent of the heavenly kingdom and the eternal king. He will arrive with great power and majesty, more splendid than he was on Mt Sinai and a fortiori than at the Incarnation. Then he will destroy all the kingdoms of the earth. This tradition of the identification of Regnum Caesaris and Regnum Diaboli, abhorrent though it was to the mentality of Eusebius, found a later supporter, though probably an unconscious one, in St Augustine, who opens the fourth chapter of *De Civ. Dei* IV with the words 'Remota igitur iustitia quid sunt regna nisi magna latrocinia?'

Interestingly and perhaps significantly Eusebius follows his treatment of the literary heritage of Hippolytus with a much lengthier account of Origen. That Origen was something of a hero for Eusebius is quite clear both from the internal evidence of *H.E.* and from what we know of Eusebius's intellectual ancestry. Book 6 opens with a lengthy account of Origen's life; cf. esp. 1–3, 8, 15, 16); chs. 23–25 say something of Origen's labours on scripture; ch. 32 deals with commentaries written by Origen at Caesarea and ch. 36 with other works written by Origen, including the *Contra Celsum*. Eusebius himself is described as *Eusebius Pamphili* and Pamphilus himself was a devoted pupil of Origen, writing a defence of him not long after his death. And Eusebius refers to a defence in at least six books he himself wrote of Origen (*H.E.* 6.36). Eusebius inherited the passion for learning, if not the theological acumen and profundity of his master; and some of the more distinctive theological positions of Origen became canonical for Eusebius.

An interesting remark by Charles on p. clxxxiv of his introduction to his masterly commentary on the book of the Apocalypse is not without significance. He is discussing the chiliastic interpretation of the work and writes: 'But the prophecy of the Millennium in ch. xx. must be taken literally, as it was by Justin Martyr, Irenaeus, Victorinus of Pettau. These writers were acquainted with the original interpretation of this chapter. But this interpretation was soon displaced by the spiritualizing interpretation of Alexandria.' Clement probably wrote some sort of (lost) commentary on the Apocalypse (cf. *H.E.* 6.14.1) and Origen projected but never actually wrote one (cf. *In Matt.* 49). But though he never produced a full-scale commentary it is not hard to guess at its lines. First of all it seems clear that Origen went against the prevailing tradition set up by Justin and Irenaeus, who both believed in the Millennium. For Justin, cf. *Trypho* 80 and 81, in the latter chapter especially the prophecy from Isa. 65.17-25 which begins, 'For behold I create a new heaven and a new earth'. This is held to be fulfilled by Rev. 20.4-6 which contains the words, 'They came to life again and reigned with Christ for a thousand years'. Justin adds to the NT witnesses to the fulfilment of Isaiah Luke 20.35-36, 'those who are accounted worthy to attain to that age and to the resurrection from the dead neither marry nor are given in marriage'. Justin in making this connection seems to identify the resurrection with the promised Millennium. It should also be noted that Justin has little hesitation in assigning the authorship of the Apocalypse to the Apostle John. Irenaeus[3] likewise, in *Adv. Haer.* 5.35, rejects the allegorical interpretation given by the Gnostics to the same Isaiah passage, which he also quotes in full in 5.34.4. 'Si autem quidam tentaverint allegorizare haec quae eiusmodi sunt', he begins in ch. 35, they are shown to be inconsistent and dishonest. Irenaeus then offers his interpretation with the help of Rev. 20 and 21.

Origen will have none of this. Apart from a slighting reference to the Millennium in *De Or.* 27.13, he goes out of his way in *De Princ.* 2.3.7[4] and 4.1.22 (cf. also 2.11.2[5] and *C. Cels.* 6.20[6] and 7.28-31[7]) to

insist on the heavenly as distinct from the earthly blessedness that
those who obey God will receive. More revealing, however, even than
his spiritualizing attitude to the Apocalypse is his exegesis of Romans
13.1, 'Let every soul be subject to the governing authorities. For
there is no authority except from God, and those that exist have been
instituted by God.' Origen's exegesis of this passage may be found in
his *In Rom. Comm.* 9.26.4 (= *P.G.* 14.1227a). There he faces the
objection of how the existence of persecuting emperors can be fitted
into such a vision. In reply he compares this abuse of power to the
abuse of the eyes, which can be used for good or evil: 'Ita ergo et
potestas omnis a deo data est ad vindictam quidem malorum, laudem
vero bonorum'. Origen is clearly of the opinion that whatever the use
made of power by the state the state is of divine institution. This was
a view that the whole outlook of Eusebius willingly endorsed. As
Charles Cochrane notes in *Christianity and Classical Culture* (Oxford,
1940), p. 184, 'To Eusebius the glorious and unexpected triumph of
the Church constituted decisive evidence of the *operatio Dei*, the
hand of God in human history'.

If Origen was a hero of Eusebius, Dionysius, bishop of Alexandria
from c. 247 to 264, himself a pupil of Origen, was even more so. He
had the added advantage from Eusebius's point of view of being a
bishop. To begin with, the actual space devoted to him by Eusebius is
large: see *H.E.* 6.40-42; 7.1-11, 20-26. Book 7, which opens with an
acknowledgment by Eusebius of his debt to Dionysius records a
letter in which he refers to the foolishness of the emperor Gallus
(251-253) who 'drove away the holy men who were praying to God to
grant him peace and health'. This is a reference, though probably not
the earliest, to prayers from the church for the good estate of the
ruler. But, of course, the really important point in Eusebius's
treatment of Dionysius is the attitude adopted by Dionysius to the
Apocalypse and its author. This is dealt with above all in *H.E.* 7.25.
The chapter begins with a long extract from Dionysius which refers
to the low esteem in which the Apocalypse was held because of the
literal exegesis it was given. So much so that some denied that the
work was of Apostolic origin at all, claiming that it was merely the
product of Cerinthus, who tried by assuming a respectable name to
recommend his own detestable doctrines. Eusebius sums up the drift
of Dionysius's argument: after examining the whole book of the
Revelation and proving the impossibility of understanding it in the
literal sense, he goes on: 'That he was John and that this work is

John's, I shall not therefore deny, for I agree that it is from the pen of a holy and inspired writer. But I am not prepared to admit that he was the apostle, the son of Zebedee and the brother of James.' Largely on the grounds of style, but partly, one suspects, on ideological grounds, Dionysius attributes the Apocalypse to another John. His evidence in favour of there having been two Johns is odd. 'I think there was another John among the Christians of Asia, as there are said to have been two tombs at Ephesus, each reputed to be John's.' This piece of evidence clearly had a considerable influence on Eusebius who quotes it again almost verbatim in *H.E.* 3.39.6. Eusebius was a stalwart and arguably uncritical supporter of the following two Dionysian propositions. (i) The book of the Apocalypse is not to be understood literally; (ii) The apostle John was not its author.

Eusebius's attitude, aside from what we may think of his treatment of Papias, should by now be fairly clear. It is marked above all by an enthusiasm for Constantine and the Constantinian settlement which gave him, to say the least, a reserve to those elements in the Christian tradition which threatened to alienate Christianity from civil society. The finale of the tenth book of *H.E.*, presumably written before 326 when the emperor's son Crispus met an untimely end, deserves quoting as an illustration of his devotion to the cause of what can only be called Caesaropapalism.

> His adversary [sc. Licinius at the battle of Chrysopolis in 324] thus finally thrown down, the mighty victor Constantine, preeminent in every virtue that true religion can confer, with his son Crispus, an emperor most dear to God and in every way resembling his father, won back their own eastern lands and reunited the Roman empire into a single whole, bringing it all under their peaceful sway, in a wide circle embracing north and south alike from east to farthest west.

Then after an almost lyrical description of the blessings enjoyed under the new regime, Eusebius ends his great work as follows:

> They having made it their task to wipe the world clean of all hatred of God, rejoice in the blessings that he had conferred upon them, and by the things they did for all men to see, displayed love of virtue, love of God, devotion and thankfulness to the almighty.

Constantine's own view of the importance of the church for the well-being of the state is hardly less pronounced, though he uses phrases that were at least patient of a purely deist interpretation. This is particularly clear from Eusebius's *Vita Constantini* 2.24 which links together the well-being of the state with due reverence for 'God, who is the source of all'. Here we have the old Roman belief—barely if at all Christianized—that the fitting worship of the divine was a *sine qua non* for the good of the empire. What a contrast it all makes to that advocate of the complete and radical secularization of the temporal, Tertullian in his Montanist period (cf. *De Cor.* 12-13; *De Pud.* 21).

Eusebius's enthusiasm for Constantine is matched by a definite reserve towards both the Apocalypse and towards Millennarianism. Much of the evidence on both of these points has already been deployed, nor do I propose to repeat it. His own doubts, however, on the Johannine authorship of the Apocalypse are not hidden. In *H.E.* 3.24.18 he writes as follows: 'Of John's writings, beside the gospel, the first of the epistles has been accepted as unquestionably his by scholars both of the present and of a much earlier period: the other two being disputed. As to the Revelation, the views of almost all people to this day are evenly divided. At the appropriate moment, the evidence of early writers shall clear up this matter too.' Unfortunately the moment did not arrive in the work as we have it, nor anywhere else. A like reserve is clear from *H.E.* 3.25.4: 'Among spurious books must be placed the "Acts of Paul", the "Shepherd", and the "Revelation of Peter"; also the alleged "Epistle of Barnabas" and the "Teachings of the Apostles", together with the Revelation of John, if this seems the right place for it: as I said before, some reject it, others include it among the recognized books'. From these two extracts it appears that there was a tradition in the early fourth century both of the non-Apostolic authorship and of the non-canonicity of the Apocalypse.

I started this paper with a question about the reliability of Papias and it has turned into one about the reliability of Eusebius. I have tried to lay bare some of the preconceptions and biases of Eusebius with a view to assessing his evidence about Papias. I have tried to show that for various reasons it was in Eusebius's interest to discredit the chiliastic tradition within the Church and to separate the apostle John from anything to do with the Apocalypse. Papias was clearly an important link in the chain that connected chiliasm with the earliest traditions in the church. Against Papias's claim that he derived his views from the Apostles themselves—a suggestion by no means improbable, a priori—Eusebius says that Papias got it all wrong. He thought he heard the Apostle John, whereas in fact all he heard was John the Presbyter, who was quite another person—a view which he believed to be endorsed by the statement of Dionysius already referred to. It is Papias's reference to chiliasm in section 12 that Eusebius finds most unpalatable:

> He says that after the resurrection of the dead there will be a period of a thousand years, when Christ's kingdom will be set up on earth in a material form. I suppose he got these notions by misinterpreting the apostolic accounts and failing to grasp what they had said in mystic and symbolic language. For he seems to have been a man of very small intelligence to judge from his books. But it is partly due to him that the great majority of churchmen after him took the same view, relying on his early date; e.g. Irenaeus and several others who clearly held the same opinion.

Here we have in Eusebius's own words precisely the form of the syllogism with which this paper began. The only difference is that whereas modern scholars like Caird and others use the words of Eusebius to discredit the inferences drawn from Papias's words about the priority of the λόγια of Matthew, Eusebius on the other hand was arguing for a slightly different point, i.e. the discrediting of Papias's views about chiliasm.

I have implied or more than implied in the above argument that not all that Eusebius has to say on the subject of Papias need be taken at its face value. Valuable though he is as an historian, he is also a propagandist. In his efforts to portray the empire as God's work on earth and as reaching its culmination he could not afford to treat favourably those writers or writings which told a different story. Hence the silence on the Montanist writings of Tertullian and the apocalyptic strain in Hippolytus. Hence the fondness for the spiritualizing versions of the gospel to be had in Origen and Dionysius. Hence too the hostility to Papias. My conclusion is that to accept the superior dismissal by Eusebius of Papias as σφόδρα σμικρὸς ὢν τὸν νοῦν is to adopt a less than serious attitude to the historiographical problems that *H.E.* 3.39.12-17 raise.

NOTES

1. The silence of Eusebius on the martyrdoms of Perpetua and Felicity may also be worth remarking. Eusebius is not averse to martyrdom, witness

his treatment of the martyrs of Lyons in *H.E.* 5.1-3 and of Simeon, bishop of Jerusalem in 3.32. Perhaps he ignores Perpetua and Felicity out of ignorance (though their subsequent fame makes this hardly likely), perhaps because the whole tone of the martyrdom makes it clear that if they were not themselves Montanist, they had Montanist sympathies.

2. The date of Hippolytus's *In Dan.* is probably the early years of the 3rd century (202-204), at which time there was a strong outbreak of millennarian feeling, perhaps occasioned by the persecution of Severus. Bardy, in his introduction to the Sources Chrétiennes edition, suggests that it amounted almost to an obsession. Hippolytus, *In Dan.* 4.18-19, relates two incidents showing contemporary feeling, one of a bishop, not a Montanist, who led his flock into the desert near Jerusalem to await the end. At roughly the same date Tertullian in *Adv. Val.* 5 mentions a prophet who interpreted the 62 weeks of years of Dan. 9.25 as a reference to the disturbances of the year AD 202. This type of thinking is evidently regarded by Eusebius with some scorn, as witness his remarks at *H.E.* 6.7: 'At the same period Jude, another author, wrote a treatise on Daniel's 70 weeks [cf. Dan 9.23-24], bringing his account to an end in the 10th year of Severus [= 202-203]. He believed that the much talked-of advent of antichrist would take place at any moment—so completely had the persecution set in motion against us at that time thrown many off their balance!'

3. Despite his being a bishop and a firm believer in Apostolic succession and on the whole (cf. *H.E.* 5.8, 20) meriting Eusebius's approval, his millennarianism, attributed by Eusebius to the malign influence of Papias (*H.E.* 3.39) is dismissed with contempt. It is in this connection interesting to note that the last five chapters of *Adv. Haer.* 5 (chs. 32–36) were, as Harvey's note (Vol. II, p. 413 n. 5) reminds us, removed from all the exemplars except that of the Cod. Voss. of the late 14th century—a striking instance of the influence of theological prejudice on the writings of the Fathers.

4. *De Princ.* 2.3.7 identifies the 'caeli caelorum' with those who 'verbo dei obedientes fuerunt et sapientiae eius iam hic capaces se obtemperantesque praebuerunt'.

5. *De Princ.* 2.11.2 directly attacks those who offer a literal interpretation of those passages used by Irenaeus to justify an earthly millennium, esp. Isa. 60.10-12; 61.5; 65.13-14; Rev. 21.10-21. He says of them: 'laborem intelligentiae recusantes et superficiem quandam legis litterae consectantes', they arrive at an earthly conception of the end. Israel, Judaea, even Jesus, are not to be understood 'carnaliter' but 'mysteria quaedam divina significant'.

6. *C. Cels.* 7.29 gives to the notion of Jerusalem an entirely other-worldly sense, and uses Col. 3.1; Heb. 12.22.

7. *C. Cels.* 6.20 sees the future with the help of 2 Cor. 4.17-18; Jn 7.38 and Ps. 148.4-5. He then rejects the notion of a physical heaven, even such as is to be found at *Phaedrus* 247c: οὐ περιαχθησόμεθα ἀπὸ τῆς τοῦ οὐρανοῦ περιφορᾶς, ἀεὶ δὲ πρὸς τῇ θέᾳ ἐσόμεθα τῶν ἀοράτων τοῦ θεοῦ.

ARGUMENTS FROM ORDER:
DEFINITION AND EVALUATION

C.M. Tuckett

Faculty of Theology
University of Manchester, Manchester M13 9PL

I

The virtual certainty of early twentieth-century scholarship that Mark came before Matthew and Luke rested very largely on the argument from order.[1]

Farmer's claim illustrates the important place which the phenomenon of order is believed to have in the study of the Synoptic problem. Before discussing arguments based on the order of events in the gospels one should define one's terms as far as possible. Such an exercise is useful in any discussion, but especially so in the present context. For study of the history of research into the Synoptic problem shows that there have been at least two arguments from order, and hence, before criticizing 'the argument from order', one must be quite clear which argument one is discussing.

It may be worthwhile to go one stage further and consider first whether it is possible to define the 'order' in question more precisely. At one level there is no problem: the sequence of the pericopes in each synoptic gospel is as well defined as the canonical text.[2] For all practical purposes this order is quite stable, and unaffected by any detailed disagreements between textual critics.[3] However, whilst the order of each gospel is a well-defined entity, it is by no means so clear that the *differences* in order between the gospels comprise so unambiguous a phenomenon and can be defined in a neutral way. Now it is quite clear that there can be, and are, better and worse attempts to give a neutral description of the phenomenon of order and of the pattern of agreement and disagreement in order between the gospels. One example of what could be called a 'worse' attempt would be Streeter's:

> Wherever Matthew departs from Mark's order Luke supports
> Mark, and whenever Luke departs from Mark, Matthew agrees
> with Mark.[4]

The sentence is clearly formulated under the presupposition of
Markan priority (MP) and can hardly be said to be an unbiased
statement of the facts.[5] Now in this case one might 'improve'
Streeter's formulation to produce a more impartial account of the
facts concerned: e.g.

> Whenever Matthew's order and Mark's order differ, Mark's order
> and Luke's order agree; and whenever Luke's order and Mark's
> order differ, Matthew's order and Mark's order agree.

This sentence does not, on its own, make any assumptions about
which gospel is prior. However, a closer analysis suggests that
differences in order may never be definable in a neutral way.
Certainly it does appear to be the case that any description of the
differences in order is not unique and this non-uniqueness goes far
deeper than simply the use of synonymous phraseology.

How does one define a disagreement in order? An agreement in
order is relatively easy to define: if two writers X and Y have two
units of tradition a and b, then if a precedes b in X and Y, there is
agreement in order. A disagreement is, at one level, a failure to agree,
i.e. if one writer has ab and the other has ba. But can one be more
precise beyond making the negative statement that there is a failure
to agree? Suppose X and Y have four pericopes a b c d in the order X:
a b c d, Y: a c b d. Clearly there is failure to agree in order. Further,
most would assume that a and d are in the same order in the two
texts. But which element, or elements, is, or are, out of order? There
are at least three ways of illustrating the parallels diagramatically:

(i)	(ii)	(iii)
X Y	X Y	X Y
a–a	a–a	a–a
b	c	b c
c–c	b–b	c b
b	c	d–d
d–d	d–d	

According to (i) b is out of order; according to (ii) c is out of order;
according to (iii) both b and c are out of order. At the purely formal
level there appears to be no way of claiming in absolute terms which

of these three is the most preferable way of describing the pattern of agreement and disagreement in order between X and Y. The way in which the parallels are initially set up inevitably affects in a significant way the description of the differences in order. A different scheme of parallelization produces a quite different set of non-parallels.[6]

This assertion thus runs counter to the general tenor of the article by Tyson[7] who claimed to be giving a totally neutral description of the phenomenon of order. However, his methodology is not totally convincing. He focusses attention solely on cases of what is called 'sequential parallelism', i.e. cases where two pericopes (using Aland's division) follow each other *immediately* in two gospels, and he enumerates all examples of this phenomenon in the three synoptic gospels. However the method is not wholly satisfactory for two reasons. First, it fails to allow for the possibility of added/deleted material leaving one pericope in a similar position in two gospels but not in sequential parallelism. For example, if X and Y have the following order of pericopes:

        X: a b c d f g
        Y: a b d e f g

most would argue that X and Y agree in their ordering of d. However, Tyson's method would only count sequential parallelism and thus would only include (ab) and (fg) as agreements in order. A concrete illustration of this is the parable of the mustard seed in Matt. 13.31-32 and Mark 4.30-32. Most would claim that Matthew and Mark agree in order here, yet Tyson's method fails to include the pericope as an agreement in order between Matthew and Mark.[8]

Let us, however, suppose a slightly different situation:

        X: a b c d f g e
        Y: a b d e f g

It is now debatable whether f and g are still in the same order in X and Y. (Is it e, or f and g, whose order has been altered?) Perhaps the situation would be clearer if we should have

        X: a b c d f g e
        Y: a b d e......f g

where the dots indicate a large separation between e and f g in Y. Most would argue here that the double unit (fg) has been moved as a whole by one writer. Yet in both these latter cases Tyson's method of quantifying the agreements in order would count both (ab) and (fg) as agreements between X and Y. This therefore leads to the second criticism of Tyson's method, viz. it does not allow for the possibility of one writer having changed the order of *two* sequential pericopes together.[9] A concrete illustration of this is the case of the parables of the mustard seed and the leaven in Matt. 13.31-33 and Luke 13.18-21. By Tyson's method this counts as an example of two pericopes in sequential parallelism; yet on almost any source hypothesis it is clear that one evangelist has changed the position of these two parables. It is therefore doubtful how satisfactory Tyson's method is for describing and quantifying the pattern of agreement and disagreement in order between the synoptic gospels.

The inherent ambiguity in any description of the disagreements in order gives some support to part of the claims made recently that any synopsis cannot really be neutral.[10] Whilst I am totally unconvinced that the way in which one assigns the gospels to the columns on the printed page affects things at all,[11] Orchard's claim that the decisions made regarding what is to be put parallel to what in a synopsis cannot be neutral does seem to be well founded. Whether these decisions are determined specifically by a presupposed solution to the Synoptic problem is perhaps more doubtful. For example, the arrangement in Huck's synopsis, and the decisions made about what to set in parallel, do not seem to be based on MP as such: rather the principle seems to be to maximize the amount of parallelization in the tradition.[12] It is arguable that Aland's synopsis is more dependent on an aspect of a solution to the Synoptic problem, viz. the Q hypothesis. For his arrangement appears to be seeking to maximize the parallelization in the order of the double tradition in Matthew and Luke. (However, his decision not to print the two great sermons, Matt. 5 - 7 and Luke 6.20ff., in parallel is rather strange.) Orchard's own arrangement of the material is self-confessedly based on his theories about Luke's redactional procedure in using Matthew.[13]

Thus although the 'order' of the pericopes in any one gospel can be precisely and uniquely defined, and whilst the existence of some agreement in order between the three gospels is clearly recognizable, the precise nature of the *dis*agreements in order (beyond the negative statement that they are failures to agree) cannot be uniquely specified. It will be important to bear this inherent indeterminacy in mind at various points in the following discussion.

II

What now is a/the 'argument from order'? In a recent article, Farmer stated that 'there are actually three arguments from order that have played an important role in the history of synoptic criticism'.[14] Since Farmer wrote, evidently a fourth should be added in view of the recent article by M. Lowe.[15] Perhaps one can deal with the latter first.

Lowe formulates the argument from order which he wishes to discuss as follows:

> It was claimed . . . that the observed coincidences of the orders of Matthew and Luke with the order of Mark suggest that the latter's gospel was the basis for the other two authors.[16]

However, this is quite unrelated to any argument based on the order of events in the gospels which has been used by previous scholars: the widespread agreement in order has never by itself been the sole basis for an argument about synoptic interrelationships. What has been used as a basis for argument has been the pattern of agreements *and disagreements* in order. Lowe constructs a complicated edifice of logical theory to show that the argument as he formulates it cannot prove MP, and is just as consistent with the claim of the Griesbach hypothesis (GH) about Mark, viz. Mark was the last gospel to be written and represents a conflation of Matthew and Luke. Further, he claims that any feature which 'contradicts' MP with regard to order does not necessarily 'contradict' the GH. Thus he concludes that the argument from order cannot prove MP against the GH's theories about Mark.

Lowe's logical theory is certainly correct in relation to the argument he has constructed. But the theory he seeks to question is simply a figment of his imagination. He seeks to discredit any proof from order that Matthew and Luke have always followed Mark's order. However, no one has ever suggested that Matthew and Luke did this. In at least one version of 'the argument from order', the argument has proceeded from observations about the ways in which Matthew's and Luke's orders *differ* from Mark's, i.e. from the fact that Matthew and Luke never agree with each other against Mark in order. The fact that Matthew and Luke do not both agree in toto with Mark's order has never been seen as a problem in itself for MP; certainly it has never been felt to 'contradict' MP. To use Lowe's own logical terms, this argument from order does not proceed from the abstract claim

If xMky, then xMty and xLky,[17]

but from the *observed* fact that, in the gospels,

If xMky, then xMty or xLky.[18]

Lowe's article is thus of little value to the contemporary debate since it is not related to any argument from order that has actually been used.

III

This leads on to the argument which, many have assumed, is 'the' argument from order to support MP. This is the argument which states that, given that there is no case in which Matthew and Luke agree in order against Mark, Mark's order must be the basis of the other two. Further, if one surrenders any idea of an Ur-gospel, the theory that Mark's order is basic swiftly becomes the theory that Mark's gospel is the basis for Matthew and Luke. It is this argument which has been dubbed the 'Lachmann fallacy', a description which appears to derive from the chapter in B.C. Butler's book where the argument was analysed.[19] Whether this is an apt description is perhaps debatable. Lachmann himself never committed the logical fallacy in question.[20] Further, one must be quite clear about what in fact is fallacious. The term 'fallacy' is perhaps a misleading one, for it suggests an illogical argument leading to a (patently) false conclusion. (Cf. mathematical 'fallacies' which 'prove' the patently false conclusion $0 = 1$.) Now it is universally recognized that Butler's analysis of the argument does not render it fallacious in the sense that the conclusion drawn, MP, is necessarily false. All that Butler showed was that, given the initial premiss in the argument, the conclusion was not unique: various other solutions would explain the facts equally well. Indeed any solution where Mark is in a 'medial' position in the tree of interrelationships satisfies the conditions. The false element in the conclusion lies in the claim that MP is the *only* possible solution.[21]

Whether anyone ever committed this logical 'fallacy' is in fact doubtful. It is very questionable whether any scholar in the past thought that this argument, in and of itself, 'proved' the priority of Mark to the exclusion of every other possibility.[22] Further, it is also very questionable how important this argument ever was in the establishing of the theory of MP.[23] But that is a matter of history.

Far more important for the contemporary debate has been the criticism brought against the argument by advocates of the GH. This claims that the failure of Matthew and Luke to agree in changing the order of any Markan pericope is too much of a coincidence to be credible. Farmer describes Streeter's statement of the facts as

> a tour de force, by which a serious problem for the Marcan hypothesis was converted into an argument in behalf of the priority of Mark.[24]

This he explains as follows:

> It is as if Matthew and Luke each knew what the other was doing, and that each had agreed to support Mark whenever the other departed from Mark . . . Since both frequently desert Mark, either by departing from his order or by omitting his material, and since neither knows what the other is doing, why do not their desertions of Mark coincide more frequently? . . . This fact of alternating support suggests some kind of conscious intention for which the Marcan hypothesis offers no ready explanation.[25]

Or, in more picturesque language, Dungan says that

> Just when Luke goes off into a special passage, there appears at Mark's side faithful Matthew, as if by magic, and just when Matthew suddenly departs on an errand of his own, in the nick of time back comes Luke, as if in response to a providential *bath qol*. How is it possible?[26]

Thus for these critics, it would appear that MP should expect *some* (but how much?) agreement between Matthew and Luke against Mark in order. (It is ironic that the occasions where Matthew and Luke do agree against Mark in wording, i.e. the minor agreements, are often fastened on by opponents of the two-document hypothesis (2DH) as the points where the theory is weakest. Yet in this case, the absence of such agreement is felt to be a problem. Within what limits should the number of Matthew–Luke agreements against Mark lie to be neither too high nor too low? Or is this a case of 'heads I win, tails you lose'?)

Now in the abstract this criticism of this argument from order might be compelling. However, the facts are less surprising when the actual texts themselves are considered. In fact it is not at all certain whether it is the case that Matthew and Luke never agree in rearranging the order of a Markan pericope. According to one perfectly plausible parallelling of pericopes, the parallels to Mark 3.13-19 (the call of the twelve) occur in different contexts in Matthew (10.2-4) and Luke (6.12-16).[27] There is thus at least one pericope where Matthew and Luke both rearrange Mark's order.[28] The coincidence whereby Matthew and Luke both avoid the other's changes of Mark is thus not quite so absolute as appears at first sight.

Even with this exception to the general rule, the failure of Matthew and Luke to agree in changing Mark's order is less surprising when the actual differences between the gospels are observed. The number of disagreements is relatively small. Thus Neirynck writes:

> Emphasis on the alternating support seems to imply that agree-
> ments and disagreements with the relative order of Mark are
> treated as comparable quantities. In fact, the disagreement against
> Mark is the exception and the absence of concurrence between
> Matthew and Luke is less surprising than the somewhat misleading
> formulation 'whenever the other departs' may suggest.[29]

If one restricts attention to strict changes in order of the same material (i.e. excluding the cases of replacement of a pericope by parallel material), then the number of changes made by Matthew and Luke, assuming MP, is relatively small. Luke changes the order of Mark 6.1-6 (// Luke 4.16-30), 1.16-20 (// Luke 5.1-11), 3.13-19 or 3.7-12 (// Luke 6.12-19) and 3.31-35 (// Luke 8.19-21).[30] Matthew, assuming one particular scheme of parallelization between Matthew and Mark,[31] changes the order of Mark 1.40-45 (// Matt. 8.1-4), 3.13-19 (// Matt. 10.2-4), 4.35–5.43 (// Matt. 8.23-34; 9.18-26) and 13.9-13 (// Matt. 10.17-22). Thus Luke changes the order of 4 Markan pericopes, Matthew changes the order of 6. These changes perhaps coincide once (Mark 3.13-19). If one takes the range of the compass of Mark prior to the passion, this covers 80 Markan pericopes (using Huck's divisions).[32] The probability of two authors independently choosing 4 and 6 respectively out of 80, and coinciding once is 0.246. The probability of their never coinciding is 0.726.[33] This is perfectly acceptable in statistical terms. (It is usually assumed that a probability has to be at least as small as 0.05 before being considered statistically significant.) There is thus nothing surprising in these figures, and nothing to suggest that the initial assumption, viz. the independence of Matthew and Luke, should be questioned. In fact, a relatively high probability is not at all surprising: the non-coincidence of the changes in order may simply be due to the fact that Matthew and Luke have different redactional aims in their alterations of Mark.[34]

There is thus no reason for thinking that the phenomenon of order poses a positive problem for MP, as Farmer and Dungan have suggested. MP remains quite consistent with the facts, and thus remains a viable solution to the Synoptic problem. Butler's analysis shows that it is not the only possible explanation of the phenomenon of the non-existence of Matthew–Luke agreements against Mark. Additional arguments are necessary in order to exclude other possible explanations of the phenomenon of order, but MP still provides a feasible explanation of the facts concerned.

IV

It has been a feature of the modern discussion that the same phenomenon of order has been used to advocate the GH. According to Farmer, this is a separate argument from the 'Lachmann fallacy',[35] and the GH's ability to explain the phenomenon of order is the hypothesis' 'central and essential strength'.[36] Farmer says that this argument from order

> is based on the observation that whenever the order of Mark is not the same as that of Matthew, it follows the order of Luke, i.e. that Mark has no independent chronology ... This seems explicable only by a conscious effort of Mark to follow the order of Matthew and Luke. Neither Matthew nor Luke could have achieved this alone. They would have had to conspire with one another to contrive this chronological neutering of Mark, i.e. robbing his chronological independence. Mark on this view can only be third and must have known Matthew and Luke. There seems to be no other satisfactory solution.[37]

The value of this argument is highly questionable. Farmer's statement of the phenomenon to which he is referring is no less biased than the formulation of Streeter cited earlier in this paper (e.g. 'the order of Mark ... *follows* the order of Luke'). In fact the 'observation' here is precisely the same as the premiss for the much criticized 'Lachmann fallacy' used to advocate MP, viz. there are agreements in order in the triple tradition between Matthew and Mark with Luke different, between Mark and Luke with Matthew different, but none between Matthew and Luke with Mark different.[38] Thus appeal is being made to the same phenomenon to support the GH and to claim that MP is false.

Now I have argued above that, assuming MP, these facts are not surprising. There is no need to postulate any 'conspiracy' between Matthew and Luke to account for the number of disagreements in order and their (general) non-coincidence. Farmer's claim, on the other hand, is that the GH alone can adequately explain the facts. ('Mark can *only* be third . . . There seems to be *no other* satisfactory solution.') But here one can refer again to Butler's analysis of the Lachmann fallacy. Butler showed convincingly that to conclude that MP was the *only* explanation of this pattern of agreements and disagreements in order was a logical error: the phenomenon was in itself ambiguous and could be explained equally well by a number of hypotheses (of which MP was one, the GH another, his own preferred Augustinian hypothesis a third). But the logic of Butler's analysis itself is really unrelated to the specific theory of MP: he simply showed that the facts in question are ambiguous and it is logically fallacious to assume that one and only one hypothesis can explain them. Thus any claim that the facts are explicable by one and only one hypothesis is a logical fallacy, whatever that hypothesis is. But this is precisely the argument of Farmer, viz. that this pattern of agreements and disagreements is *only* explicable by the GH. This argument from order to support the GH thus represents a reappearance of 'the Lachmann fallacy' in a slightly different guise. Since the phenomenon itself is ambiguous,[39] one must produce quite different arguments to support the claim that one or other of the possibilities where Mark is in a 'medial' position is to be preferred. The absence of Matthew-Luke agreements against Mark cannot of itself decide the issue.

V

This leads to the final 'argument from order' which has always held a firm place in the study of the Synoptic problem. This argument was that used by Lachmann, and amongst advocates of MP, it was used by scholars such as Holtzmann, Wrede, Wernle, Woods, Sanday and others.[40] This is the argument which seeks to explain the *dis*agreements in order as part of a rational, coherent plan on the part of the secondary evangelist(s). Such a form of argument must inevitably assume a source hypothesis. The attempt is then made to make this hypothesis credible by explaining the development of the tradition which the hypothesis implies. The coherence and consistency of the implied redactional activity will then be a measure of the validity of the hypothesis. Thus, assuming MP, the argument would seek to show that the changes which Matthew and Luke must have made to Mark's order can be seen to be intelligible and reasonably coherent as a redactional plan, consistent with what we know of their general tendencies. A similar argument to support the GH would seek to show that Luke's alterations of Matthew's order, and Mark's use of Matthew and Luke to produce his order, are also part of some intelligible redactional activity by Luke and Mark respectively. Such a form of argument can make no claim to being probative, but the nature of the case makes this inevitable. Given two differing versions A and B, one cannot tell which way dependence lies without looking at the contents of A and B and asking which change (A changed to B, or B changed to A) is more likely.[41]

On the GH detailed explanations of the redactional activity of Luke and Mark implied by the hypothesis are not often given. With regard to Mark, the explanation is usually offered that Mark followed the order of one source at a time alternately.[42] Such an explanation does work at one level, though it fails to account for the details of why Mark changed from one source to another precisely when he did;[43] further it does not in itself explain *why* Mark should have adopted this redactional procedure which involved omitting so much of the material available to him.[44] With regard to Luke, the only detailed attempt to explain Luke's redactional procedure in rearranging Matthew that I am aware of is the discussion in B. Orchard's *Matthew, Luke & Mark* (pp. 39-68), and I have tried to give reasons elsewhere for why I cannot accept his explanations in detail.[45] (However, it may be that the GH is right, but that Luke's reasons for altering Matthew's order are other than Orchard suggests. This simply illustrates the inherent inconclusiveness of any discussion in the Synoptic problem, since any pattern of synoptic interrelationships is theoretically possible.)

It is incumbent upon the defender of any source hypothesis to account for the changes which the secondary writers (on the hypothesis) must have made to their source(s). Thus in the final section of this paper I offer some possible reasons for why Matthew and Luke might have changed Mark's order in the way that MP implies they must have done. (This argument works unashamedly within the presuppositions of MP, though not all theories about the redactional tendencies of Matthew and Luke are necessarily dependent on the 2DH for their validity.) Insofar as the reasons suggested here are convincing, they will function as some support for the correctness of the source hypothesis presupposed.

I start with the difference in order between Matthew and Mark. Frequently, it is stated that most of Matthew's rearrangement of Mark is in order to collect a cycle of miracle stories in chs. 8–9.[46] This may be seen partly as an attempt to show Jesus as Messiah of deed as well as of word after the Sermon on the Mount,[47] partly to prepare the way for Jesus' claims in 11.5.[48] Such a blanket statement is, however, too simplistic.[49] Not only does it make Matt. 8–9 too monochrome (see below), but it also fails to account for the detailed changes in order which Matthew made (assuming MP) within this section. (E.g. within chs. 8–9, the relative order of the Markan pericopes used is not maintained.) A more precise set of reasons is thus necessary to make MP more credible here.

It is clear that the differences in order between Matthew and Mark are confined to the first half of the gospels. As always there is the problem of defining precisely the changes in order made (see section I above). In this case the matter is of some importance, and it becomes significant where precisely Matthew's Sermon on the Mount is placed in relation to the Markan order. The arrangement in Huck's synopsis places the Sermon after the summary in Mark 1.39. This implies that, assuming MP, Matthew has changed the order of Mark 1.29-31 and 1.32-34 to come later (Matt. 8.14-17), after the healing of the leper. Perhaps more convincing is the argument of Neirynck who claims that the Sermon should be placed between Mark 1.21 and 1.22.[50] This has the effect of bringing Mark 1.22 and Matt. 7.28f. into parallel order. It also implies that there is no alteration of the relative order of Mark 1.29-34; rather, the pericope whose order is changed is that of the healing of the leper (Matt. 8.1-4 // Mark 1.40-45):

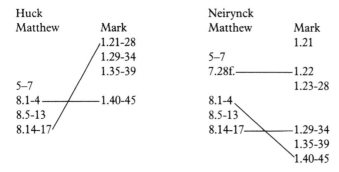

By using Neirynck's model a relatively simple explanation of the change in order now seems available, assuming MP. The story of the leper shows Jesus fulfilling the requirements of the OT law by commanding the healed leper to go to the priests and offer the appropriate sacrifices. Indeed this forms the climax of the story in Matthew.[51] (In Mark the climax is the wide fame which Jesus enjoyed [1.45], but this does not appear in Matthew: on MP this change is thus due to Matthew's redaction [MattR], but in any case this feature is identifiable as the climax in Matthew's story without reference to the Markan parallel.) This now fits in extremely well with Matthew's overall tendency, clearly evidenced throughout his gospel, to portray Jesus as the fulfilment of, and in a line of positive continuity with, the OT dispensation. (One can say this on almost any source hypothesis.) Matt. 5.17 (whose final form may owe a lot to MattR) sums this up well. It is thus quite in keeping with Matthew's overall interests to have re-ordered Mark's account so that the first miracle after the Sermon on the Mount (where 5.17 acts as a kind of 'title') shows Jesus as maintaining a thoroughly positive attitude to the OT.

The remaining changes of Mark's order in Matt. 8–9 involve the transfer of Mark 4.35–5.20 to Matt. 8.23-34 and Mark 5.21-43 to Matt. 9.18-26. Possible reasons for these changes are closely tied to one's theories about the structure of Matt. 8–9 as a whole. Certainly it is too imprecise to say that these two chapters form a 'collection of miracles'.[52] At the very least this fails to account for the presence of the controversy stories in Matt. 9.9-17.[53] Several recent studies have been made of this section in Matthew.[54] In general there is widespread agreement that the three stories in 8.1-17 form a subsection where the primary interest is in the person of Jesus as the miracle worker and as the one who fulfils scripture.[55] Similarly there is agreement that a major interest in 9.18-31 is the 'faith' required of those who respond to Jesus.[56] Matthew's version of the healing of the woman with the haemorrhage clearly underlines this feature, and if one assumes MP, Matthew has severely abbreviated Mark's account to highlight the woman's faith. This may well explain why this story (and the related story of Jairus's daughter) is placed in this subsection along with the story of the two blind men (where again the motif of faith is clearly highlighted).[57] The following story of the healing of the deaf-dumb demoniac (9.32-34) may also belong here, since Matthew appears to use these exorcism stories, and stories of curing dumbness/blindness, as paradigms to illustrate various responses to Jesus.[58] If then this whole section 9.18-34 is intended to illustrate the proper response to Jesus as being one of faith, there is little difficulty in seeing Matthew's redaction of, and transposition of, Mark 5.21-43 in Matt. 9.18-26 as perfectly consistent with this.

The central section in Matt. 8.18–9.17 gives rise to more dispute. Following Bornkamm's study it seems clear that 8.18-27 concern discipleship, and the story of the stilling of the storm has been redacted by Matthew to act as a 'parable' of the costs and dangers of discipleship.[59] The transposition of Mark 4.35-41 to follow the call story in Matt. 8.18-22 is thus, at one level, intelligible. Matt. 8.28-34 may also now belong within this theme for Matthew: Matthew's version of the story ends with the abrupt rejection of Jesus by the healed demoniacs' compatriots (8.34). The positive note of Mark 5.20 is lacking in Matthew. (Again, if we assume MP this is due to MattR explicitly; but on any source hypothesis the ending and climax of Matthew's version quite clearly involve the rejection of Jesus.) The story now acts in Matthew as an illustration of the saying in 8.20 about the Son of man having 'nowhere to lay his head',[60] and thus continues the theme of the costly nature of discipleship, following the one who finds no welcome with men.[61] The transfer of this story which Matthew must have made, assuming MP, would be coherent with the dominant themes which seem to be emerging in this section of Matthew's gospel. The same theme of discipleship may also explain the presence of the next two pericopes in Matthew (9.1-8, 9-13, though no change in the Markan order is involved here). Clearly this theme fits the story of the call of Matthew, but also the story of the healing of the paralytic is, in its Matthean version, implicitly concerned with discipleship: the fact that the crowds praise God for giving such authority 'to men' (plur.) implies that Jesus' miraculous powers can be disseminated to others, i.e. the disciples.[62] Thus the whole section in 8.18–9.17 is concerned with various aspects of the theme of discipleship.[63] The various transpositions which MP must assume fit in here if Matthew's intention is to create a small subsection centred on this theme.

Apart from the changes already considered, there are two further differences in order between Matthew and Mark. On MP, Matthew transfers the call of the twelve in Mark 3.13-19 to Matt. 10.2-4. This is not difficult to explain: Matthew has a clear tendency to systematize and to collect his material into thematic blocks. Chapter 10 is Matthew's great mission discourse, and it is relatively easy to see why he has placed the call of the twelve at this point, immediately prior to their being sent out. The remaining change concerns the anticipation (on MP) of the predictions of Jewish persecutions from Mark 13.9-13 to Matt. 10.17-22. This too is easily intelligible if, as seems likely, Matthew is writing for a situation of intense Jewish hostility. Jewish persecutions are, for Matthew, not an immediate prelude to the Parousia, but a matter of present experience,[64] or perhaps even a thing of the past.[65] There seems little difficulty in seeing this change in order as due to MattR.

Overall, Matthew's changes to Mark's order can be seen as part of a reasonably coherent and consistent pattern of redactional activity, consonant with what one can discern of Matthew's interests and concerns elsewhere.

Luke's changes of Mark's order are less numerous,[66] and also fairly easy to explain.[67] The transfer of the story of the rejection at Nazareth from Mark 6.1-6 to Luke 4.16-30[68] needs little explanation, given the very important programmatic significance which the story clearly has for Luke's two-volume work. The change in order is thus part of the (redactional) stress which is clearly laid on it (though perhaps the altered position may also be due in part to the presence of a rejection story in Luke's source at this point.) The change in order of Mark 3.13-19 (or 3.7-12) is usually taken to be due to Luke's desire to create an audience for the Great Sermon.[69] The change in position and wording of the saying about 'true relatives' (Luke 8.19-21; cf. Mark 3.31-35) produces an appropriate ending to the parables chapter, where, in Luke, the discussion is not so much about parables as about the Word of God.[70]

Reasons for the change in order of 5.1-11 are less clear. It is sometimes said that Luke has delayed the call story until after the account of Jesus' miracles in Capernaum to make Peter's response more plausible.[71] Against this can be placed the fact that there is a miracle inherent in the story itself. Nevertheless the later position of the call story does help to reduce the arbitrariness of Peter's response. There is, however, the problem of the inherent ambiguity in describing the change in order: has Luke pushed the call story back in order, or has he brought the material of Mark 1.21-39 forward? Part of the reason for the different order may be a desire by Luke to link the events in Capernaum more closely to the Nazareth story. In Luke's version all the events in 4.31-41 are portrayed as exorcisms. This is unexceptional in 4.31-37, and in the mass healings (4.41), but the fever in v. 39 is also 'rebuked', i.e. Luke is using exorcistic language here too.[72] This may now tie up closely with Luke's interpretation of the Isa. 61 quotation in Luke 4.17f. Acts 10.38 gives what appears to be Luke's understanding of the 'liberation' promise in Isa. 61 // Luke 4 as referring to Jesus' 'healing all who were oppressed by the devil'. Luke's order in Luke 4 may thus be due to his desire to bring out this facet of Jesus' ministry by bringing forward the events in Capernaum and redacting the material so that the language is predominantly exorcistic.[73] The change in order may thus be due to Luke's interpretation of the Isa. 61 material and is thus at least as much an anticipation of Mark 1.21-39 as a postponement of Mark 1.16-20.

There may be yet other factors which are also relevant. The Nazareth story for Luke clearly prefigures the future rejection of the gospel by the Jews and the mission of the later church to the Gentiles. But also 5.1–6.11 may represent a new section in the gospel where the sphere of Jesus' activity spreads outwards.[74] Many have seen the call story in 5.1-11 as having in view the future expansion of the church: for the person called here is the one who will later inaugurate the Gentile mission.[75] It would thus be quite appropriate to preface this section, which is concerned with the expansion of Jesus' mission, with the call of the one who will start the great expansion in the later church's mission. Thus for a variety of reasons Luke may well have altered the Markan order in this way.

The changes in order which must have happened according to the theory of MP are thus all intelligible as redactional changes by Matthew and Luke. They form a pattern which is reasonably coherent, and consistent with what can be discerned elsewhere of the evangelists' interests. These observations can never provide a strict proof of the correctness of the theory of MP. The changes in order might have taken place for quite different reasons; alternatively, the GH might be right and Luke and Mark did alter the order of their source(s) in the way that hypothesis implies, perhaps for reasons as yet undetermined. Nevertheless, if the above arguments are accepted as a plausible set of reasons for why Matthew and Luke might have changed Mark's order, they may legitimately be used as a contributory factor in maintaining belief in the priority of Mark.

NOTES

1. W.R. Farmer, 'The Lachmann Fallacy', *NTS* 14 (1968), pp. 441-43, on p. 442.

2. I realize that the division of the text into pericopes is in itself in part an arbitrary procedure, and that any such division is non-unique. See D. Dungan, 'Theory of Synopsis Construction', *Biblica* 61 (1980), pp. 305-29, esp. pp. 314f., 322f.

3. The situation is, of course, quite different with regard to the detailed wording of the text.

4. B.H. Streeter, *The Four Gospels* (London, 1924), p. 161.

5. See J.B. Tyson, 'Sequential Parallelism in the Synoptic Gospels', *NTS* 22 (1976), pp. 276-308, on p. 276; D. Dungan, 'Mark—The Abridgement of Matthew and Luke', *Jesus and Man's Hope*, I (1970), pp. 51-97, on p. 60, says that Streeter's formulation was 'stated in an inexcusably prejudicial manner'.

6. A similar point is made in more general terms by A.D. Jacobson, 'The Literary Unity of Q', *JBL* 101 (1982), pp. 365-89, on p. 367: 'It would appear that the data to be explained by a source hypothesis (i.e. the agreements and disagreements of various kinds) are generated by the hypothesis itself', though it is not clear if he has in mind the fact that the data itself is not uniquely specifiable (as claimed here), or if he is simply referring to the fact that the same data can often be adequately explained by different source hypotheses.

7. *Op. cit.* (n. 5).

8. Tyson explicitly states that this is a 'relocation' (*op. cit.*, p. 296). He does not allow for the possibility of added/deleted material (e.g. Matt. 13.24-30 and Mark 4.26-29) as breaking the sequential nature of the parallelism but preserving the common order.

9. Although such a possibility is observable from Tyson's tables, as *two* sequences each involving two pericopes, his final analysis simply adds the numbers of pericopes in sequential parallelism together indiscriminately. Thus Tyson's statistical results do not distinguish between the examples

given above, and the possibility of two texts having the four pericopes a b f g in immediate sequential parallelism.

10. See Dungan, *op. cit.* (n. 2); B. Orchard, 'Are All Gospel Synopses Biassed?', *TZ* 34 (1978), pp. 149-62.

11. Contra Orchard, *op. cit.*, pp. 150-52.

12. Dungan, *op. cit.*, pp. 326f., points to a number of places where some bias towards MP may be suspected, e.g. in Huck's decision to invert the order of Luke 6.12-16 and 17-19, thus following the order of Mark as basic. In an earlier draft of this article, in a paper submitted to the Synoptic Problem Seminar at the SNTS meeting at Durham, 1979, Dungan also referred to Huck's decision not to print the parallel to Matt. 10.17-22 from Mark 13 in the text opposite Matt. 10, but only as a footnote at the bottom of the page. These criticisms are justified, but they relate more to the issue of how frequently a text should be printed in a synopsis and where some abbreviations might be acceptable, rather than to the more fundamental principle of how the parallels should initially be set up.

13. *Op. cit.*, pp. 156f., 162; also his *Matthew, Luke & Mark* (Manchester, 1976), pp. 39-68, and his *A Synopsis of the Four Gospels* (Edinburgh, 1983).

14. 'Modern Developments of Griesbach's Hypothesis', *NTS* 23 (1977), pp. 275-95, on p. 293.

15. M. Lowe, 'The Demise of Arguments from Order for Markan Priority', *NovT* 24 (1982), pp. 27-36.

16. *Ibid.*, p. 27. Although Lowe refers to 'arguments' (plural) in his title, he seems to have in mind only one argument (perhaps as used by several people).

17. Following Lowe's own abbreviated language. 'xMky' means 'x comes before y in Mark'.

18. This is exactly the same as what Lowe regards as the claim of the GH about Mark. This simply illustrates what I shall argue in section IV of this paper: that the argument from order used to advocate the GH appeals to exactly the same facts as at least one argument from order used to advocate MP.

19. *The Originality of St. Matthew* (Cambridge, 1951), pp. 62-71.

20. This is explicitly acknowledged by Butler, *op. cit.*, p. 63; Farmer, *op. cit.* (n. 1), p. 442.

21. See, on the side of modern advocates of MP, G. Styler, Excursus IV in C.F.D. Moule, *The Birth of the New Testament* (3rd edn, London, 1981), p. 290; F. Neirynck, 'The Argument from Order and St. Luke's Transpositions', *ETL* 49 (1973), pp. 784-815, reprinted in *The Minor Agreements of Matthew and Luke against Mark* (Louvain, 1974) (all page refs. to the latter), pp. 302f.

22. I have tried to demonstrate this in my article, 'The Argument from Order and the Synoptic Problem', *TZ* 36 (1980), pp. 338-54.

23. Farmer's claim to this effect (cf. n. 1 above) is due to his confusing

different arguments from order in the history of research. See my 'Argument from Order', pp. 339ff.

24. *The Synoptic Problem* (2nd edn, Dillsboro, N.C., 1976), p. 213.

25. *Ibid.*, pp. 213, 214.

26. *Op. cit.* (n. 5), p. 63. However, it should be noted that Farmer and Dungan both appear to be confusing two separate phenomena, i.e. changes in order by Matthew/Luke and omissions of Markan material. The 'argument from order' under consideration here has always been confined in the past to changes in order. Some attempt to interrelate the two is also made by E.P. Sanders, 'The Argument from Order and the Relationship between Matthew and Luke', *NTS* 15 (1969), pp. 249-61, who points to places where Matthew re-orders, and Luke omits, the same material in Mark, as some contributory evidence that Matthew and Luke are not independent (though Sanders never suggests that this should prejudice belief in MP). However, Neirynck, *op. cit.*, p. 295, points out that the Lukan omissions are in each case much more extensive than the one element re-ordered by Matthew, and probably cannot be used in the way Sanders suggests. With regard to the omissions made by Matthew and Luke, assuming MP, it is not the case that these never coincide: e.g. Mark 3.20-21; 4.26-29; 7.31-37; 8.22-26 are omitted by both Matthew and Luke. Thus there is no conspiracy to support Mark alternately. It has been argued that, in fact, the number of common omissions is slightly higher than the expected number if such omissions were being made randomly; but this is not surprising since the fact that a pericope is omitted by one writer suggests that it might be unacceptable to some, and hence there may be an increased probability that the same pericope may be omitted by another writer. See S. McLoughlin, 'A Reply' [to H. Meynell, 'A Note on the Synoptic Problem'], *Down. Rev.* 90 (1972), pp. 201-206, on pp. 201f.

27. Noted by Sanders, *op. cit.*, p. 256. Sanders's other alleged examples of this phenomenon are, however, unconvincing: see the critique by Neirynck, *op. cit.*, pp. 296f., though Neirynck perhaps glosses over this pericope too quickly (he calls Luke's version 'only an inversion within the *same* section of Mk III' [my italics]).

28. Although, due to the inherent ambiguity in describing changes in order, one could say that Luke has rearranged Mark 3.7-12.

29. *Op. cit.*, p. 299, referring to Farmer, *Synoptic Problem*, pp. 213f.

30. Some of these are arguably cases where Luke is not using Mark at all but is dependent on independent traditions. I have excluded texts such as Luke 7.36-50; 10.25-28; 13.18-19, for this reason. For at least the latter two as representing non-Markan traditions, see my *The Revival of the Griesbach Hypothesis* (Cambridge, 1983), pp. 81, 126.

31. See below.

32. The passion narrative is perhaps a special case since there is uncertainty about the extent to which Luke has access to independent traditions.

33. I.e. $4 \times \frac{6}{80} \times \frac{74}{79} \times \frac{73}{78} \times \frac{72}{77}$, and $\frac{74}{80} \times \frac{73}{79} \times \frac{72}{78} \times \frac{71}{77}$ respectively.

34. Cf. G.D. Fee, 'A Text-Critical Look at the Synoptic Problem', *NovT* 22 (1980), pp. 12-28, on pp. 14f. Also Styler, *op. cit.*, p. 310. Styler makes the valid point that not all Matthew's changes are random: some may be for the *same* reason, and hence the number of independent changes may be effectively rather smaller. Styler limits attention to Mark 1.16–6.44, and calculates the chances of Matthew and Luke not agreeing to re-order as 'about 10:1'. I cannot see how this figure is arrived at, and it is uncertain whether one should limit attention to this smaller section of Mark. It is a feature of the work of J.C. O'Neill, 'The Synoptic Problem', *NTS* 21 (1975) pp. 273-85, that he seems to dismiss the possibility of *any* change in order as being due to conscious redactional activity by a secondary writer (see esp. pp. 275f.): thus all differences in order have to be explained by independent incorporation of the same material at various stages in the pre-redactional tradition-history. But placing such severe restrictions on the possible redactional activity of the evangelists seems unnecessary, if not misleading.

35. 'Modern Developments', p. 293.

36. *Ibid.*, p. 280.

37. *Ibid.*, p. 293. Cf. also his *Synoptic Problem*, p. 212, though the later statement makes the argument more stringent.

38. Farmer notes as an exeption the dating of the cleansing of the temple.

39. This ambiguity was noted as long ago as 1844 by an advocate of the GH, viz. F.J. Schwarz, *Neue Untersuchungen über das Verwandtschaftverhältniss der synoptischen Evangelien mit besonderer Berücksichtigung der Hypothese vom schöpferischen Urevangelisten* (Tübingen, 1844), p. 307, who saw that this meant 'dass Markus entweder der Urevangelist ist, oder dass er seine beiden Vorgänger benützt hat'. (Cited also by Neirynck, *op. cit.*, p. 300.)

40. For justification and references, see my 'Argument from Order'.

41. I have tried to argue this more fully in my *Revival*, pp. 9-15.

42. So already Griesbach; Farmer, 'Modern Developments', pp. 293f.; cf. Dungan, 'Mark—The Abridgement', p. 63, and T.R.W. Longstaff, 'A Critical Response to J.C. O'Neill', *NTS* 23 (1977), pp. 116-17, both appealing to the example of Arrian as a precedent.

43. It was the great merit of Griesbach himself to try to give such reasons: see his famous 'Commentatio', now available in English translation in B. Orchard and T.R.W. Longstaff (eds.), *Griesbach Studies. Synoptic and Text-Critical Studies 1776–1976* (Cambridge, 1978), pp. 103ff., especially the notes on pp. 209-12. These reasons were criticized in detail by B. Weiss, 'Zur Entstehungsgeschichte der synoptischen Evangelien', *Theol. Stud. u. Krit.* (1861), pp. 646-713, esp. pp. 680f. None of these criticisms has, as far as I am aware, been discussed in the contemporary revival of the GH. See my 'The Griesbach Hypothesis in the 19th Century', *JSNT* 3 (1979), pp. 29-60, for

further details.

44. For the theory that Mark is seeking to avoid discrepancies in his sources, see my *Revival*, pp. 52ff.

45. *Revival*, pp. 31-40.

46. E.g. W.G. Kümmel, *Introduction to the New Testament* (Eng. Tr.; London, 1975), p. 59, is typical.

47. Cf. J. Schniewind, *Das Evangelium nach Matthäus* (Göttingen, 1936), p. 106.

48. So already Lachmann, Eng. Tr. in N.H. Palmer, 'Lachmann's Argument', *NTS* 13 (1967), pp. 368-78, on p. 373; E. Schweizer, *The Good News according to Matthew* (Eng. Tr.; London, 1976), p. 69; H.J. Held, 'Matthew as Interpreter of the Miracle Stories', in G. Bornkamm, G. Barth, H.J. Held, *Tradition and Interpretation in Matthew* (Eng. Tr.; London, 1963), p. 251, and others.

49. See the critique by C. Burger, 'Jesu Taten nach Matthäus 8 und 9', *ZThK* 70 (1973), pp. 272-87.

50. F. Neirynck, 'The Sermon on the Mount in the Gospel Synopsis', *ETL* 53 (1976), pp. 350-57. The phenomenon of the link verses in Matthew is discussed by Neirynck in great detail, in 'La rédaction matthéenne et la structure du premier évangile', in I. de la Potterie (ed.), *De Jésus aux Évangiles* (BETL, 25; Gembloux, 1967), pp. 41-73, esp. pp. 63-72; also 'The Gospel of Matthew and Literary Criticism', in M. Didier (ed.), *L'Évangile selon Matthieu. Rédaction et Théologie* (BETL, 29; Gembloux, 1972), pp. 37-69, esp. pp. 61-67. He shows that there is no need to see anything other than MattR of Mark in the summary and link verses in Matthew.

51. For the prominence of this in Matthew, see Held, *op. cit.*, p. 256; Schweizer, *op. cit.*, p. 211; H.B. Green, *The Gospel according to Matthew* (Oxford, 1975), p. 99.

52. See n. 46 above.

53. For some these simply reveal the relics of Matthew's source: cf. F.H. Woods, 'The Origin and Mutual Relation of the Synoptic Gospels', *Studia Biblica et Ecclesiastica* II (1890), pp. 59-104, esp. p. 71; Held, *op. cit.*, p. 249; Kümmel, *op. cit.*, p. 60. But according to MP, Matthew has felt free to make wholescale changes to Mark to create his pattern. It would be odd if Matthew had felt bound by his source to retain elements which did not fit his pattern. Rather, one should perhaps question whether one has correctly understood Matthew's pattern, before claiming that some elements do not fit an alleged pattern.

54. Apart from Held's programmatic study of all the miracle stories in Matthew, see W.G. Thompson, 'Reflections on the Composition of Mt 8:1–9:34', *CBQ* 33 (1971), pp. 365-88; Burger, *op. cit.*; J.D. Kingsbury, 'Observations on the "Miracle Chapters" of Matthew 8–9', *CBQ* 40 (1978), pp. 559-73. There is widespread agreement between these authors, but it is

noteworthy that MP is not necessarily a basis for the argument. For example Thompson deliberately shuns the method of comparing Matthew with his alleged source and concentrates solely on analysing the Matthean story-line in and of itself to discover the dominant themes.

55. Held, *op. cit.*, pp. 253ff.; Thompson, *op. cit.*, pp. 368-70; Kingsbury, *op. cit.* p. 562. Burger, *op. cit.*, p. 284, Green, *op. cit.*, p. 98 (and many others) would see the main theme here in the fact that Jesus cures three people who are in some sense 'outcasts' from full Jewish society. However, Held's analysis does seem to show convincingly that the primary interest in Matthew's account is in the person of *Jesus*, not in the people cured.

56. Held, *op. cit.*, pp. 178ff.; Thompson, *op. cit.*, pp. 379-84; Burger, *op. cit.*, pp. 286f.; Kingsbury, *op. cit.*, p. 562. O.L. Cope, *Matthew: A Scribe Trained for the Kingdom of Heaven* (Washington, 1976), pp. 65-73, sees the section 9.10-34 as a unit, governed by the Hos. 6.6 citation in v. 13 and centred on the theme of mercy taking precedence over Torah piety. But is is very uncertain whether 'mercy' is really an appropriate term for the permission given to the disciples not to fast (9.14-17); and the issue of cultic impurity associated with the people healed in 9.18-34 never surfaces as an issue in *Matthew's* account (whatever may have been the case in the pre-Matthean tradition).

57. Clearly so on any source hypothesis, but on MP this is presumably a redactional duplication and adaptation of Mark's Bartimaeus story.

58. See W.R.G. Loader, 'Son of David, Blindness, Possession and Duality in Matthew', *CBQ* 44 (1982), pp. 570-85.

59. See *Tradition* (n. 49) pp. 52-57.

60. Burger, *op. cit.*, p. 285.

61. Thompson thinks that the theme of discipleship links the whole section in 8.18–9.17, but that this is 'somewhat submerged' in 8.28–9.8 (*op. cit.*, p. 371). This therefore may not be necessary.

62. Held, *op. cit.*, p. 274, and others cited there. Matthew clearly implies by his arrangement that the disciples are to continue the work of Jesus in all its aspects: 10.1 echoes 4.23 and 9.35; 10.7 echoes 4.17; 10.8 picks up chs. 8–9. See Held, *op. cit.* p. 250.

63. Hence contra Burger *op. cit.*, p. 286, and Kingsbury, *op. cit.*, p. 562, who both see 9.1-17 as to do with the separation of the church from Judaism. This rather forces the meaning of 9.1-8; also, in 9.14 the fasting question is posed by the disciples of the Baptist, yet Matthew is generally thoroughly positive about the Baptist: see W. Wink, *John the Baptist in the Gospel Tradition* (Cambridge, 1968), esp. pp. 33ff.

64. Cf. W. Marxsen, *Der Evangelist Markus* (Göttingen, 1959), p. 138; D.R.A. Hare, *The Theme of Jewish Persecution of Christians in the Gospel according to St. Matthew* (Cambridge, 1967), p. 100; M.D. Goulder, *Midrash and Lection in Matthew* (London, 1974), p. 347.

65. W.G. Thompson, 'An Historical Perspective in the Gospel of Matthew',

JBL 93 (1974), pp. 243-62.

66. I leave aside those cases where I would argue that Luke has a non-Marken version of a pericope (cf. n. 30 above). In these cases the different ordering may be due to the presence of the parallel version in one of Luke's non-Markan sources, together with his general tendency not to intermingle his Markan and non-Markan material.

67. On MP, or on the Augustinian hypothesis, these alterations are changes from the order of Mark. On the GH they are changes from the order of Matthew. The GH must explain all these changes by LkR, as MP must, as well as many more.

68. I have argued elsewhere that Luke 4 is dependent in part on Mark 6, as well as possibly on Q. See my 'Luke 4,16-30, Isaiah and Q', in J. Delobel (ed.), *LOGIA. Les Paroles du Jésus—The Sayings of Jesus* (BETL, 59; Louvain, 1982), pp. 343-54.

69. See Kümmel, *op. cit.*, p. 59; I.H. Marshall, *The Gospel of Luke* (Exeter, 1978), p. 237. For arguments against the existence of a non-Markan (?Q) source here (so e.g. H. Schürmann, *Das Lukasevangelium* [Freiburg, 1969], p. 323), see Neirynck, *op. cit.* (n. 21), pp. 315-17.

70. See Marshall, *op. cit.*, p. 330; W.C. Robinson, 'On Preaching the Word of God (Luke 8:4-21)', in L.E. Keck, J.L. Martyn (eds.), *Studies in Luke–Acts* (London, 1966), pp. 131-38. On almost any source hypothesis the redactional activity of Luke will be the same.

71. Cf. Kümmel, *op. cit.*, p. 59; H. Conzelmann, *The Theology of St Luke* (Eng. Tr.; London 1960), p. 191; P.J. Achtemeier, 'The Lucan Perspective on the Miracles of Jesus', *JBL* 94 (1975), pp. 547-62, esp. p. 555.

72. This is LkR whether Luke's source is Mark or Matthew.

73. See U. Busse, *Die Wunder des Propheten Jesu. Die Rezeption, Komposition und Interpretation der Wundertradition im Evangelium des Lukas* (Stuttgart, 1979), pp. 66-90. However, I am doubtful if this is the original idea in the use of Isa. 61 to refer to Jesus, or if this stress on exorcism is a very dominant motif in the whole of the rest of Luke–Acts. This is one reason why I would argue that the use of Isa. 61 in Luke 4 represents a pre-Lukan tradition. See further n. 68.

74. Cf. Schürmann, *op. cit.*, p. 261: 'Der neue Abschnitt, der Jesu breite Volkstätigkeit im ganzen Judenland schildert . . . '

75. Cf. J.M. Creed, *The Gospel according to St. Luke* (London, 1930), p. 73; R. Pesch, *Der reiche Fischfang* (Düsseldorf, 1969), p. 142.

INDEXES

INDEX OF BIBLICAL REFERENCES